1994 CASE SUPPLEMENT

to

COX, BOK, GORMAN AND FINKIN

CASES AND MATERIALS

ON

LABOR LAW

ELEVENTH EDITION

By

ROBERT A. GORMAN
Kenneth W. Gemmill Professor of Law
University of Pennsylvania

MATTHEW W. FINKIN
Professor of Law and Professor in the Institute of
Labor and Industrial Relations
University of Illinois

Westbury, New York
THE FOUNDATION PRESS, INC.
1994

TEXT IS PRINTED ON 10% POST CONSUMER RECYCLED PAPER  PRINTED WITH SOY INK™ ∞

ANALYTICAL TABLE OF CONTENTS

*

TABLE OF CASES

Principal cases are in italic type. Non-principal cases are in roman type. References are to Pages.

1994 CASE SUPPLEMENT

to

CASES AND MATERIALS

ON

LABOR LAW

*

Part One

EVOLUTION OF LABOR RELATIONS LAWS

VIII. JURISDICTION, ORGANIZATION
AND PROCEDURE OF THE NLRB

A. NLRB JURISDICTION

Page 106. Add the following case after the Note:

NATIONAL LABOR RELATIONS BOARD v. HEALTH
CARE & RETIREMENT CORP. OF AMERICA

___ U.S. ___, 114 S.Ct. 1778, ___ L.Ed.2d ___ (1994).

JUSTICE KENNEDY delivered the opinion of the Court.

The National Labor Relations Act affords employees the rights to organize and to engage in collective bargaining free from employer interference. The Act does not grant those rights to supervisory employees, however, so the statutory definition of supervisor becomes essential in determining which employees are covered by the Act. In this case, we decide the narrow question whether the National Labor Relations Board's test for determining if a nurse is a supervisor is consistent with the statutory definition.

I

* * *

In this case, the Board's General Counsel issued a complaint alleging that respondent, the owner and operator of the Heartland Nursing Home in Urbana, Ohio, had committed unfair labor practices in disciplining four licensed practical nurses. At Heartland, the Director of Nursing has overall responsibility for the nursing department. There is also an Assistant Director of Nursing, 9 to 11 staff nurses (including both registered nurses and the four licensed practical nurses involved in this case), and 50 to 55 nurses' aides. The staff nurses are the senior ranking employees on duty after 5 p.m. during the week and at all times on weekends—approximately 75% of the time. The staff nurses have responsibility to ensure adequate staffing; to make daily work assignments; to monitor the aides' work to ensure proper performance; to

1

counsel and discipline aides; to resolve aides' problems and grievances; to evaluate aides' performances; and to report to management. In light of these varied activities, respondent contended, among other things, that the four nurses involved in this case were supervisors, and so not protected under the Act. The administrative law judge (ALJ) disagreed, concluding that the nurses were not supervisors. The ALJ stated that the nurses' supervisory work did not "equate to responsibly directing the aides *in the interest of the employer*," noting that "the nurses' focus is on the well-being of the residents rather than of the employer." 306 N.L.R.B. 68, 70 (1992) (internal quotation marks omitted) (emphasis added). The Board stated only that "the judge found, and we agree, that the Respondent's staff nurses are employees within the meaning of the Act." 306 N.L.R.B. 63, 63, n. 1 (1992).

* * * We granted certiorari, 510 U.S. ___ (1993), to resolve the conflict in the Courts of Appeals over the validity of the Board's rule. See, e.g., Waverly–Cedar Falls Health Care Center, Inc. v. NLRB, 933 F.2d 626 (CA8 1991); NLRB v. Res–Care, Inc., 705 F.2d 1461 (CA7 1983); Misericordia Hospital Medical Center v. NLRB, 623 F.2d 808 (CA2 1980).

II

We must decide whether the Board's test for determining if nurses are supervisors is rational and consistent with the Act. See Fall River Dyeing & Finishing Corp. v. NLRB, 482 U.S. 27, 42, 107 S.Ct. 2225, 2235, 9 L.Ed.2d 22 (1987). We agree with the Court of Appeals that it is not.

A

The Board's interpretation, that a nurse's supervisory activity is not exercised in the interest of the employer if it is incidental to the treatment of patients, is similar to an approach the Board took, and we rejected, in NLRB v. Yeshiva Univ., 444 U.S. 672, 100 S.Ct. 856, 63 L.Ed.2d 115 (1980). There, we had to determine whether faculty members at Yeshiva were "managerial employees." Managerial employees are those who "formulate and effectuate management policies by expressing and making operative the decisions of their employer." NLRB v. Bell Aerospace Co., 416 U.S. 267, 288, 94 S.Ct. 1757, 40 L.Ed.2d 134 (1974) (internal quotation marks omitted). Like supervisory employees, managerial employees are excluded from the Act's coverage. Id., at 283, 94 S.Ct. at 1766 ("so clearly outside the Act that no specific exclusionary provision was thought necessary"). The Board in *Yeshiva* argued that the faculty members were not managerial, contending that faculty authority was "exercised in the faculty's own interest rather than in the interest of the university." 444 U.S., at 685, 100 S.Ct. at 863. To support its position, the Board placed much reliance on the faculty's independent professional role in designing the curriculum and in discharging their professional obligations to the students. We found the Board's reasoning unpersuasive:

> "In arguing that a faculty member exercising independent judgment acts primarily in his own interest and therefore does not represent the interest of his employer, the Board assumes that the professional interests of the faculty and the interests of the institution are distinct, separable entities with which a faculty member could not simultaneously be aligned. The Court of Appeals found no justification for this distinction, and we perceive none. In fact, the faculty's professional interests—as applied to governance at a university like Yeshiva—cannot be separated from those of the institution.... The "business" of a university is education." Id., at 688, 100 S.Ct. at 865.

The Board's reasoning fares no better here than it did in *Yeshiva*. As in *Yeshiva*, the Board has created a false dichotomy—in this case, a dichotomy between acts taken in connection with patient care and acts taken in the interest of the employer. That dichotomy makes no sense. Patient care is the business of a nursing home, and it follows that attending to the needs of the nursing home patients, who are the employer's customers, is in the interest of the employer. See Beverly California, supra, at 1553. We thus see no basis for the Board's blanket assertion that supervisory authority exercised in connection with patient care is somehow not in the interest of the employer.

Our conclusion is supported by the case that gave impetus to the statutory provision now before us. In *Packard Motor*, we considered the phrase "in the interest of an employer" contained in the definition of "employer" in the original 1935 Act. We stated that "every employee, from the very fact of employment in the master's business, is required to act in his interest." 330 U.S., at 488, 67 S.Ct., at 791–792. We rejected the argument of the dissenters who, like the Board in this case, advanced the proposition that the phrase covered only "those who acted for management ... in formulating and executing its labor policies." Id., at 496, 67 S.Ct., at 795 (Douglas, J., dissenting); cf. Reply Brief for NLRB 4 (filed July 23, 1993) (nurses are supervisors when "in addition to performing their professional duties and responsibilities, they also possess the authority to affect the job status or pay of employees working under them"). * * *

Not only is the Board's test inconsistent with *Yeshiva, Packard Motor*, and the ordinary meaning of the phrase "in the interest of the employer," it also renders portions of the statutory definition in § 2(11) meaningless. Under § 2(11), an employee who in the course of employment uses independent judgment to engage in one of the 12 listed activities, including responsible direction of other employees, is a supervisor. Under the Board's test, however, a nurse who in the course of employment uses independent judgment to engage in responsible direction of other employees is not a supervisor. Only a nurse who in the course of employment uses independent judgment to engage in one of the activities related to another employee's job status or pay can qualify as a supervisor under the Board's test. See Reply Brief for NLRB 4 (filed July 23, 1993) (nurses are supervisors when they affect "job status or pay of employees working under them"). The Board provides no plausible justification, however, for reading the responsible direction portion of § 2(11) out of the statute in nurse cases, and we can perceive none.

The Board defends its test by arguing that phrases in § 2(11) such as "independent judgment" and "responsibly to direct" are ambiguous, so the Board needs to be given ample room to apply them to different categories of employees. That is no doubt true, but it is irrelevant in this particular case because interpretation of those phrases is not the underpinning of the Board's test. The Board instead has placed exclusive reliance on the "in the interest of the employer" language in § 2(11). With respect to that particular phrase, we find no ambiguity supporting the Board's position. It should go without saying, moreover, that ambiguity in one portion of a statute does not give the Board license to distort other provisions of the statute. Yet that is what the Board seeks us to sanction in this case.

The interpretation of the "in the interest of the employer" language mandated by our precedents and by the ordinary meaning of the phrase does not render the phrase meaningless in the statutory definition. The language ensures, for example, that union stewards who adjust grievances are not considered supervisory employees and deprived of the Act's protections. But the language cannot support the Board's argument that supervision of the care of patients is not in the interest of the employer. The welfare of the patient, after all, is no less the object and concern of the employer than it is of the nurses. And the statutory dichotomy the Board has created is no more justified in the health care field than it would be in any other business where supervisory duties are a necessary incident to the production of goods or the provision of services.

B

Because the Board's test is inconsistent with both the statutory language and this Court's precedents, the Board seeks to shift ground, putting forth a series of non-statutory arguments. None of them persuades us that we can ignore the statutory language and our case law.

The Board first contends that we should defer to its test because, according to the Board, granting organizational rights to nurses whose supervisory authority concerns patient care does not threaten the conflicting loyalties that the supervisor exception was designed to avoid. Brief for Petitioner 25. We rejected the same argument in *Yeshiva* where the Board contended that there was "no danger of divided loyalty and no need for the managerial exclusion" for the Yeshiva faculty members. 444 U.S., at 684, 100 S.Ct., at 863. And we must reject that reasoning again here. * * * Even on the assumption, moreover, that the statute permits consideration of the potential for divided loyalties so that a unique interpretation is permitted in the health care field, we do not share the Board's confidence that there is no danger of divided loyalty here. Nursing home owners may want to implement policies to ensure that patients receive the best possible care despite potential adverse reaction from employees working under the nurses' direction. If so, the statute gives nursing home owners the ability to insist on the undivided loyalty of its nurses notwithstanding the Board's impression that there is no danger of divided loyalty.

The Board also argues that "[t]he statutory criterion of having authority 'in the interest of the employer' ... must not be read so broadly that it overrides Congress's intention to accord the protections of the Act to professional employees." Brief for Petitioner 26; see 29 U.S.C. § 152(12). The Act does not distinguish professional employees from other employees for purposes of the definition of supervisor in § 2(11). The supervisor exclusion applies to "any individual" meeting the statutory requirements, not to "any non-professional employee." In addition, the Board relied on the same argument in *Yeshiva*, but to no avail. * * *

Finally, as a reason for us to defer to its conclusion, the Board cites legislative history of the 1974 amendments to other sections of the Act. Those amendments did not alter the test for supervisory status in the health care field, yet the Board points to a statement in a Committee Report expressing apparent approval of the Board's then-current application of its supervisory employee test to nurses. S.Rep. No. 93–766, p. 6 (1974); see Yeshiva, supra, at 690, n. 30, 10 S.Ct., at 866, n. 30. As an initial matter, it is far from clear that the Board in fact had a consistent test for nurses before 1974. Compare Avon Convalescent Center, 200 N.L.R.B. 702 (1972) with Doctors' Hospital of Modesto, Inc., 183 N.L.R.B. 950 (1970). In any event, the isolated statement in the 1974 Committee Report does not represent an authoritative interpretation of the phrase "in the interest of the employer," which was enacted by Congress in 1947. "It is the function of the courts and not the Legislature, much less a Committee of one House of the Legislature, to say what an enacted statute means." Pierce v. Underwood, 487 U.S. 552, 566, 108 S.Ct. 2541, 2551, 1 L.Ed.2d 490 (1988). Indeed, in American Hospital Assn. v. NLRB, 499 U.S. 606, 111 S.Ct. 1539, 113 L.Ed.2d 675 (1991), the petitioner pointed to isolated statements from the same 1974 Senate Report cited here and argued that they revealed Congress' intent with respect to a provision of the original 1935 Act. We dismissed the argument, stating that such statements do not have "the force of law, for the Constitution is quite explicit about the procedure that Congress must follow in legislating." Id., at 616, 111 S.Ct., at 1545; see also Betts, 492 U.S., at 168, 109 S.Ct., at 2861–2862. In this case as well, we must reject the Board's reliance on the 1974 Committee Report. If the Congress wishes to enact the policies of the Board, it can do so without indirection. See generally Central Bank of Denver v. First Interstate Bank, ___ U.S. ___, ___–___, 114 S.Ct. 1439, 1452–1453, 12 L.Ed.2d 119 (1994).

III

An examination of the professional's duties (or in this case the duties of the four non-professional nurses) to determine whether one or another of the 12 listed activities is performed in a manner that makes the employee a supervisor is, of course, part of the Board's routine and proper adjudicative function. In cases involving nurses, that inquiry no doubt could lead the Board in some cases to conclude that supervisory status has not been demonstrated. The Board has not sought to sustain its decision on that basis here, however. It has chosen instead to rely on an industry-wide interpretation of the phrase "in the interest of the employer" that contravenes precedents of this Court and has no relation to the ordinary meaning of that language. * * *

We note further that our decision casts no doubt on Board or court decisions interpreting parts of § 2(11) other than the specific phrase "in the interest of the employer." Because the Board's interpretation of "in the interest of the employer" is for the most part confined to nurse cases, our decision will have almost no effect outside that context. Any parade of horribles about the meaning of this decision for employees in other industries is thus quite misplaced; indeed, the Board does not make that argument.

In sum, the Board's test for determining the supervisory status of nurses is inconsistent with the statute and our precedents. The Board did not petition this Court to uphold its order in this case under any other theory. See Brief for Respondent 21, n. 25. If the case presented the question whether these nurses were supervisors under the proper test, we would have given a lengthy exposition and analysis of the facts in the record. But as we have indicated, the Board made and defended its decision by relying on the particular test it has applied to nurses. Our conclusion that the Court of Appeals was correct to find the Board's test inconsistent with the statute therefore suffices to resolve the case. The judgment of the Court of Appeals is Affirmed.

JUSTICE GINSBURG, with whom JUSTICE BLACKMUN, JUSTICE STEVENS, and JUSTICE SOUTER join, dissenting.

* * *

I

As originally enacted in 1935, the National Labor Relations Act (Act), 29 U.S.C. § 151 et seq., did not expressly exclude supervisors from the class of "employees" entitled to the Act's protections. See Sections 7, 2(3), 49 Stat. 452, 450. The Board decided in Packard Motor Co., 61 N.L.R.B. 4 (1945), that in the absence of an express exclusion, supervisors must be held within the Act's coverage. This Court agreed, stating that the language of the Act allowed no other interpretation. Packard Motor Car Co. v. NLRB, 330 U.S. 485, 67 S.Ct. 789, 91 L.Ed. 1048 (1947).

Congress responded by excluding supervisors in the Labor Management Relations Act of 1947. The Senate Committee Report noted that the Senate's definition of "supervisor" had been framed with a view to assuring that "the employees ... excluded from the coverage of the act would be truly supervisory." S.Rep. No. 105, 80th Cong., 1st Sess., 19 (1947) (hereinafter Senate Report), Legislative History 425; see also H.Conf.Rep. No. 510, 80th Cong., 1st Sess., 35 (1947), Legislative History 539 ("supervisor" limited "to individuals generally regarded as foremen and persons of like or higher rank"). * * * The purpose of § 2(11)'s definition of "supervisor," then, was to limit the term's scope to "the front line of management," the "foremen" who owed management "undivided loyalty," id., at 5, Legislative History 411, as distinguished from workers with "minor supervisory duties."

At the very time that Congress excluded supervisors from the Act's protection, it added a definition of "professional employees." See 29 U.S.C. § 152(12). The inclusion of that definition, together with an amendment to § 9(b) of the Act limiting the placement of professionals and nonprofessionals in the same bargaining unit, see n. 1, supra, confirm that Congress did not intend its exclusion of supervisors largely to eliminate coverage of professional employees.

Nevertheless, because most professionals supervise to some extent, the Act's inclusion of professionals is in tension with its exclusion of supervisors. The Act defines a supervisor as "any individual" with authority to use "independent judgment" "to ... assign ... other employees, or responsibly to direct them." Professionals, by definition, exercise independent judgment, see 29 U.S.C. § 152(12), and most professionals have authority to assign tasks to other employees and "responsibly to direct" their work. See NLRB v. Res–Care, Inc., 705 F.2d 1461, 1465 (CA7 1983) (Posner, J.) ("Most professionals have some supervisory responsibilities in the sense of directing another's work—the lawyer his secretary, the teacher his teacher's aide, the doctor his nurses, the registered nurse her nurse's aide, and so on."). If possession of such authority and the exercise of independent judgment were sufficient to classify an individual as a statutory "supervisor," then few professionals would receive the Act's protections, contrary to Congress' express intention categorically to include "professional employees."

II

A

The NLRB has recognized and endeavored to cope with the tension between the Act's exclusion of supervisors and its inclusion of professional employees. See, e.g., Northcrest Nursing Home, 313 N.L.R.B. No. 54, p. 2 (1993). To harmonize the two prescriptions, the Board has properly focused on the policies that motivated Congress to exclude supervisors. Accounting for the exclusion of supervisors, the Act's drafters emphasized that employers must have the "undivided loyalty" of those persons, "traditionally regarded as part of management," on whom they have bestowed "such genuine management prerogatives as the right to hire or fire, discipline, or make effective recommendations with respect to such action." See Senate Report, at 409–411 (quoted in Northcrest Nursing Home, 313 N.L.R.B. No. 54, p. 1). Accordingly, the NLRB classifies as supervisors individuals who use independent judgment in the exercise of managerial or disciplinary authority over other employees. Id., at 3–4. But because professional employees often are not in management's "front line," the "undivided loyalty" concern is somewhat less urgent for this class of workers. The Board has therefore determined that the exercise of professional judgment "to assign and direct other employees in the interest of providing high quality and efficient service" does not, by itself, "confer supervisory status." Id., at 4.

The NLRB has essayed this exposition of its inquiry: "In determining the existence of supervisory status, the Board must first determine whether the individual possesses any of the 12 indicia of supervisory authority and, if so, whether the exercise of that authority entails 'independent judgment' or is 'merely routine.' If the individual independently exercises supervisory authority, the Board must then determine if that authority is exercised 'in the interest of the employer.'" Id., at 3.

As applied to the health-care field, the Board has reasoned that to fit the formulation "in the interest of the employer," the nurse's superintendence of others must reflect key managerial authority, and not simply control attributable to the nurse's "professional or technical status," direction incidental to "sound patient care." Id., at 3, 6. Cf. Children's Habilitation Center, Inc. v. NLRB, 887 F.2d 130, 134 (CA7 1989) (Posner, J.) (authority does not fit within the "interest of the employer" category if it is "exercised in accordance with professional rather than business norms," i.e., in accordance with "professional standards rather than ... the company's profit-maximizing objectives").

B

The NLRB's "patient care analysis" is not a rudderless rule for nurses, but an application of the approach the Board has pursued in other contexts. The Board has employed the distinction between authority arising from professional knowledge, on one hand, and authority encompassing front-line management prerogatives, on the other, to resolve cases concerning the supervisory status of, for example, doctors,[6] faculty members,[7] pharmacists,[8] librarians,[9] social workers,[10] lawyers,[11] television station directors,[12] and, as this Court has noted, architects and engineers. See NLRB v. Yeshiva University, 444 U.S. 672, 690, n. 30, 100 S.Ct. 856, 866, n. 30, 63 L.Ed.2d 115 (1980) (citing cases). Indicating approval of the NLRB's general approach to the Act's coverage of professionals, the Court stated in *Yeshiva* :

6. See The Door, 297 N.L.R.B. 601, 602, n. 7 (1990) ("routine direction of employees based on a higher level of skill or experience is not evidence of supervisory status").

7. See Detroit College of Business, 296 N.L.R.B. 318, 320 (1989) (professional employees " 'frequently require the ancillary services of nonprofessional employees in order to carry out their professional, not supervisory, responsibilities,' " but "it was not Congress' intention to exclude them from the Act 'by the rote application of the statute without any reference to its purpose or the individual's place on the labor-management spectrum' "), quoting New York Univ., 221 N.L.R.B. 1148, 1156 (1975).

8. See Sav–On Drugs, Inc., 243 N.L.R.B. 859, 862 (1979) ("pharmacy managers do exercise discretion and judgment" in assigning and directing clerks, but "such exercise ... falls clearly within the ambit of their professional responsibilities, and does not constitute the exercise of supervisory authority in the interest of the Employer").

9. See Marymount College of Virginia, 280 N.L.R.B. 486, 489 (1986) (rejecting classification of catalog librarian as a statutory supervisor, although librarian's authority over technician's work included "encouraging productivity, reviewing work for typographical errors, and providing answers to the technician's questions based on the catalog librarian's professional knowledge").

10. See Youth Guidance Center, 263 N.L.R.B. 1330, 1335, and n. 23 (1982) ("senior supervising social workers" and "supervising social workers" not statutory supervisors; "the Board has carefully and consistently avoided applying the statutory definition of 'supervisor' to professionals who give direction to other employees in the exercise of professional judgment which is incidental to the professional's treatment of patients and thus is not the exercise of supervisory authority in the interest of the employer").

11. See Neighborhood Legal Services, Inc., 236 N.L.R.B. 1269, 1273 (1978): "To the extent that the attorneys in question train, assign, or direct work of legal assistants and paralegals for whom they are professionally responsible, we do not find the exercise of such authority to confer supervisory status within the meaning of Section 2(11) of the Act, but rather to be an incident of their professional responsibilities as attorneys and thereby as officers of the court." The Board continued: "We are careful to avoid applying the definition of 'supervisor' to professionals who direct other employees in the exercise of their professional judgment, which direction is incidental to the practice of their profession, and thus is not the exercise of supervisory authority in the interest of the Employer." Id., at 1273, n. 9.

12. See Golden–West Broadcasters–KTLA, 215 N.L.R.B. 760, 762, n. 4 (1974): "An employee with special expertise or training who directs or instructs another in the proper performance of his work for which the former is professionally responsible is not thereby rendered a supervisor.... This is so even when the more senior or more expert employee exercises some independent discretion where, as here, such discretion is based upon special competence or upon specific articulated employer policies."

"The Board has recognized that employees whose decisionmaking is limited to the routine discharge of professional duties in projects to which they have been assigned cannot be excluded from coverage even if union membership arguably may involve some divided loyalty. Only if an employee's activities fall outside the scope of the duties routinely performed by similarly situated professionals will he be found aligned with management. We think these decisions accurately capture the intent of Congress...." Id., at 690, 100 S.Ct., at 866 (footnote omitted).

Notably, in determining whether, in a concrete case, nurses are supervisors within the meaning of the Act, the Board has drawn particularly upon its decisions in "leadperson" controversies. "Leadpersons" include skilled employees who do not qualify as statutory "professionals," but, like professional employees, have some authority to assign or direct other workers. * * *

III

Following the pattern revealed in NLRB decisions, the administrative law judge, affirmed by the Board, determined that the four licensed practical nurses in this case were not supervisors. The ALJ closely examined the organization and operation of nursing care at Heartland and found the nurses' direction of aides "closely akin to the kind of directing done by leadmen or straw bosses, persons ... Congress plainly considered to be 'employees.'" 306 N.L.R.B., at 70. Backing up this finding, the ALJ pointed out that, although the nurses "gave orders (of certain kinds) to aides, and the aides followed those orders," id., at 72, the nurses "spent only a small fraction of their time exercising that authority." Id., at 69. Essentially, the nurses labored "to ensure that the needs of the residents were met," and to that end, they "checked for changes in the health of the residents, administered medicine, ... received status reports from the nurses they relieved, and gave such reports to aides coming on duty and to the nurses' reliefs," pinch-hit for aides in "bathing, feeding or dressing residents," and "handled incoming telephone calls from physicians and from relatives of residents who wanted information about a resident's condition." Ibid.

The ALJ noted, too, that "when setting up the aide-resident assignments," the nurses "followed old patterns"; indeed, "the nurses routinely let the aides decide among themselves which aide was to cover which residents." Id., at 70. The administrator and the director of nursing were "always on call" and nurses in fact called them at their homes "when non-routine matters arose." Id., at 72.

Throughout the hearing, the ALJ reported, he gained "the impression that Heartland's administrator believed that the nurses' views about anything other than hands-on care of the residents were not worth considering." Ibid.... "The actions of Heartland's administrator," the

ALJ concluded, repeatedly and unmistakably demonstrated that "to Heartland's management, Heartland's nurses were just hired hands." Ibid. I see no tenable basis for rejecting the ALJ's ultimate ruling that the nurses' jobs did not entail genuine, front-line supervisory status of the kind that would exclude them from the Act's protection.

IV

A

The phrase ultimately limiting the § 2(11) classification "supervisor" is, as the Court recognizes, "in the interest of the employer." To give that phrase meaning as a discrete and potent limitation, the Board has construed it, in diverse contexts, to convey more than the obligation all employees have to further the employer's business interests, indeed more than the authority to assign and direct other employees pursuant to relevant professional standards. See, e.g., Northcrest Nursing Home, 313 N.L.R.B. No. 54 (1993) (nurses); Youth Guidance Center, 263 N.L.R.B. 1330, 1335, and n. 23 (1982) (social workers); Sav–On Drugs, Inc., 243 N.L.R.B. 859, 862 (1979) (pharmacists); Neighborhood Legal Services, Inc., 236 N.L.R.B. 1269, 1273, and n. 9 (1978) (attorneys).[13]
* * *

Maintaining professional standards of course serves the interest of an enterprise, and the NLRB is hardly blind to that obvious point. See Northcrest Nursing Home, 313 N.L.R.B. No. 54, p. 4 (interest of employer and employees not likely to diverge on charge nurse decisions concerning methods of attending to patients' needs). But "the interest of the employer" may well tug against that of employees, on matters such as "hiring, firing, discharging, and fixing pay"; "in the interest of the employer," persons with authority regarding "things of that sort" are properly ranked "supervisor."

The Court does not deny that the phrase "in the interest of the employer" was intended to limit, not to expand, the category "supervisor."[15] Yet the reading the Court gives to the phrase allows it to provide

13. The Board, as the decisions cited in text demonstrate, takes no unique approach in cases involving nurses. * * * Nor, contrary to the Court's report, see ante, at 2, did counsel for the NLRB admit to deviant interpretation of the phrase, "interest of the employer," in nurses' cases. When asked whether "it is uniquely nurses" who do not act "in the interest of the employer" when attending to "the needs of the customer," counsel replied, "No, it is not uniquely nurses." Tr. of Oral Arg. 52. While counsel continued, when pressed, to say that "the Board has not applied a theory that's phrased in the same terms to other categories of professionals," ibid., counsel appears to have been referring to

the precisely particularized, "patient care" version of the inquiry. Counsel added: "What the Board has done is draw an analogy between ... what nurses do and what other minor supervisory employees do.... The Board's rule in this case is fully consistent with the traditional rule that it has applied." Id., at 53.

15. The Court does maintain, however, that Congress meant to embrace our statement in Packard Motor Car Co. v. NLRB, 330 U.S. 485, 67 S.Ct. 789, 91 L.Ed. 1040 (1947), that "every employee, from the very fact of employment in the master's business, is required to act in his interest." Id., at 488, 67 S.Ct., at 791–792; see ante, at

only one example of workers who would not fit the description: "The language ensures ... that union stewards who adjust grievances are not considered supervisory employees and deprived of the Act's protections." Ante, at 8. Section 2(11)'s expression, "in the interest of the employer," however, modifies all 12 of the listed supervisory activities, not just the adjustment of grievances. Tellingly, the single example the Court gives, "union stewards who adjust grievances," rests on the very distinction the Board has endeavored to apply in all quarters of the workplace: one between "management" interests peculiar to the employer, and the sometimes conflicting interests of employees.[16]

Congress adopted the supervisor exclusion to bind to management those persons "vested with ... genuine management prerogatives," Senate Report, at 4, Legislative History 410, i.e., those with the authority and duty to act specifically "in the interest of the employer" on matters as to which management and labor interests may divide. The Board has been faithful to the task Congress gave it, I believe, in distinguishing the employer's hallmark managerial interest—its interest regarding labor-management relations—from the general interest of the enterprise, shared by its professional and technical employees, in providing high-quality service.

B

In rejecting the Board's approach, the Court relies heavily on NLRB v. Yeshiva University, 444 U.S. 672, 100 S.Ct. 856, 63 L.Ed.2d 115 (1980). The heavy weight placed on Yeshiva is puzzling, for the Court in that case noted with approval the Board's decisions differentiating professional team leaders (or "project captains") from "supervisors."

1782–1783. But Congress' purpose, in enacting § 2(11), was to overturn the Court's holding in *Packard Motor Car*. Thus it is more likely that Congress was taken by Justice Douglas' dissenting view that "acting in the interest of the employer" fits employees who act for management "not only in formulating but also in executing its labor policies." 330 U.S., at 496, 67 S.Ct. at 795. Moreover, Congress had included the phrase, "in the interest of the employer," the year before *Packard Motor Car*, in a predecessor bill to the Labor Management Relations Act that defined the term "supervisor" almost identically. See n. 14, supra. Finally, the Court acknowledged in *Packard Motor Car* that the phrase "interest of the employer" may also be read more narrowly, in contradistinction to employees' interests in improving their compensation and working conditions. 330 U.S., at 489, 490, 67 S.Ct., at 792. *Packard Motor Car*, then, does not support the conclusion that the words, "interest of the employer," have a plain meaning inconsistent with the interpretation the Board has given them in supervisor cases.

16. The Court suggests that the Board has "read the responsible direction portion of § 2(11) out of the statute in nurse cases." Ante, at 8 (referring to the words "responsibly to direct" in § 2(11)'s list of supervisory activities). The author of the amendment that inserted those words explained, however, that persons having authority "responsibly to direct" other employees are persons with "essential managerial duties" who rank "above the grade of 'straw bosses, lead men, set-up men, and other minor supervisory employees,' as enumerated in the Senate report." 93 Cong. Rec. 4804 (1947) (remarks of Sen. Flanders), Legislative History 1303. As explained above, the Board has used this same analogy to straw bosses and leadpersons to determine whether particular nurses are supervisors. See supra, at 10.

* * * No plausible equation can be made between the self-governing Yeshiva faculty, on one hand, and on the other, the licensed practical nurses involved in this case, with their limited authority to assign and direct the work of nurses' aides, pursuant to professional standards.

V

The Court's opinion has implications far beyond the nurses involved in this case. If any person who may use independent judgment to assign tasks to others or direct their work is a supervisor, then few professionals employed by organizations subject to the Act will receive its protections.[17] The Board's endeavor to reconcile the inclusion of professionals with the exclusion of supervisors, in my view, is not just "rational and consistent with the Act," NLRB v. Curtin Matheson Scientific, Inc., 494 U.S. 775, 796, 110 S.Ct. 1542, 1554, 108 L.Ed.2d 801 (1990); it is required by the Act. I would therefore reverse the contrary judgment of the Court of Appeals.

Page 107. Add to the Problems for Discussion:

7. In *Health Care & Retirement Corp., supra,* Justice Kennedy rejects the materiality of a Senate Committee Report that, he said, expressed "apparent approval" of the Board's approach to the supervisory status of nurses when the health care amendments were fashioned in 1974: The Committee Report cannot color what Congress meant in 1947, he opined, and, an "isolated statement" does not reveal the intent of the legislature. What the Committee Report said was:

> Various organizations representing health care professionals have urged an amendment to Section 2(11) of the Act so as to exclude such professionals from the definition of "supervisor." The Committee has studied this definition with particular reference to health care professionals, such as registered nurses, interns, residents, fellows, and salaried physicians and concludes that the proposed amendment is unnecessary because of existing Board decisions. The Committee notes that the Board has carefully avoided applying the definition of "supervisor" to a health care professional who gives direction to other employees in the exercise of professional judgment, which direction is incidental the [sic] the professional's treatment of patients, and thus is not the exercise of supervisory authority in the interest of the employer.

Is the above immaterial to the judicial disposition of the Board's approach to the question?

17. As the Board repeatedly warned in its presentations to this Court: "If all it took to be a statutory supervisor were a showing that an employee gives discretionary direction to an aide, even though done pursuant to the customary norms of the profession, the coverage of professionals would be a virtual nullity." Brief for the National Labor Relations Board 27; see also id., at 12, Reply Brief for the National Labor Relations Board 7–8.

8.   Justice Kennedy says that the question before the Court in that case was "narrow" and that the Court's resolution of it "will have almost no effect outside . . . [the] context of health care." Justice Ginsberg disagrees. Which is more persuasive? Note that while all occupations grew by 19% in the period 1979–1992, professional and technical jobs grew by 43% and 58% respectively in that period; and are expected to exceed the rate of growth for all occupations for the immediate future.

Part Two

THE ESTABLISHMENT OF THE COLLECTIVE BARGAINING RELATIONSHIP

I. PROTECTION OF THE RIGHT OF SELF–ORGANIZATION

A. INTERFERENCE, RESTRAINT AND COERCION

1. *Restrictions on Solicitation and Distribution*

Page 128. Substitute the following case for *Babcock & Wilcox*:

LECHMERE, INC. v. NATIONAL LABOR RELATIONS BOARD

___ U.S. ___, 112 S.Ct. 841, 117 L.Ed.2d 79 (1992).

JUSTICE THOMAS delivered the opinion of the Court.

This case requires us to clarify the relationship between the rights of employees under § 7 of the National Labor Relations Act, 49 Stat. 452, as amended, 29 U.S.C. § 157, and the property rights of their employers.

I

This case stems from the efforts of Local 919 of the United Food and Commercial Workers Union, AFL–CIO, to organize employees at a retail store in Newington, Connecticut, owned and operated by petitioner Lechmere, Inc. The store is located in the Lechmere Shopping Plaza, which occupies a roughly rectangular tract measuring approximately 880 feet from north to south and 740 feet from east to west. Lechmere's store is situated at the Plaza's south end, with the main parking lot to its north. A strip of 13 smaller "satellite stores" not owned by Lechmere runs along the west side of the Plaza, facing the parking lot. To the Plaza's east (where the main entrance is located) runs the Berlin Turnpike, a four-lane divided highway. The parking lot, however, does not abut the Turnpike; they are separated by a 46–foot–wide grassy strip, broken only by the Plaza's entrance. The parking lot is owned jointly by Lechmere and the developer of the satellite stores. The grassy

15

strip is public property (except for a four-foot-wide band adjoining the parking lot, which belongs to Lechmere).

The union began its campaign to organize the store's 200 employees, none of whom was represented by a union, in June 1987. After a full-page advertisement in a local newspaper drew little response, nonemployee union organizers entered Lechmere's parking lot and began placing handbills on the windshields of cars parked in a corner of the lot used mostly by employees. Lechmere's manager immediately confronted the organizers, informed them that Lechmere prohibited solicitation or handbill distribution of any kind on its property,[1] and asked them to leave. They did so, and Lechmere personnel removed the handbills. The union organizers renewed this handbilling effort in the parking lot on several subsequent occasions; each time they were asked to leave and the handbills were removed. The organizers then relocated to the public grassy strip, from where they attempted to pass out handbills to cars entering the lot during hours (before opening and after closing) when the drivers were assumed to be primarily store employees. For one month, the union organizers returned daily to the grassy strip to picket Lechmere; after that, they picketed intermittently for another six months. They also recorded the license plate numbers of cars parked in the employee parking area; with the cooperation of the Connecticut Department of Motor Vehicles, they thus secured the names and addresses of some 41 nonsupervisory employees (roughly 20% of the store's total). The union sent four mailings to these employees; it also made some attempts to contact them by phone or home visits. These mailings and visits resulted in one signed union authorization card.

Alleging that Lechmere had violated the National Labor Relations Act by barring the nonemployee organizers from its property, the union filed an unfair labor practice charge with respondent National Labor Relations Board (Board). Applying the criteria set forth by the Board in *Fairmont Hotel Co.*, 282 N.L.R.B. 139 (1986), an administrative law judge (ALJ) ruled in the union's favor. 295 N.L.R.B. No. 15, ALJ slip op. (1988). He recommended that Lechmere be ordered, among other things, to cease and desist from barring the union organizers from the parking lot and to post in conspicuous places in the store signs proclaiming in part:

---

1. Lechmere had established this policy several years prior to the union's organizing efforts. The store's official policy statement provided, in relevant part:

"Non-associates [i.e., nonemployees] are prohibited from soliciting and distributing literature at all times anywhere on Company property, including parking lots. Non-associates have no right of access to the non-working areas and only to the public and selling areas of the store in connection with its public use." Brief for Petitioner 7.

On each door to the store Lechmere had posted a 6 in. by 8 in. sign reading: "TO THE PUBLIC. No Soliciting, Canvassing, Distribution of Literature or Trespassing by Non–Employees in or on Premises." App. 115–116. Lechmere consistently enforced this policy inside the store as well as on the parking lot (against, among others, the Salvation Army and the Girl Scouts).

"WE WILL NOT prohibit representatives of Local 919, United Food and Commercial Workers, AFL–CIO ("the Union") or any other labor organization, from distributing union literature to our employees in the parking lot adjacent to our store in Newington, Connecticut, nor will we attempt to cause them to be removed from our parking lot for attempting to do so." *Id.,* App. to ALJ slip op.

The Board affirmed the ALJ's judgment and adopted the recommended order, applying the analysis set forth in its opinion in *Jean Country,* 291 N.L.R.B. 11 (1988), which had by then replaced the short-lived *Fairmont Hotel* approach. 295 N.L.R.B. No. 15, Board slip op. A divided panel of the United States Court of Appeals for the First Circuit denied Lechmere's petition for review and enforced the Board's order. 914 F.2d 313 (1990). This Court granted certiorari, 499 U.S. ___, 111 S.Ct. 1305, 113 L.Ed.2d 240 (1991).

II

A

Section 7 of the NLRA provides in relevant part that "[e]mployees shall have the right to self-organization, to form, join, or assist labor organizations." 29 U.S.C. § 157. Section 8(a)(1) of the Act, in turn, makes it an unfair labor practice for an employer "to interfere with, restrain, or coerce employees in the exercise of rights guaranteed in [§ 7]." 29 U.S.C. § 158(a)(1). By its plain terms, thus, the NLRA confers rights only on *employees,* not on unions or their nonemployee organizers. In NLRB v. Babcock & Wilcox Co., 351 U.S. 105, 76 S.Ct. 679, 100 L.Ed.2d 975 (1956), however, we recognized that insofar as the employees' "right of self-organization depends in some measure on [their] ability * * * to learn the advantages of self-organization from others," id., at 113, 76 S.Ct., at 684, § 7 of the NLRA may, in certain limited circumstances, restrict an employer's right to exclude nonemployee union organizers from his property. It is the nature of those circumstances that we explore today.

Babcock arose out of union attempts to organize employees at a factory located on an isolated 100–acre tract. The company had a policy against solicitation and distribution of literature on its property, which it enforced against all groups. About 40% of the company's employees lived in a town of some 21,000 persons near the factory; the remainder were scattered over a 30–mile radius. Almost all employees drove to work in private cars and parked in a company lot that adjoined the fenced-in plant area. The parking lot could be reached only by a 100–yard–long driveway connecting it to a public highway. This driveway was mostly on company-owned land, except where it crossed a 31–foot–wide public right-of-way adjoining the highway. Union organizers attempted to distribute literature from this right-of-way. The union also secured the names and addresses of some 100 employees (20% of the total), and sent them three mailings. Still other employees were contacted by telephone or home visit.

The union successfully challenged the company's refusal to allow nonemployee organizers onto its property before the Board. While acknowledging that there were alternative, nontrespassory means whereby the union could communicate with employees, the Board held that contact at the workplace was preferable. *The Babcock & Wilcox Co.,* 109 N.L.R.B. 485, 493–494 (1954). "[T]he right to distribute is not absolute, but must be accommodated to the circumstances. Where it is impossible or unreasonably difficult for a union to distribute organizational literature to employees entirely off of the employer's premises, distribution on a nonworking area, such as the parking lot and the walkways between the parking lot and the gate, may be warranted." Id., at 493. Concluding that traffic on the highway made it unsafe for the union organizers to distribute leaflets from the right-of-way, and that contacts through the mails, on the streets, at employees' homes, and over the telephone would be ineffective, the Board ordered the company to allow the organizers to distribute literature on its parking lot and exterior walkways. Id., at 486–487.

The Court of Appeals for the Fifth Circuit refused to enforce the Board's order, NLRB v. Babcock & Wilcox Co., 222 F.2d 316 (1955), and this Court affirmed. While recognizing that "the Board has the responsibility of 'applying the Act's general prohibitory language in the light of the infinite combinations of events which might be charged as violative of its terms,'" 351 U.S., at 111–112, 76 S.Ct., at 683–684 (quoting NLRB v. Stowe Spinning Co., 336 U.S. 226, 231, 69 S.Ct. 541, 543, 93 L.Ed. 638 (1949)), we explained that the Board had erred by failing to make the critical distinction between the organizing activities of employees (to whom § 7 guarantees the right of self-organization) and nonemployees (to whom § 7 applies only derivatively). Thus, while "[n]o restriction may be placed on the employees' right to discuss self-organization among themselves, unless the employer can demonstrate that a restriction is necessary to maintain production or discipline," 351 U.S., at 113, 76 S.Ct., at 684 (emphasis added) (citing Republic Aviation Corp. v. NLRB, 324 U.S. 793, 803, 65 S.Ct. 982, 987, 89 L.Ed. 1372 (1945)), "no such obligation is owed nonemployee organizers," 351 U.S., at 113, 76 S.Ct., at 684. As a rule, then, an employer cannot be compelled to allow distribution of union literature by nonemployee organizers on his property. As with many other rules, however, we recognized an exception. Where "the location of a plant and the living quarters of the employees place the employees beyond the reach of reasonable union efforts to communicate with them," ibid., employers' property rights may be "required to yield to the extent needed to permit communication of information on the right to organize," id., at 112, 76 S.Ct., at 684.

Although we have not had occasion to apply *Babcock's* analysis in the ensuing decades, we have described it in cases arising in related contexts. Two such cases, Central Hardware Co. v. NLRB, 407 U.S. 539, 92 S.Ct. 2238, 33 L.Ed.2d 122 (1972), and Hudgens v. NLRB, 424 U.S. 507, 96 S.Ct. 1029, 47 L.Ed.2d 196 (1976), involved activity by union supporters on employer-owned property. The principal issue in both cases was whether, based upon Food Employees v. Logan Valley Plaza, Inc., 391 U.S. 308, 88 S.Ct. 1601, 20 L.Ed.2d 603 (1968), the First Amendment protected such activities. In both cases we rejected the First Amendment claims, and in *Hudgens* we made it clear that *Logan Valley* was overruled. Having decided the cases on constitutional grounds, we remanded them to the Board for consideration of the union supporters' § 7 claims under *Babcock*. In both cases, we quoted approvingly *Babcock* 's admonition that accommodation between employees' § 7 rights and employers' property rights "must be obtained with as little destruction of the one as is consistent with the maintenance of the other," 351 U.S., at 112, 76 S.Ct., at 684. See *Central Hardware,* supra, at 544, 92 S.Ct., at 2241; *Hudgens,* supra, at 521, 522, 96 S.Ct., at 1037, 1038. There is no hint in *Hudgens* and *Central Hardware,* however, that our invocation of *Babcock* 's language of "accommodation" was intended to repudiate or modify *Babcock* 's holding that an employer need not accommodate nonemployee organizers unless the employees are otherwise inaccessible. Indeed, in *Central Hardware* we expressly noted that nonemployee organizers cannot claim even a limited right of access to a nonconsenting employer's property until "[a]fter the requisite need for access to the employer's property has been shown." 407 U.S., at 545, 92 S.Ct., at 2241.

If there was any question whether *Central Hardware* and *Hudgens* changed § 7 law, it should have been laid to rest by Sears, Roebuck & Co. v. San Diego County District Council of Carpenters, 436 U.S. 180, 98 S.Ct. 1745, 56 L.Ed.2d 209 (1978). As in *Central Hardware* and *Hudgens,* the substantive § 7 issue in *Sears* was a subsidiary one; the case's primary focus was on the circumstances under which the NLRA pre-empts state law. Among other things, we held in *Sears* that arguable § 7 claims do not pre-empt state trespass law, in large part because the trespasses of nonemployee union organizers are "far more likely to be unprotected than protected," 436 U.S., at 205; permitting state courts to evaluate such claims, therefore, does not "create an unacceptable risk of interference with conduct which the Board, and a court reviewing the Board's decision, would find protected," ibid. This holding was based upon the following interpretation of *Babcock:*

> "While *Babcock* indicates that an employer may not always bar nonemployee union organizers from his property, his right to do so remains the general rule. To gain access, the union has the burden of showing that no other reasonable means of communicating its organizational message to the employees exists or that the employer's access rules discriminate against union solicitation. That the burden imposed on the union is a heavy one is evidenced by the fact

[handwritten marginnote: Non–Employees can't get access unless :]

that the balance struck by the Board and the courts under the *Babcock* accommodation principle has rarely been in favor of trespassory organizational activity." 436 U.S., at 205, 98 S.Ct., at 1761 (emphasis added; footnotes omitted).

We further noted that, in practice, nonemployee organizational trespassing had generally been prohibited except where "unique obstacles" prevented nontrespassory methods of communication with the employees. Id., at 205–206, n. 41, 98 S.Ct., at 1761–1762, n. 41.

B

Jean Country, as noted above, represents the Board's latest attempt to implement the rights guaranteed by § 7. It sets forth a three-factor balancing test:

> "[I]n all access cases our essential concern will be [1] the degree of impairment of the Section 7 right if access should be denied, as it balances against [2] the degree of impairment of the private property right if access should be granted. We view the consideration of [3] the availability of reasonably effective alternative means as especially significant in this balancing process." 291 N.L.R.B., at 14.

The Board conceded that this analysis was unlikely to foster certainty and predictability in this corner of the law, but declared that "as with other legal questions involving multiple factors, the 'nature of the problem, as revealed by unfolding variant situations, inevitably involves an evolutionary process for its rational response, not a quick, definitive formula as a comprehensive answer.'" Ibid. (quoting Electrical Workers v. NLRB, 366 U.S. 667, 674, 81 S.Ct. 1285, 1289, 6 L.Ed.2d 592 (1961)).

Citing its role "as the agency with responsibility for implementing national labor policy," the Board maintains in this case that *Jean Country* is a reasonable interpretation of the NLRA entitled to judicial deference. Brief for Respondent 18, and n. 8; Tr. of Oral Arg. 22. It is certainly true, and we have long recognized, that the Board has the "special function of applying the general provisions of the Act to the complexities of industrial life." NLRB v. Erie Resistor Corp., 373 U.S. 221, 236, 83 S.Ct. 1139, 1149, 10 L.Ed.2d 308 (1963); see also Phelps Dodge Corp. v. NLRB, 313 U.S. 177, 196–197, 61 S.Ct. 845, 853–854, 85 L.Ed. 1271 (1941). Like other administrative agencies, the NLRB is entitled to judicial deference when it interprets an ambiguous provision of a statute that it administers. See, *e.g.*, NLRB v. Food & Commercial Workers, 484 U.S. 112, 123, 108 S.Ct. 413, 420, 98 L.Ed.2d 429 (1987); cf. Chevron U.S.A. Inc. v. Natural Resources Defense Council, Inc., 467 U.S. 837, 842–843, 104 S.Ct. 2778, 2781–2782, 81 L.Ed.2d 694 (1984).

Before we reach any issue of deference to the Board, however, we must first determine whether *Jean Country*—at least as applied to nonemployee organizational trespassing—is consistent with our past interpretation of § 7. "Once we have determined a statute's clear meaning, we adhere to that determination under the doctrine of *stare decisis,* and we judge an agency's later interpretation of the statute against our prior determination of the statute's meaning." Maislin Industries, U.S., Inc. v. Primary Steel, Inc., 497 U.S. __, __, 110 S.Ct. 2759, 2768, 111 L.Ed.2d 94 (1990).

In *Babcock,* as explained above, we held that the Act drew a distinction "of substance," 351 U.S., at 113, 76 S.Ct., at 684, between the union activities of employees and nonemployees. In cases involving *employee* activities, we noted with approval, the Board "balanced the conflicting interests of employees to receive information on self-organization on the company's property from fellow employees during nonworking time, with the employer's right to control the use of his property." Id., at 109–110, 76 S.Ct., at 682–683. In cases involving *nonemployee* activities (like those at issue in *Babcock* itself), however, the Board was not permitted to engage in that same balancing (and we reversed the Board for having done so). By reversing the Board's interpretation of the statute for failing to distinguish between the organizing activities of employees and nonemployees, we were saying, in *Chevron* terms, that § 7 speaks to the issue of nonemployee access to an employer's property. *Babcock* 's teaching is straightforward: § 7 simply does not protect nonemployee union organizers *except* in the rare case where "the inaccessibility of employees makes ineffective the reasonable attempts by nonemployees to communicate with them through the usual channels," 351 U.S., at 112, 76 S.Ct., at 684. Our reference to "reasonable" attempts was nothing more than a commonsense recognition that unions need not engage in extraordinary feats to communicate with inaccessible employees—*not* an endorsement of the view (which we expressly rejected) that the Act protects "reasonable" trespasses. Where reasonable alternative means of access exist, § 7's guarantees do not authorize trespasses by nonemployee organizers, *even* (as we noted in *Babcock,* id., at 112, 76 S.Ct., at 684) "under * * * reasonable regulations" established by the Board.

Jean Country, which applies broadly to "all access cases," 291 N.L.R.B., at 14, misapprehends this critical point. Its principal inspiration derives not from *Babcock,* but from the following sentence in *Hudgens:* "[T]he locus of th[e] accommodation [between § 7 rights and private property rights] may fall at differing points along the spectrum depending on the nature and strength of the respective § 7 rights and private property rights asserted in any given context." 424 U.S., at 522, 96 S.Ct. 1037. From this sentence the Board concluded that it was appropriate to approach every case by balancing § 7 rights against property rights, with alternative means of access thrown in as nothing more than an "especially significant" consideration. As explained above, however, *Hudgens* did not purport to modify *Babcock,* much less to alter it fundamentally in the way *Jean Country* suggests. To say that our cases require accommodation between employees' and employers' rights is a true but incomplete statement, for the cases also go far in establishing the *locus* of that accommodation where nonemployee organizing is at issue. So long as nonemployee union organizers have reasonable access to employees outside an employer's property, the requisite accommodation has taken place. It is *only* where such access is infeasible that it becomes necessary and proper to take the accommodation inquiry to a second level, balancing the employees' and employers' rights as described in the *Hudgens* dictum. See *Sears,* 436 U.S., at 205, 98 S.Ct., at 1761; *Central Hardware,* 407 U.S., at 545, 92 S.Ct., at 2241. At least as applied to nonemployees, *Jean Country* impermissibly conflates these two stages of the inquiry—thereby significantly eroding *Babcock*'s general rule that "an employer may validly post his property against nonemployee distribution of union literature," 351 U.S., at 112, 76 S.Ct., at 684. We reaffirm that general rule today, and reject the Board's attempt to recast it as a multifactor balancing test.

C

The threshold inquiry in this case, then, is whether the facts here justify application of *Babcock*'s inaccessibility exception. The ALJ below observed that "the facts herein convince me that reasonable alternative means [of communicating with Lechmere's employees] *were* available to the Union," 295 N.L.R.B. No. 15, ALJ slip op., at 9 (emphasis added).[2] Reviewing the ALJ's decision under *Jean Country,* however, the Board reached a different conclusion on this point, asserting that "there was no reasonable, effective alternative means available for the Union to communicate its message to [Lechmere's] employees." 295 N.L.R.B. No. 15, Board slip op., at 4–5.

We cannot accept the Board's conclusion, because it "rest[s] on erroneous legal foundations," *Babcock,* 351 U.S., at 112, 76 S.Ct., at 684; see also NLRB v. Brown, 380 U.S. 278, 290–292, 85 S.Ct. 980, 987–988, 13 L.Ed.2d 839 (1965). As we have explained, the exception to *Babcock*'s rule is a narrow one. It does not apply wherever nontrespassory access to employees may be cumbersome or less-than-ideally effective, but only where "the *location of a plant and the living quarters of the employees* place the employees *beyond the reach* of reasonable union efforts to communicate with them," 351 U.S., at 113, 76 S.Ct., at 684 (emphasis added). Classic examples include logging camps, see NLRB v.

---

2. Under the (pre-*Jean Country*) *Fairmont Hotel* analysis applied by the ALJ, it was only where the employees' § 7 rights and an employer's property rights were deemed "relatively equal in strength," *Fairmont Hotel Co.* 282 N.L.R.B. 139, 142 (1986), that the adequacy of nontrespassory means of communication became relevant.

Because the ALJ found that the § 7 rights involved here outweighed Lechmere's property rights, he had no need to address the latter issue. He did so, he explained, only because of the possibility that his evaluation of the relative weights of the rights might not be upheld. 295 N.L.R.B. No. 15, ALJ slip op., at 9.

Lake Superior Lumber Corp., 167 F.2d 147 (CA6 1948); mining camps, see *Alaska Barite Co.,* 197 N.L.R.B. 1023 (1972), enforced mem., 83 LRRM 2992 (CA9), cert. denied, 414 U.S. 1025 (1973); and mountain resort hotels, see NLRB v. S & H Grossinger's Inc., 372 F.2d 26 (CA2 1967). *Babcock*'s exception was crafted precisely to protect the § 7 rights of those employees who, by virtue of their employment, are isolated from the ordinary flow of information that characterizes our society. The union's burden of establishing such isolation is, as we have explained, "a heavy one," *Sears,* supra, at 205, 98 S.Ct. 1761, and one not satisfied by mere conjecture or the expression of doubts concerning the effectiveness of nontrespassory means of communication.

The Board's conclusion in this case that the union had no reasonable means short of trespass to make Lechmere's employees aware of its organizational efforts is based on a misunderstanding of the limited scope of this exception. Because the employees do not reside on Lechmere's property, they are presumptively not "beyond the reach," *Babcock,* supra, at 113, 76 S.Ct. at 684, of the union's message. Although the employees live in a large metropolitan area (Greater Hartford), that fact does not in itself render them "inaccessible" in the sense contemplated by *Babcock.* See *Monogram Models, Inc.,* 192 N.L.R.B. 705, 706 (1971). Their accessibility is suggested by the union's success in contacting a substantial percentage of them directly, via mailings, phone calls, and home visits. Such direct contact, of course, is not a necessary element of "reasonably effective" communication; signs or advertising also may suffice. In this case, the union tried advertising in local newspapers; the Board said that this was not reasonably effective because it was expensive and might not reach the employees. 295 N.L.R.B. No. 15, Board slip op., at 4–5. Whatever the merits of that conclusion, other alternative means of communication were readily available. Thus, signs (displayed, for example, from the public grassy strip adjoining Lechmere's parking lot) would have informed the employees about the union's organizational efforts. (Indeed, union organizers picketed the shopping center's main entrance for months as employees came and went every day.) *Access* to employees, not *success* in winning them over, is the critical issue—although success, or lack thereof, may be relevant in determining whether reasonable access exists. Because the union in this case failed to establish the existence of any "unique obstacles," *Sears,* 436 U.S., at 205–206, n. 41, 98 S.Ct., at 1761–1762, n. 41, that frustrated access to Lechmere's employees, the Board erred in concluding that Lechmere committed an unfair labor practice by barring the nonemployee organizers from its property.

* * *

The judgment of the First Circuit is therefore reversed, and enforcement of the Board's order denied.

It is so ordered.

Whit & Blackmun Dissenting :

JUSTICE WHITE, with whom JUSTICE BLACKMUN joins, dissenting. * * *

In the case before us, the Court holds that *Babcock* itself stated the correct accommodation between property and organizational rights; it interprets that case as construing §§ 7 and 8(a)(1) of the National Labor Relations Act to contain a general rule forbidding third-party access, subject only to a limited exception where the union demonstrates that the location of the employer's place of business and the living quarters of the employees place the employees beyond the reach of reasonable efforts to communicate with them. The Court refuses to enforce the Board's order in this case, which rested on its prior decision in *Jean Country,* 291 N.L.R.B. 11 (1988), because, in the Court's view, *Jean Country* revealed that the Board misunderstood the basic holding in *Babcock,* as well as the narrowness of the exception to the general rule announced in that case.

For several reasons, the Court errs in this case. First, that *Babcock* stated that inaccessibility would be a reason to grant access does not indicate that there would be no other circumstance that would warrant entry to the employer's parking lot and would satisfy the Court's admonition that accommodation must be made with as little destruction of property rights as is consistent with the right of employees to learn the advantages of self-organization from others. Of course the union must show that its "reasonable efforts", without access, will not permit proper communication with employees. But I cannot believe that the Court in *Babcock* intended to confine the reach of such general considerations to the single circumstance that the Court now seizes upon. If the Court in *Babcock* indicated that nonemployee access to a logging camp would be required, it did not say that only in such situations could nonemployee access be permitted. Nor did *Babcock* require the Board to ignore the substantial difference between the entirely private parking lot of a secluded manufacturing plant and a shopping center lot which is open to the public without substantial limitation. Nor indeed did *Babcock* indicate that the Board could not consider the fact that employees' residences are scattered throughout a major metropolitan area; *Babcock* itself relied on the fact that the employees in that case lived in a compact area which made them easily accessible.

Moreover, the Court in *Babcock* recognized that actual communication with nonemployee organizers, not mere notice that an organizing campaign exists, is necessary to vindicate § 7 rights. 351 U.S., at 113, 76 S.Ct., at 684. If employees are entitled to learn from others the advantages of self-organization, ibid., it is singularly unpersuasive to suggest that the union has sufficient access for this purpose by being

<u>able to hold up signs from a public grassy strip adjacent to the highway leading to the parking lot.</u>

Second, the Court's reading of *Babcock* is not the reading of that case reflected in later opinions of the Court. We have consistently declined to define the principle of *Babcock* as a general rule subject to narrow exceptions, and have instead repeatedly reaffirmed that the standard is a neutral and flexible rule of accommodation. In Central Hardware Co. v. NLRB, 407 U.S. 539, 544, 92 S.Ct. 2238, 2241, 33 L.Ed.2d 122 (1972), we explicitly stated that the "guiding principle" for adjusting conflicts between § 7 rights and property rights enunciated in *Babcock* is that contained in its neutral "accommodation" language. Hudgens v. NLRB, 424 U.S. 507, 96 S.Ct. 1029, 47 L.Ed.2d 196 (1976), gave this Court the occasion to provide direct guidance to the NLRB on this issue. In that case, we emphasized *Babcock*'s necessity-to-accommodate admonition, pointed out the differences between *Babcock* and *Hudgens,* and left the balance to be struck by the Board. "The locus of that accommodation * * * may fall at differing points along the spectrum depending on the nature and strength of the respective § 7 rights and private property rights asserted in any given context. In each generic situation, the primary responsibility for making this accommodation must rest with the Board in the first instance." 424 U.S., at 522, 96 S.Ct., at 1038. <u>*Hudgens* did not purport to modify *Babcock* and surely indicates that *Babcock* announced a more flexible rule than the narrow, iron-clad rule that the Court now extracts from that case. If *Babcock* means what the Court says it means, there is no doubt tension between that case and *Hudgens*. If that is so, *Hudgens* as the later pronouncement on the question, issued as a directive to the Board, should be controlling.</u>[1]

---

1. In Sears, Roebuck & Co. v. Carpenters, 436 U.S. 180, 98 S.Ct. 1745, 56 L.Ed.2d 209 (1978), we once again reaffirmed the accommodation language, as refined by *Hudgens*. <u>The language we quoted in text in *Sears* was that of *Hudgens,* not *Babcock.*</u> Thus, notwithstanding the majority's assertion that *Sears* laid to rest any question whether *Hudgens* changed § 7 law, ante, at 846, <u>*Sears* in fact endorsed the *Hudgens* refinement of the § 7 property rights accommodation analysis, recognizing that the accommodation may fall at differing points, and that the Board should evaluate the nature and strength of property and § 7 rights.</u>

Sears was a pre-emption case, and only peripherally involved substantive principles of § 7 accommodation by the NLRB. Unlike *Hudgens,* in *Sears* we did not remand for ultimate disposition by the Board, but rather remanded to the state court. <u>Thus, we had no occasion in that case, as we did in *Hudgens,* to provide further guidance to the Board in its interpretation of the NLRA</u> (and of *Babcock, Hudgens,* and other decisions). Our "general rule" language recounting the rarity of NLRB decisions allowing access should be taken for what it was, a descriptive recounting of what "experience * * * teaches", *Sears,* supra, at 205, about the way that the NLRB had exercised its authority, and not any prescription from this Court as to the analysis the Board should apply. That analysis had already been cited. 436 U.S., at 204, 98 S.Ct., at 1761. <u>Contrary to what the majority suggests, *Sears* did not clear up any false ambiguity created by *Hudgens;* to the extent that it addressed the relevant issues, it reaffirmed the refined and more detailed guidance offered by *Hudgens*.</u>

The majority today asserts that "[i]t is *only* where [reasonable alternative] access is infeasible that it becomes necessary and proper to take the accommodation inquiry to a second level, balancing the employees' and employers' rights." Ante, at 848. Our cases, however, are more consistent with the *Jean Country* view that reasonable alternatives are an important factor in finding the least destructive accommodation between § 7 and property rights. The majority's assertion to this effect notwithstanding, our cases do not require a prior showing regarding reasonable alternatives as a precondition to any inquiry balancing the two rights. The majority can hardly fault the Board for a decision which "conflates * * * two stages of the inquiry," ante, at 848, when no two-stage inquiry has been set forth by this Court.

Third, and more fundamentally, *Babcock* is at odds with modern concepts of deference to an administrative agency charged with administering a statute. See Chevron U.S.A. Inc. v. Natural Resources Defense Council, Inc., 467 U.S. 837, 104 S.Ct. 2778, 81 L.Ed.2d 694 (1984). When reviewing an agency's construction of a statute, we ask first whether Congress has spoken to the precise question at issue. *Chevron*, supra, at 842, 104 S.Ct., at 2781. If it has not, we do not simply impose our own construction on the statute; rather, we determine if the agency's view is based on a permissible construction of the statute. 467 U.S., at 843, 104 S.Ct., at 2781. *Babcock* did not ask if Congress had specifically spoken to the issue of access by third parties and did not purport to explain how the NLRA specifically dealt with what the access rule should be where third parties are concerned. If it had made such an inquiry, the only basis for finding statutory language that settled the issue would have been the language of § 7, which speaks only of the rights of employees; i.e., the Court might have found that § 7 extends no access rights at all to union representatives. But *Babcock* itself recognized that employees have a right to learn from others about self-organization, 351 U.S., at 113, 76 S.Ct., at 685, and itself recognized that in some circumstances, §§ 7 and 8 required the employer to grant the union access to parking lots. So have later Courts and so does the Court today.

That being the case, the *Babcock* Court should have recognized that the Board's construction of the statute was a permissible one and deferred to its judgment. Instead, the Court simply announced that as far as access is concerned, third parties must be treated less favorably than employees. Furthermore, after issuing a construction of the statute different from that of the Board, rather than remanding to the Board to determine how third parties should be dealt with, the *Babcock* Court essentially took over the agency's job, not only by detailing how union organizer access should be determined but also by announcing that the records before it did not contain facts that would satisfy the newly coined access rule.

Had a case like *Babcock* been first presented for decision under the law governing in 1991, I am quite sure that we would have deferred to the Board, or at least attempted to find sounder ground for not doing so. Furthermore, had the Board ruled that third parties must be treated differently than employees and held them to the standard that the Court now says *Babcock* mandated, it is clear enough that we also would have accepted that construction of the statute. But it is also clear, at least to me, that if the Board later reworked that rule in the manner of *Jean Country,* we would also accept the Board's change of mind. See NLRB v. Curtin Matheson Scientific, Inc., 494 U.S., at ___, 110 S.Ct., at ___; NLRB v. J. Weingarten, Inc., 420 U.S. 251, 265–266, 95 S.Ct. 959, 967–968, 43 L.Ed.2d 171 (1975).

As it is, the Court's decision fails to recognize that *Babcock* is at odds with the current law of deference to administrative agencies and compounds that error by adopting the substantive approach *Babcock* applied lock, stock, and barrel. And unnecessarily so, for, as indicated above, *Babcock* certainly does not require the reading the Court gives it today, and in any event later cases have put a gloss on *Babcock* that the Court should recognize.

Finally, the majority commits a concluding error in its application of the outdated standard of *Babcock* to review the Board's conclusion that there were no reasonable alternative means available to the union. Unless the Court today proposes to turn back time in the law of judicial deference to administrative agencies, the proper standard for judicial review of the Board's rulings is no longer for " 'erroneous legal foundations,' " ante at 11, but for rationality and consistency with the statute. Litton Financial Printing Div. v. NLRB, 501 U.S. ___, 111 S.Ct. 2215, 115 L.Ed.2d 177 (1991); *NLRB v. Curtin Matheson Scientific, Inc.,* supra; Fall River Dyeing & Finishing Corp. v. NLRB, 482 U.S. 27, 42, 107 S.Ct. 2225, 96 L.Ed.2d 22 (1987); NLRB v. Financial Institution Employees, 475 U.S. 192, 202, 106 S.Ct. 1007, 1012, 89 L.Ed.2d 151 (1986); *Beth Israel Hospital,* 437 U.S., at 501, 98 S.Ct., at 2473. "The judicial role is narrow: * * * the Board's application of the rule, if supported by substantial evidence on the record as a whole, must be enforced." Ibid. The Board's conclusion as to reasonable alternatives in this case was supported by evidence in the record. Even if the majority cannot defer to that application, because of the depth of its objections to the rule applied by the NLRB, it should remand to the Board for a decision under the rule it arrives at today, rather than sitting in the place Congress has assigned to the Board.

The more basic legal error of the majority today, like that of the Court of Appeals in *Chevron,* is to adopt a static judicial construction of the statute when Congress has not commanded that construction. Cf. *Chevron,* supra, at 842, 104 S.Ct., at 2781. By leaving open the question of how § 7 and private property rights were to be accommodated under the NLRA, Congress delegated authority over that issue to the Board, and a court should not substitute its own judgment for a reasonable construction by the Board. Cf. id., at 844, 104 S.Ct., at 2781.

Under the law that governs today, it is *Babcock* that rests on questionable legal foundations. The Board's decision in *Jean Country,* by contrast, is both rational and consistent with the governing statute. The Court should therefore defer to the Board, rather than resurrecting and extending the reach of a decision which embodies principles which the law has long since passed by.

It is evident, therefore, that, in my view, the Court should defer to the Board's decision in *Jean Country* and its application of *Jean Country* in this case. With all due respect, I dissent.

———

JUSTICE STEVENS, dissenting.

For the first two reasons stated in Justice White's opinion, ante, at 850–852, I would affirm the judgment of the Court of Appeals enforcing the Board's order. I agree with Justice White that the Court's strict construction of NLRB v. Babcock & Wilcox Co., 351 U.S. 105, 76 S.Ct. 679, 100 L.Ed. 975 (1956), is not consistent with Hudgens v. NLRB, 424 U.S. 507, 96 S.Ct. 1029, 47 L.Ed.2d 196 (1976), and our other cases interpreting *Babcock.* I do not, however, join his opinion to the extent that it suggests that the *Babcock* case was incorrectly decided, ante, at 852–853. That decision rejected the Board's view that the rules applicable to union organizing draw no distinction between employees and nonemployees. I believe that central holding in *Babcock* was correct and is not inconsistent with the current law of deference to administrative agencies. Accordingly, I also respectfully dissent.

———

After the Supreme Court's decision in *Lechmere,* the court of appeals remanded to the NLRB to consider, in light of the Court's decision, the question whether the Lechmere Company had violated section 8(a)(1) by directing the non-employee union organizers to leave the grassy public area adjacent to the privately owned mall parking lot. The Board reaffirmed its previous ruling that Lechmere's action had indeed violated the Act: "The Supreme Court's vindication of the [employer's] private-property rights, if anything, elevates the gravity of [the employer's] attempt to bar union access to public property." 308 N.L.R.B. 1074 (1992).

Problems for Discussion

1. Do you agree with the Supreme Court's application of the *Chevron* doctrine to the decision of the NLRB in this case? When the Court concluded

[handwritten marginalia at top: they should have determined if agency's view was based on a permissible construction of the statute]

that the Board had improperly interpreted unambiguous language in the statute, did the Court act properly in deciding on its own (as the Court had earlier done in *Babcock*) whether there was sufficient proof of inadequate access by the union to the Lechmere workers? *[handwritten: No, not under Chevron!]*

2. After *Lechmere,* can the Board no longer interpret the "alternative *[handwritten: No]*
access" test so as to allow union access to the property of an employer not in the *[handwritten: still not clear.]*
category of the remote logging camp, mining camp or seagoing vessel? Does the NLRA compel such a narrow reading of the employees' section 7 rights? Is not the Board in a particularly good position to know whether a union can communicate its message through reasonable means away from company property, even when employees do not live on the company's premises? *[handwritten: Yes]*

3. How, after *Lechmere,* should the following cases be decided?

(a) A hospital has ejected a union organizer from a cafeteria that was open to members of the public. The organizer, who was initially allowed to sit in the cafeteria for hours at a time, chatting with employees, was ordered to leave only after hospital representatives learned that he was doing union business. See Oakwood Hospital v. NLRB, 983 F.2d 698 (6th Cir.1993). *[handwritten: ejected]*

(b) The union organizers can show that Lechmere, on the average of once or twice each month, allows the sale of Girl Scout cookies and charity raffles, and appeals by organizations like the Salvation Army, on its adjacent parking lot, after requests for permission to do so. See Susquehanna United Super Inc., 308 N.L.R.B. 201 (1992). *[handwritten: ejected]*

(c) The persons seeking to distribute materials on the Lechmere parking lot are employees of a competing discount department store nearby, which has a collective bargaining agreement with the Retail Clerks Union; these persons wish to distribute handbills to Lechmere customers, stating that Lechmere pays substandard wages and is therefore driving down the wages of workers elsewhere. *[handwritten: ejected !!]*

(d) The Woodmere Store is located in a large shopping mall. The mall owns the buildings and the parking lots; it is bordered by high speed roads. Woodmere's unionized warehouse workers engaged in an economic strike and were permanently replaced. The replaced strikers stationed themselves at Woodmere's parking lot entrance. They wore sashes stating "Don't Shop at Woodmere" and handed out leaflets to customers describing their dispute and demanding their jobs. The Mall management, at Woodmere's request, has directed them to leave. Has Woodmere committed any unfair labor practice? See Report of the NLRB General Counsel, June 2, 1994.

4. A large Coca Cola plant is located on a large privately owned tract of land closed to the public. The Company has long and consistently enforced a posted rule that reads: "Persons who are not employees of the Coca Cola Company are not permitted on Company property to solicit, or distribute materials to, Company employees at any time." Rather than utilize its own employees to perform janitorial work at the plant, Coca Cola subcontracts such work to the Kleen–Up Company, which regularly has 150 employees at the location in question. While in the parking lot used by Company employees and employees of subcontractors, just before the beginning of her shift doing janitorial work for Kleen–Up, Betty Brite begins to distribute material to her fellow Kleen–Up employees, urging them to join the Machinists Union. The Coca Cola

foreman promptly forbids her to do so, and threatens her with discipline unless she stops. This continues for several days.

The Union has asked you whether Brite's rights under the NLRA have been violated. Give your advice. See Southern Services, Inc. v. NLRB, 954 F.2d 700 (11th Cir.1992).

Page 133. Add citation at the close of Problem 6:

Automotive Plastics Technologies, Inc., 313 N.L.R.B. No. 50 (1993).

Page 133. Add to Problem 7:

Compare Willmar Elec. Serv., Inc. v. NLRB, 968 F.2d 1327 (D.C.Cir.1992), cert. denied, ___ U.S. ___, 113 S.Ct. 1252, 122 L.Ed.2d 651 (1993). The Board, after oral argument, reconsidered and reaffirmed its position. Sunland Construction Co., 309 N.L.R.B. 1224 (1992), and Town & Country Electric, Inc., 309 N.L.R.B. 1250 (1992). But the Fourth Circuit has adhered to the position it took in *Zachry.* Ultrasystems Western Constructors, Inc. v. NLRB, 18 F.3d 251 (4th Cir.1994).

2. Election Propaganda
(a) Threats of Reprisal

Page 158. Add new Problem 3A:

Assume that Able Tool & Die's management assembles its employees and reads to them the following corporate by-law the board of directors had adopted ten years earlier:

> *Section 2—Corporate Dissolution.* Able Tool & Die hereby expresses as a matter of corporate policy that operations will cease and the corporation will be dissolved in the event of unionization of its employees. As hereby authorized by the Board of Directors, this by-law may be announced to the employees of Able Tool & Die at any time deemed appropriate by the Board.

Has the Company committed an unfair labor practice? Wiljef Transp., Inc. v. NLRB, 946 F.2d 1308 (7th Cir.1991).

(b) Factual Misrepresentations

Page 175. Insert at the end of the Problems:

The most recent notable chapter in the Board's regulation of factual misrepresentations is its decision in AWB METAL, INC., 306 N.L.R.B. 109 (1992), *enf'd,* 4 F.3d 993 (6th Cir.1993). There, the company circulated a leaflet, within 24 hours preceding the election, that misrepresented the wage rates negotiated by the union at another of the company's plants. The Board majority declined to set aside the company's election victory; it relied upon *Midland National Life* and found no condemnable forgery. In an extended dissenting opinion, set forth below, Member Raudabaugh proposed a modest modification in the *Midland* standard. [Would you concur in his suggestion?]

While I agree generally with the holding in [*Midland National Life Insurance*] that elections are not to be set aside on the basis of misleading campaign statements, I would not apply it to a situation where the misrepresentation occurs within 24 hours of the opening of the polls.[2]   Applying this rule to the instant case, I would invalidate the election and direct a second election.

It is undisputed that less than 24 hours prior to the election, the Petitioner circulated a handbill containing misrepresentations with respect to contractual wage rates recently negotiated between Machinists Local Lodge 1312 and the Employer at its plant in Trenton, Ohio.   The handbill directed the employees' attention to the attached pages of the contract, which listed the starting wages for all job classifications in the two-tiered wage system and invited them to compare the "amazing superior level and difference in * * * wages provided at the * * * Ohio plant and your plant at Indianapolis." The Petitioner, however, omitted a page from the contract containing a critical footnote explaining that the starting wages for most of the lower tiered employees were actually 30 percent lower than the wages listed and would not reach the enumerated amount until after 5 years of employment with the Employer.   The Regional Director concluded that this misrepresentation did not involve the use of forged documents—the only ground for setting an election aside under *Midland*.   Thus, he recommended overruling the Employer's objections and certifying the Petitioner.

Like the majority, I have no desire to return to the era of *Hollywood Ceramics* when the Board routinely scrutinized and analyzed preelection campaign statements if there was a claim that they included misstatements of fact warranting invalidation of an election.   The premise underlying *Hollywood Ceramics* was that Board intervention was necessary to protect employees from their presumed inability to filter out exaggerations or misrepresentations.   I agree with the view that employees are intelligent enough to assess the statements of all sides in an organizational campaign.   However, this view is valid only if the employees have had the opportunity to assess the statements of both sides.   If one side makes a misrepresentation in circumstances where there is no opportunity to reply, the employees never get to hear the other side.   They will then go to the polls with the misrepresentation fresh in their minds and with no effective response to it.   In such circumstances, I would not permit the offending party to reap the electoral fruits of the misconduct.

I wish to emphasize that my approach does not return to the days of *Hollywood Ceramics*.   If the alleged misrepresentation occurs more than 24 hours before the election, the Board need not deal with it.   Similarly, the 24–hour rule would not leave ambiguous the issue of whether there was an adequate opportunity to respond.   If the statement was made before the 24–hour period, I would hold, as a matter of law, that there was an adequate opportunity to respond. If it was made thereafter, I would hold, as a matter of law, that there was no such opportunity * * *.

Applying this rule to the facts of this case, I would find that the Petitioner's misrepresentation of the contractual wage rates of certain of the Employer's unionized work force, which was admittedly circulated in a leaflet during the 24 hours before the election, constituted objectionable conduct warranting the setting aside of the election and the direction of a second election.[8]

2. The term "misrepresentation" as used herein, means a substantial departure from the truth, such that it may reasonably be expected to have an impact on the election.

8. I stress that my proposed rule would prohibit last-minute misrepresentations by both unions and employers alike.

3. Other Forms of Interference, Restraint or Coercion

Page 189. Add Problem 7:

7. A week prior to a decertification election, the Company announced that it would hold a raffle for all employees who voted in the election. The raffle ticket would be given to them after they had voted, but they were assured that no list of voters would be kept, that participation would be voluntary, and that the raffle would be held regardless of the outcome. First prize was a television set and second prize a discman, which employees could in any event purchase at a discount for approximately $600 and $175 respectively. The union lost the election, 44 votes for to 76 votes against. Has the Company committed an unfair labor practice? See Sony Corp. of America, 313 N.L.R.B. No. 55 (1993).

4. Union Misconduct Affecting Self–Organization

Page 193. Add new Problem 4:

4. At a rally on the eve of a representation election, attended by about a third of the employees involved, the Union announced that it had filed a class action lawsuit on behalf of the employees. The Union's lawyer explained the theory of the suit—that it would be "a long and difficult battle"—but that if they were to prevail each employee might collect as much as $35,000. The union won the election. Should the election be set aside? See Nestle Dairy Systems, Inc., 311 N.L.R.B. 987 (1993).

B. COMPANY DOMINATION OR ASSISTANCE

Page 216. Insert before Problems:

Concurrence is important in this case.

ELECTROMATION, INC.
309 N.L.R.B. 990 (1992).

[The NLRB decided this case after oral argument was heard and briefs filed by the parties as well as by a number of organizations serving as amicus curiae.]

This case presents the issue of whether "Action Committees" composed, in part, of the Respondent's employees constitute a labor organization within the meaning of Section 2(5) of the Act and whether the Respondent's conduct vis a vis the "Action Committees" violated Section 8(a)(2) and (1) of the Act. In the notice of hearing of May 14, 1991, the Board framed the pertinent issues as follows:

(1) At what point does an employee committee lose its protection as a communication device and become a labor organization?

(2) What conduct of an employer constitutes domination or interference with the employee committee?

For the reasons below, we find that the Action Committees were not simply "communication devices" but instead constituted a labor organization within the meaning of Section 2(5) of the Act and that the Respondent's conduct towards the Action Committees constituted domination and interference in violation of Section 8(a)(2) and (1). These findings rest on the totality of the record evidence, and they are not intended to suggest that employee committees formed under other circumstances for other purposes would necessarily be deemed "labor organizations" or that employer actions like some of those at issue here would necessarily be found, in isolation or in other contexts, to constitute unlawful support, interference, or domination.

I.

The Respondent is engaged in the manufacture of electrical components and related products. It employs approximately 200 employees. These employees were not represented by any labor organization at the time of the events described herein.

[In response to financial difficulties, the employer-Respondent in late 1988 substituted a year-end payment for the anticipated 1989 wage increase, and made changes in its attendance bonus policy. This provoked a petition from the employees, and led to a meeting between the company President, John Howard, and several employees, at which there were discussions of several economic issues. Howard then met with company supervisors, and he and they decided that "it was very unlikely that further unilateral management action to resolve these problems was going to come anywhere near making everybody happy ... and we thought that the best course of action would be to involve the employees in coming up with solutions to these issues"; they decided that "action committees" would be a way to involve employees. Howard met once again with the employee group, and proposed the creation of action committees to deal with each of the five areas that he had identified as the subject of employee complaints; he stated that if these committees "came up with solutions that . . . we believed were within budget concerns and they generally felt would be acceptable to the employees, that we would implement these suggestions or proposals." Although the reaction of the employee group was initially unfavorable, they ultimately endorsed the idea.]

On January 19, the Respondent posted a memorandum directed to all employees announcing the formation of five Action Committees and posted sign-up sheets for each Action Committee. The memorandum explained that each Action Committee would consist of six employees and one or two members of management, as well as the Respondent's Employees Benefits Manager, Loretta Dickey, who would coordinate all the Action Committees. The sign-up sheets explained the responsibilities and goals of each Committee. No employees were involved in the drafting of the policy goals expressed in the sign-up sheets. The Respondent determined the number of employees permitted to sign-up for the Action Committees. The Respondent informed two employees who had signed up for more than one committee that each would be limited to participation on one committee. After the Action Committees were organized, the Respondent posted a notice to all employees announcing the members of each Committee and the dates of the initial Committee meetings. The Action Committees were designated as (1) Absenteeism/Infractions, (2) No Smoking Policy, (3) Communication Network, (4) Pay Progression for Premium Positions, and (5) Attendance Bonus Program.

The Action Committees began meeting in late January and early February.[6] The Respondent's coordinator of the Action Committees, Dickey, testified that management expected that employee members on the Committees would "kind of talk back and forth" with the other employees in the plant, get their ideas, and that, indeed, the purpose of the Respondent's postings was to ensure that "anyone [who] wanted to know what was going on, they could go to these people" on the Action Committees. Other management representatives, as well as Dickey, participated in the Action Committees' meetings, which were scheduled to meet on a weekly basis in a conference room on the Respondent's premises. The Respondent paid employees for their time spent participating and supplied necessary materials. Dickey's role in the meetings was to facilitate the discussions.

On February 13, the Union made a demand to the Respondent for recognition. There is no evidence that the Respondent was aware of organizing efforts by the Union until this time. On about February 21, Howard informed Dickey of the recognition demand and, at the next scheduled meeting of each Action Committee, Dickey informed the members that the Respondent could no longer participate but that the

---

6. The no-smoking committee was never organized and held no meetings.

employees could continue to meet if they so desired. The Absentee-ism/Infraction and the Communication Network Committees each decided to continue their meetings on company premises; the Pay Progression Committee disbanded; and the Attendance Bonus Committee decided to write up a proposal they had discussed previously and not to meet again. The Attendance Bonus Committee's proposal was one of two proposals that the employees had developed concerning attendance bonuses. The first one, developed at the committee's second or third meeting, was pronounced unacceptable by the Respondent's controller, a member of that committee, because it was too costly. Thereafter the employees devised a second proposal, which the controller deemed fiscally sound. The proposal was not presented to President Howard because the Union's campaign to secure recognition had intervened.

On March 15, Howard informed employees that "due to the Union's campaign, the Company would be unable to participate in the committee meetings and could not continue to work with the committees until after the election," which was to be held on March 31 * * *.

[The Administrative Law Judge held that the action committees were "labor organizations" within the NLRA definition, and that the company dominated and impermissibly assisted them.]

In its exceptions and brief, the Respondent contends that the Action Committees were not statutory labor organizations and did not interfere with employee free choice. It notes that no proposals from any committee were ever implemented, that the committees were formed in the absence of knowledge of any union activity, and that they followed a tradition of similar employer-employee meetings.

II.

[The Board quoted the text of sections 2(5) and 8(a)(2) of the NLRA.]

* * * [We] seek guidance from the legislative history to discern what kind of activity Congress intended to prohibit when it made it an unfair labor practice for an employer to "dominate or interfere with the formation or administration of any labor organization" or to contribute support to it.[9]

---

9. A number of the amici have suggested that, even if the language and legislative history of the provisions at issue show a clear congressional intent to impose a broad prohibition extending to activities like those of the Respondent and the employee committees at issue in this case, and even if that understanding of congressional intent was expressed in an opinion of the Supreme Court, the Board is free to adjust the breadth of the prohibition in light of changing economic realities. In particular, the amici argue that, for the sake of American competitiveness in world markets, it is desirable to allow employers to create and support employee/management committees in the manner that the Respondent did with respect to the Action Committees here. While we agree that when the Board has the latitude to change a particular construction of the statute we may appropriately take into account changing industrial realities, we do not agree that we are free so to act either when congressional intent to the

The legislative history reveals that the provisions outlawing company dominated labor organizations were a critical part of the Wagner Act's purpose of eliminating industrial strife through the encouragement of collective bargaining. Early in his opening remarks Senator Wagner stated:

> Genuine collective bargaining is the only way to attain equality of bargaining power * * *. The greatest obstacles to collective bargaining are employer-dominated unions, which have multiplied with amazing rapidity since the enactment of [the National Industrial Recovery Act]. Such a union makes a sham of equal bargaining power * * *. (O)nly representatives who are not subservient to the employer with whom they deal can act freely in the interest of employees. For these reasons the very first step toward genuine collective bargaining is the abolition of the employer dominated union as an agency for dealing with grievances, labor disputes, wages, rates, or hours of employment.

* * *

* * * Congress concluded that ridding collective bargaining of employer-dominated organizations, the formation and administration of which had been fatally tainted by employer "domination" or "interference," would advance the Wagner Act's goal of eliminating industrial strife. That conclusion was based on the nation's experience under the NIRA, recounted by witnesses at the Senate hearings, that employer interference in setting up or running employee "representation" groups actually robbed employees of the freedom to choose their own representatives. Senator Wagner here made a distinction, important for this inquiry, between interference and minimal conduct—"merely suggesting to his employees that they organize a union or committee"—that the nation's experience had shown did not rob employees of their right to a representative of their own choosing. As Senator Wagner stated:

> The question is entirely one of fact and turns upon whether or not the employee organization is entirely the agency of the workers * * *. The organization itself should be independent of the employer-employee relationship.

In sum, Congress brought within its definition of "labor organization" a broad range of employee groups, and it sought to ensure that such groups were free to act independently of employers in representing employee interests.

III.

Before a finding of unlawful domination can be made under Section 8(a)(2) a finding of "labor organization" status under Section 2(5) is

contrary is absolutely clear or the Supreme Court has decreed that a particular reading of the statute is required to reflect such an intent, or both * * *.

required. Under the statutory definition set forth in Section 2(5), the organization at issue is a labor organization if (1) employees participate, (2) the organization exists, at least in part, for the purpose of "dealing with" employers, and (3) these dealings concern "conditions of work" or concern other statutory subjects, such as grievances, labor disputes, wages, rates of pay, or hours of employment. Further, if the organization has as a purpose the representation of employees, it meets the statutory definition of "employee representation committee or plan" under Section 2(5) and will constitute a labor organization if it also meets the criteria of employee participation and dealing with conditions of work or other statutory subjects. Any group, including an employee representation committee, may meet the statutory definition of "labor organization" even if it lacks a formal structure, has no elected officers, constitution or bylaws, does not meet regularly, and does not require the payment of initiation fees or dues. Fire Alert Co., 182 NLRB 910, 912 fn. 12 (1970), enfd. 77 LRRM 2895 (10th Cir.1971); Armco, Inc., 271 NLRB 350 (1984). Thus, a group may be an "employee representation committee" within the meaning of Section 2(5) even if there is no formal framework for conducting meetings among the represented employees (i.e. those employees whose conditions of employment are the subject of committee dealings) or for otherwise eliciting the employees' views.
* * *

In considering the interplay between Section 2(5) and Section 8(a)(2), we are guided by the Supreme Court's opinion in NLRB v. Cabot Carbon Co., 360 U.S. 203 (1959). In Cabot Carbon the Court held that the term "dealing with" in Section 2(5) is broader than the term "collective bargaining" and applies to situations that do not contemplate the negotiation of a collective bargaining agreement.[21] * * *

Notwithstanding that "dealing with" is broadly defined under Cabot Carbon, it is also true that an organization whose purpose is limited to performing essentially a managerial or adjudicative function is not a labor organization under Section 2(5). In those circumstances, it is irrelevant if the impetus behind the organization's creation emanates from the employer. See General Foods Corp., 231 NLRB 1232 (1977) (employer created job enrichment program composed of work crews of entire employee complement); Mercy–Memorial Hospital, 231 NLRB 1108 (1977) (committee decided validity of employees' complaints and did not discuss or deal with employer concerning the complaints); John

---

21. As Member Devaney notes, witnesses cautioned the Senate committee that limiting "labor organization" to groups that engage in collective bargaining with an employer might fail to capture employer-dominated organizations, many of which never wrested a single concession, let alone a bargaining agreement, from the employer. Referring again to the abuses Congress meant to proscribe in enacting the Wagner Act, we view "dealing with" as a bilateral mechanism involving proposals from the employee committee concerning the subjects listed in Sec. 2(5), coupled with real or apparent consideration of those proposals by management. A unilateral mechanism, such as a "suggestion box," or "brainstorming" groups or meetings, or analogous information exchanges does not constitute "dealing with."

Ascuaga's Nuggett, 230 NLRB 275, 276 (1977) (employees' organization resolved employees' grievances and did not interact with management).

Although Section 8(a)(2) does not define the specific acts that may constitute domination, a labor organization that is the creation of management, whose structure and function are essentially determined by management, * * * and whose continued existence depends on the fiat of management, is one whose formation or administration has been dominated under Section 8(a)(2). In such an instance, actual domination has been established by virtue of the employer's specific acts of creating the organization itself and determining its structure and function.[24] However, when the formulation and structure of the organization is determined by employees, domination is not established, even if the employer has the potential ability to influence the structure or effectiveness of the organization. See Duquesne University, 198 NLRB 891, 892–893 (1972). * * *

The Board's analysis of Section 2(5) and Section 8(a)(2) generally has met with judicial approval. * * * [25] The Board, however, has been less than successful in the Sixth Circuit. See, e.g., NLRB v. Scott & Fetzer Co., 691 F.2d 288 (6th Cir.1982); Airstream, Inc. v. NLRB, 877 F.2d 1291 (6th Cir.1989).

* * * As noted previously (fn. 24), Board precedent and decisions of the Supreme Court indicate that the presence of antiunion motive is not critical to finding an 8(a)(2) violation. We also see no basis in the statutory language, the legislative history, or decisions apart from Scott & Fetzer to require a finding that the employees believe their organization to be a labor union. * * *

Of course, Section 2(5) literally requires us to inquire into the "purpose" of the employee entity at issue because we must determine whether it exists "for the purpose of dealing" with conditions of employment. But "purpose" is different from motive; and the "purpose" to which the statute directs inquiry does not necessarily entail subjective

---

24. Sec. 8(a)(2) does not require a finding of antiunion animus or a specific motive to interfere with Sec. 7 rights. In NLRB v. Newport News Shipbuilding Co., 308 U.S. 241 (1939), the Supreme Court found that an employer had dominated a statutory labor organization even though the "Committee" in question operated to the apparent satisfaction of the employees who had signified their desire for its continuance. The Court also noted that there was no evidence that the employer objected to its employees joining labor unions and that there had been no discrimination against them because of membership in outside unions. See also Garment Workers' Union (Bernhard–Altmann Texas Corp.) v. NLRB, 366 U.S. 731 (1961) (good-faith belief in union's

majority status is no defense under Sec. 8(a)(2) to the grant of exclusive recognition to a union that does not have support of the majority of employees) * * *.

25. In NLRB v. Northeastern University, 601 F.2d 1208 (1st Cir.1979); Hertzka & Knowles v. NLRB, 503 F.2d 625 (9th Cir. 1974); and Chicago Rawhide Mfg. Co. v. NLRB, 221 F.2d 165 (7th Cir.1955), the courts denied enforcement in circumstances where the impetus behind the organizations emanated from the employees themselves. Without passing on the merits of the underlying Board decisions in those cases, we find those cases distinguishable from the cases cited in our discussion herein, and from the instant case.

hostility towards unions. Purpose is a matter of what the organization is set up to do, and that may be shown by what the organization actually does. If a purpose is to deal with an employer concerning conditions of employment, the Section 2(5) definition has been met regardless of whether the employer has created it, or fostered its creation, in order to avoid unionization or whether employees view that organization as equivalent to a union.[27]

IV.

Applying these principles to the facts of this case, we find, in agreement with the judge, that the Action Committees constitute a labor organization within the meaning of Section 2(5) of the Act; and that the Respondent dominated it, and assisted it, i.e., contributed support, within the meaning of Section 8(a)(2).

First, there is no dispute that employees participated in the Action Committees. Second, we find that the activities of the committees constituted dealing with an employer. Third, we find that the subject matter of that dealing—which included the treatment of employee absenteeism and employee remuneration in the form of bonuses and other monetary incentives—concerned conditions of employment. Fourth, we find that the employees acted in a representational capacity within the meaning of Section 2(5). Taken as a whole, the evidence underlying these findings shows that the Action Committees were created for, and actually served, the purpose of dealing with the Respondent about conditions of employment.

* * * The evidence thus overwhelmingly demonstrates that a purpose of the Action Committees, indeed their only purpose, was to address employees' disaffection concerning conditions of employment through the creation of a bilateral process involving employees and management in order to reach bilateral solutions on the basis of employee-initiated proposals. This is the essence of "dealing with" within the meaning of Section 2(5).[28]

* * * [W]e find that employee-members of the Action Committees acted in a representational capacity and that the Action Committees

---

27. In this we differ from Member Raudabaugh's view that employee perception of an employee committee is a significant element in evaluating its lawfulness. Much of the harm implicit in employer—dominated organizations is that, when they are successful, they appear to employees to be the result of an exercise of statutory freedoms, when in fact they are coercive by their very nature. Thus, we cannot agree that employee perceptions of the nature of an employee committee are significant indicators of their lawfulness.

28. We find no basis in this record to conclude that the purpose of the Action Committees was limited to achieving "quality" or "efficiency" or that they were designed to be a "communication device" to promote generally the interests of quality or efficiency. We, therefore, do not reach the question of whether any employer initiated programs that may exist for such purposes, as described by amici in this proceeding, may constitute labor organizations under Sec. 2(5). Cf. General Foods Corp., supra.

were an "employee representation committee or plan" as set forth in Section 2(5).

There can also be no doubt that the Respondent's conduct vis a vis the Action Committees constituted "domination" in their formation and administration. It was the Respondent's idea to create the Action Committees. When it presented the idea to employees on January 18, the reaction, as the Respondent's President Howard admitted, was "not positive." Howard then informed employees that management would not "just unilaterally make changes" to satisfy employees' complaints. As a result, employees essentially were presented with the Hobson's choice of accepting the status quo, which they disliked, or undertaking a bilateral "exchange of ideas" within the framework of the Action Committees, as presented by the Respondent. The Respondent drafted the written purposes and goals of the Action Committees which defined and limited the subject matter to be covered by each Committee, determined how many members would compose a committee and that an employee could serve on only one committee, and appointed management representatives to the Committees to facilitate discussions.[30] Finally, much of the evidence supporting the domination finding also supports a finding of unlawful contribution of support. In particular, the Respondent permitted the employees to carry out the committee activities on paid time within a structure that the Respondent itself created.[31]

On these facts, we find that the Action Committees were the creation of the Respondent and that the impetus for their continued existence rested with the Respondent and not with the employees. Accordingly, the Respondent dominated the Action Committees in their formation and administration and unlawfully supported them.

* * *

MEMBER DEVANEY, concurring.

30. As Member Devaney notes in his concurrence, the "bargaining" going on through the Action Committees was not between the employees and management. Rather, each committee contained supervisors or managers and the committee charged with compensation issues had its proposals evaluated by the Respondent's controller before they were presented to the Respondent. Thus, the situation here put the Respondent in the position of sitting on both sides of the bargaining table with an "employee committee" that it could dissolve as soon as its usefulness ended and to which it owed no duty to bargain in good faith.

31. We do not hold that paying employee members of a committee for their meeting time and giving that committee space to meet and supplies is per se a violation of Sec. 8(a)(2). Here, however, the Respondent's assistance was in furtherance of its unlawful domination of the Action Committees and cannot be separated from that domination. Because the Respondent's conduct in supplying materials and furnishing space to the Action Committees occurred in the context of the Respondent's domination of these groups, this case is distinguishable from instances where an employer confers such benefits in the context of an amicable, arm's-length relationship with a legitimate representative organization. See Duquesne University, 198 NLRB at 891. (Certain employer benefits resulting from "friendly cooperation" with a lawfully recognized labor organization do not constitute an 8(a)(2) violation (dictim).)

I agree that the Respondent violated Section 8(a)(2) and (1) by "dominating or supporting" the Action Committees, which were "labor organizations" under Section 2(5). I write separately in response to concerns, raised by the parties and amici on both sides of the issue, over the lawfulness under Section 8(a)(2) of contemporary employee participation programs.

Like my colleagues, I acknowledge that a genuine "employee participation program" is not before the Board today, and, in agreeing that the Respondent violated Section 8(a)(2), I do not pass on the status of any other arrangement. It is my position, however, notwithstanding the concerns of some amici, that legislative history, binding judicial precedent, and Board precedent provide significant latitude to employers seeking to involve employees in the workplace. In my view, Section 8(a)(2) prohibits a specific form of employer conduct. It is not a broad-based ban on employee/employer communications. * * *

The record here indicates overwhelmingly that the Action Committees are not "normal relations and innocent communications" between employer and employee that Congress intended to leave undisturbed. Instead, the facts demonstrate why Congress couched the prohibition of company unions in broad terms. The Action Committees do not correspond to the historical "employee representation plans." Yet the Action Committees' effect on Section 7 rights is precisely the harm Congress sought to avert in Section 8(a)(2). In this regard, the Respondent, in spite of the expressed reluctance of employees and with no assurance of majority support, established the Action Committees for the purpose of "bargaining" with them over terms and conditions of employment. The Respondent itself chose the Action Committee members and charged them with representing their fellows, overriding employee preferences as to how the representatives would be chosen. By these acts, the Respondent substituted its will for that of a majority of employees and usurped their right to choose their own representative. In addition, the Action Committees effectively put the Respondent on both sides of the bargaining table; the company excluded the subject of wages from the committees' agenda, in spite of employee preference that it be discussed, and the controller "pre-screened" employee proposals so that the Respondent would have only palatable proposals to consider. Thus, the Action Committees gave employees the illusion of a bargaining representative without the reality of one. Further, the subject matter of the Action Committees, as set out by the Respondent, did not consist of concerns about productivity, efficiency, materials conservation, safety, and the like: instead, the Committees were set up to bargain over terms and conditions of employment. Nor did they constitute employee participation or empowerment committees: they were intended to give the impression that decisions resulting from their activities were "bilateral," yet the Respondent was in control of their subject matter and of the content of their proposals. By establishing committees that purported to act as the agent of employees in the bilateral consideration of problems, but in reality acted as its own agent, the Respondent unlawfully "dominated and supported" a labor organization in violation of Section 8(a)(2). * * *

MEMBER OVIATT, concurring.

* * * I join in the majority opinion, but I do so as much for what the opinion does not condemn as an unfair labor practice as for what it does find to be a violation of Section 8(a)(2) and (1). Thus, I write separately to stress the wide range of lawful activities which I view as untouched by this decision.

In my view, the critical question in most cases of alleged violations of Section 8(a)(2) through domination or support of an entity that includes employees among its membership is whether the entity is created with any purpose to deal with "grievances, labor disputes, wages, rates of pay, hours of employment, or conditions of work" as set forth in the Section 2(5) definition of "labor organization." In this case, I have no doubt that the subject matter of the Action Committees falls comfortably within the definition. The Committee's purpose was to address and find solutions for issues related to absenteeism, pay progression, attendance bonuses, and no-smoking policies. These are plainly among the subject matters about which labor organizations traditionally bargain since they involve "wages" or "conditions of work."

There is, however, an important area of industrial relations where committees and groups of employees and managerial personnel act together with the purpose of communicating, addressing and solving problems in the workplace that do not implicate the matters identified in Section 2(5). Among the employee-participation groups that may be established by management are so-called "quality circles" whose purpose is to use employee expertise by having the group examine certain operational problems such as labor efficiency and material waste. See, Beaver, Are Worker Participation Plans "Labor Organizations" Within the Meaning of Section 2(5)? A Proposed Framework of Analysis, Lab.L.J. 226 (1985). Other such committees have been dubbed "quality-of-work-life programs." These involve management's attempt to draw on the creativity of its employees by including them in decisions that affect their work lives. These decisions may go beyond improvements in productivity and efficiency to include issues involving worker self-fulfillment and self-enhancement. See, Fulmer and Coleman, Do Quality-of Work–Life Programs Violate Section 8(a)(2)?, 35 Lab.L.J. 675 (1984). Others of these programs stress joint problem-solving structures that engage management and employees in finding ways of improving operating functions. See, Lee, Collective Bargaining and Employee Participation: An Anomalous Interpretation of the National Labor Relations Act, 38 Lab.L.J. 206, 207 (1987). And then there are employee-management committees that are established by a company with the purpose of creating better communications between employer and employee by exploring employee attitudes, communicating certain information to employees, and making management more aware of employee problems. See, Beaver, supra.

Where there is a labor union on the scene, these employee-management cooperative programs may act as a complement to the union. They can not, however, lawfully usurp the traditional role of the Union in representing the employees in collective bargaining about grievances, wages, hours, and terms and conditions of work. Where no labor union represents the employees, these programs are often established to open lines of communication so that the operation may take advantage of employee technical knowledge and expertise. See, Note, New Standards For Domination and Support Under 8(a)(2), 82 Yale Law Journal 510, 511 (1973).

Certainly, I find nothing in today's decision that should be read as a condemnation of cooperative programs and committees of the type I have outlined above. The statute does not forbid direct communication between the employer and its employees to address and solve significant productivity and efficiency problems in the workplace. In my view, committees and groups dealing with these subjects alone plainly fall outside the Section 2(5) definition of "labor organization" since they are not concerned with grievances, labor disputes, wages, rates of pay, hours of employment or conditions of work. Indeed, in this age of increased global competition I consider it of critical importance that management and employees be able, indeed, are encouraged, to engage in cooperative endeavors to improve production methods and product quality.

It is with this understanding of the scope of the majority decision that I join in its reasoning and result.[5]

Member Raudabaugh also would give persuasive weight to the fact that an employer expressly assures employees that, notwithstanding the existence of an employee participatory program, they are free to "select traditional union representation * * *." No authority is cited for giving weight to this kind of a statement when the Board is adjudicating an

---

5. Like the majority, I reject Member Raudabaugh's efforts to rewrite Sec. 8(a)(2). In my view his 4–part test significantly erodes Congressional intent as understood by the Supreme Court. Thus, Member Raudabaugh would be guided in part by the extent to which the "employees do not view the committee" as a substitute for collective bargaining. Under Member Raudabaugh's approach the employees' perception must be "reasonable." This, however, simply encourages a separate contest over "reasonableness," a factor not contemplated by Congress or the statute.

8(a)(2) case. Such an assurance would be hollow indeed if the employees have already been unlawfully influenced not to choose an outside organization by the establishment of an in-house committee in violation of 8(a)(2). Further, exactly what the Employer said, how he said it, and to whom and when it was said, could well be disputed, creating the potential for additional trial issues. Thus, Member Raudabaugh's test, however well-intentioned, provides a road map for increased litigation, not cooperation. In my view, today's Employer does not need to be confronted with the possibility of more litigation and the costs associated therewith, but should be free, within the limits of our Statute, to encourage problem solving through cooperation so as to better compete in the world marketplace.

Finally, as the majority opinion shows, Newport News Shipbuilding, supra, is still good law. That case, and Garment Workers Union (Bernhard Altmann), supra, wisely reject the employer good-faith-motive principle embraced by Member Raudabaugh. The employer's subjective intent in no way dissipates the impact on the employees of the presence of an employer-dominated, in-house committee that substitutes for a legitimate labor organization's collective bargaining function. Sec. 8(a)(2) addresses that impact, not the employer's intentions.

MEMBER RAUDABAUGH, concurring.

I. Introduction

My colleagues find a violation of Section 8(a)(2) in this case. I concur. However, because I believe that this case genuinely raises the broader issue of whether Section 8(a)(2) should be reinterpreted and because of the significance of this issue as applied to employee participation programs, I write this separate concurrence.[1]

* * * Cooperative programs are seen by many as a necessary response to competition in a global economy. That is the reason this case was selected for oral argument. That is the reason so much attention has been focused on it. And that is the reason I expressly address the issues of law and policy that have been raised by the parties and the amici concerning employee participation programs in situations like that of the instant case where employees are not represented by an exclusive collective-bargaining representative.

* * *

1. I have used the term "employee participation programs" (EPPs) to refer to labor-management cooperative efforts. Although such programs cover a broad gamut, they all involve the concept of employee participation. See Eaton and Voos, "Un-ions and Contemporary Innovations in Work Organization, Compensation, and Employee Participation," Unions and Economic Competitiveness (M.E. Sharpe, Inc., 1992) at 208–210 for a description of the different forms of EPPs.

IV.   The 2(5) Definition of "Labor Organization"

* * * The most important decision interpreting [section 2(5)] is the Supreme Court's opinion in NLRB v. Cabot Carbon Co., 360 U.S. 203 (1959).   The Court held that the term "dealing" in Section 2(5) is broader than the term "collective-bargaining" and includes such activities as presenting grievances and making recommendations.   That holding set the parameters for an analysis of whether EPPs are labor organizations.   * * *

The Court's construction of the term "dealing" is very broad. Consistent with the breadth of the Court's holding, the Board's exceptions to the Cabot Carbon standard have been narrow.   For example, the Board has found that if the employee committee can itself resolve grievances, with no need to go to the employer, there is no "dealing." Similarly, the Board has determined that if employees are divided into work crews which have the power to resolve employment-related problems, there is no "dealing" between those crews and the employer.

It would appear that most EPPs would fit within the broad Cabot Carbon standard of "dealing with."   Most EPPs involve the presentation of proposals or ideas to management, and a management response to those proposals or ideas.   * * * As noted, most EPPs involve some interaction between the committee and management.   It is rare for full grievance-handling authority to be delegated to a committee without any further interaction with management.   To date, it is uncommon for production teams to have managerial functions fully delegated to them without interaction with management.

* * * In sum, I believe that most EPPs will possess the three elements of the Section 2(5) definition of "labor organization."   This conclusion is consistent with clear legislative history.   As my colleagues have observed in the principal opinion, Congress deliberately abandoned a narrow definition of "labor organization" and chose a broader one that expressly covered employee representation committees and plans.   Accordingly, in my opinion, any reinterpretation of Section 8(a)(2) which relies on excluding EPPs from Section 2(5) would be beyond the Board's authority.

* * * In sum, if EPPs are to be lawful, Section 2(5) will have to be changed legislatively unless Section 8(a)(2) can be reinterpreted so as to accommodate such programs.   I now turn to that 8(a)(2) issue.

V.   Section 8(a)(2)

Section 8(a)(2) makes it an unfair labor practice for an employer "to dominate or interfere with the formation or administration of any labor organization or contribute financial or other support to it."   The legislative history of the Wagner Act of 1935 shows that employer conduct with regard to employee committees was placed in the same category as creating "company unions" and was one of the evils that Section 8(a)(2) was designed to combat.

The only Supreme Court decision interpreting this aspect of Section 8(a)(2) is NLRB v. Newport News Shipbuilding Co., 308 U.S. 241 (1939). Any analysis of Section 8(a)(2), in the context of EPPs, must come to grips with the Supreme Court's construction of the Act in that case.

* * * It is not surprising that courts advocating a change in the interpretation of Section 8(a)(2) make no reference to Newport News.[27] The Court's decision appears to leave little room for contemporary EPPs. The Court set forth a requirement that the employee committee be independent of the employer.   Since the employer had controlled the committee, it was irrelevant, for remedial purposes, that: (1) the employer had a lawful motive in establishing and working with the committees, (2) the plan had obviated serious labor disputes, and (3) employees approved of the committees.

Contemporary EPPs are often set up by employers with the lawful motives of enhancing morale, communication, product quality, and increasing productivity.   To achieve these goals, the employers usually

---

27. Various courts of appeals have posed new interpretations of Sec. 8(a)(2) in the context of labor management cooperation.   These decisions, however, have failed adequately to address either the legislative history or the Supreme Court's ruling in this area and thus, provide insufficient guidance.

The first of these decisions was rendered by the Court of Appeals for the Seventh Circuit in Chicago Rawhide Mfg. Co. v. NLRB, 221 F.2d 165 (7th Cir.1955).   In that case, the company and a group of employees together created an association (Employee Committees) for handling grievances and other employment matters.   The company permitted elections and committee meetings to be held on company property during work hours, and made financial contributions to the shop recreation committee. The Board found unlawful support by the company.   The Seventh Circuit, however, refused to enforce the Board's order on the ground that the Board had failed to distin-

guish between unlawful support and lawful cooperation.   The court stated:

> Support, even though innocent, can be identified because it constitutes at least some degree of control or influence.   Cooperation only assists the employees or their representatives in carrying out their independent intention.   If this line between cooperation and support is not recognized, the employer's fear of accusations of domination may defeat the principal purpose of the Act, which is cooperation between management and labor. [221 F.2d at 167.]

The court cites no support for this rationale.   The decision is silent with respect to the legislative history of the Act and the Newport News decision.

Several other courts of appeal have taken the Seventh Circuit's approach with the same absence of discussion of legislative history and Supreme Court precedent. * * *

retain some degree of control over the EPPs. The plans often obviate serious labor disputes. Further, because they are generally designed to be in the interest of employees and the employer, they are acceptable to both. Newport News suggests that such EPPs are unlawful under Section 8(a)(2). The question, then, is whether Newport News retains its vitality. Because of legislative changes occurring after the issuance of the decision, I have concluded that it does not.

I believe that Newport News is to be understood in the context of the Wagner Act of 1935, the legislation upon which the decision is based. * * * The adversarial model, upon which the Wagner Act was based, is at odds with a cooperative model of labor relations. In the adversarial model, there is an inherent conflict between management and labor which may lead to industrial strife and unrest. Collective bargaining is the means by which this conflict can be constructively contained. In that collective-bargaining struggle, each side has different interests, and each faces the other across a wide divide. As one commentator has phrased it:

> The term "adversarial model" is used to describe a system in which management and labor maintain a strict separation, and approach collective bargaining as competing entities with opposing interests, involved in a struggle over limited resources. * * *

By 1947, the labor-management world had undergone major change. The Taft–Hartley amendments of that year were enacted not to further strengthen unions but in response to legislative concern that unions had become too strong. The focus of Taft–Hartley was to assure employees of their right to make a free choice for or against unionization. * * * In short, Taft–Hartley emphasized (1) employee free choice rather than governmental encouragement of unionism; and (2) the encouragement of peaceful methods for resolving labor-management disputes, rather than strikes and lockouts. There was a concomitant de-emphasis of the concept that employees and employers are forever locked in an adversarial struggle and there was a rejection of the notion that the government's role was to assure that employees have power through unionism.

In light of the Taft–Hartley Act and the socio-economic changes on which it was based, I believe that there is a substantial doubt that the Supreme Court would now decide Newport News exactly as the Court decided it in 1938. That decision could not take into account the substantial changes wrought by the enactment of Taft–Hartley in 1947. Today, if employees freely choose to participate in an EPP, that would seem consistent with their Taft–Hartley right to refrain from choosing traditional union representation. Similarly, if employers and employees can amicably resolve their differences through cooperation, that would seem consistent with Taft–Hartley's encouragement of peaceful methods of resolving disputes. Finally, since EPPs are based on a recognition that employers and employees have mutual interests and need not always be adversaries, that would seem to reflect the shift away from the philosophy underlying the Wagner Act.

In short, Taft–Hartley recognizes that adversarial labor relations and collective bargaining through unions are not the only approaches to workplace relations.   * * * Newport News is not a straightjacket, and the NLRB, as the agency charged with interpreting the Act to reflect industrial reality, can and should interpret the Act to reflect the changes described herein.

This view of legislative intent is further supported by more recent legislative developments.   In 1975, Congress passed the National Productivity and Quality of Working Life Act which emphasizes the importance of such cooperative efforts to improving the productivity of U.S. industry.   That Act states that the "laws, rules, regulations and policies of the U.S. shall be interpreted as to give full force and effect to this policy." [38]   In 1978,[39] Congress passed the Labor–Management Cooperation Act which recognizes labor-management cooperation as a means of achieving organizational effectiveness.   This statute established a grant program to be administered by the Federal Mediation and Conciliation Service for organizations that develop labor-management committees at the plant level and on an area and industry basis.

The Board has an obligation to take such legislation into account when construing the Act.   * * *

For the reasons stated above, I believe that the Act can be interpreted to accommodate at least some EPPs.   I recognize that others, including particularly the courts, may have a different view.   If so, those who favor EPPs will have to resort to the legislative process.   My view is not a rejection of collective bargaining and the underlying adversarial model but a recognition of changed statutory language making room for a variety of choices for shaping workplace relations with employee free choice charting the course.

VI.   The Test for Evaluating EPPs Under Section 8(a)(2)

I conclude that Newport News does not foreclose a fresh interpretation of Section 8(a)(2), at least with respect to EPPs.   Of course, this is not to say that all EPPs are lawful.   As discussed above, they are labor organizations and hence an employer may not "dominate, interfere with, or support them."   The question before me is how to interpret these words in a way that will accommodate labor-management cooperation and the Section 7 rights of employees.   In my view, the answer to the question turns on the following factors: (1) the extent of the employer's

---

38. National Productivity and Quality of Work Life Act of 1975, 15 U.S.C. § 2401 et seq.

39. The Labor–Management Cooperation Act of 1978, 29 U.S.C. §§ 173(e),

175(a), 175(b) (grants confined to employers with collective-bargaining relationships), 186(c).

involvement in the structure and operation of the committees; (2) whether the employees, from an objective standpoint, reasonably perceive the EPP as a substitute for full collective bargaining through a traditional union; (3) whether employees have been assured of their Section 7 right to choose to be represented by a traditional union under a system of full collective bargaining, and (4) the employer's motives in establishing the EPP. I would consider all four factors in any given case. No single factor would necessarily be dispositive.

With respect to the first factor, the fact that an employer initiates the idea of an EPP is not sufficient to condemn it. Under Section 8(c) of the Act, an employer is free to voice an opinion on labor-management matters. Thus, for example, an employer can tell its employees that it favors or disfavors traditional union representation. By the same token, an employer should be able to tell its employees that it favors an EPP. I also note that the original version of the Wagner Act made it unlawful for an employer to "initiate" or "influence the function of" a labor organization. The provision was rejected. Thus, even under the Wagner Act, it would appear that such conduct was lawful.

However, the employer cannot coerce an employee into becoming part of an EPP. Consistent with Taft–Hartley, the choice must be that of the employee. Similarly, if the employees on a committee are to be the representatives of other employees, they must be selected by the employees, not by the employer.

In addition, although the employer can set forth the broad purpose of the committee, the committee must be free to consider any and all matters that are germane to that purpose. Thus, for example, the employer may say that the purpose of the committee is to enhance product quality or improve production efficiency. However, the committee must be free to consider any and all matters which are germane to those broad goals.

Further, managers and supervisors can be on the committee. In this regard, I note that the original version of the Wagner Act made it unlawful for the employer to "participate in" the labor organization. The provision was rejected. Thus, even under the Wagner Act, such conduct was lawful. However, managers and supervisors cannot be given a dominant role.

In addition, the employer can give support to the committee by providing it with meeting rooms, writing materials, secretarial assistance, etc., and it would be permissible to allow the committee to meet on company time.

Finally, the mere fact that the employer may suggest the rules and policies of the labor organization is not sufficient to condemn the EPP. In this regard, I note that the original version of the Wagner Act made it unlawful for an employer to "influence . . . the rules and other policies of a labor organization." The provision was rejected.

The second factor seeks to accommodate the Section 7 right of employees to choose traditional unions to represent them in resolving their disputes with their employer. If the committee is set up in response to employee grievances and complaints, and if it functions as a vehicle for presenting those matters to the employer, it can reasonably be viewed as a substitute for traditional union representation. However, if the committee is set up by the employer to accomplish its own entrepreneurial interests, e.g., enhanced product quality and improved production efficiency, it can reasonably be viewed as a vehicle for addressing employer interests, rather than as a substitute for traditional union representation. Similarly, to the extent that employees reasonably perceive the committee as their representative concerning employment related matters, the committee may be viewed as a substitute for collective bargaining. Conversely, to the extent that the employees do not view the committee in this way, the committee would not be viewed as a substitute for collective bargaining.

The third factor also seeks to accommodate Section 7 rights. I would consider it significant that the employer expressly assures its employees that, notwithstanding the EPP, they are free to select traditional union representation and full collective bargaining.

As to the fourth factor, if the employer establishes the EPP for a purpose of stifling an ongoing union campaign, the impact on Section 7 rights is obvious. Conversely, if the employer's motive in establishing the committee is solely to enhance lawful entrepreneurial goals, there would be no impact, under this factor, on Section 7 rights.

I believe that these four factors properly balance interests in labor-management cooperation and employee Section 7 rights. In addition, they reflect the Taft–Hartley goals of (1) insuring employee free choice and (2) promoting harmony and cooperation in the sphere of labor-management relations. Finally, they reflect the national interest in taking steps to insure that American firms successfully compete in a global economy.[47]

VII.   The Instant Case

I now apply the foregoing analysis to the instant case.

Based on my analysis of Section 2(5), and on the facts recited by my colleagues, it is clear that the committees are labor organizations.

---

47. Member Oviatt has expressed concern that the test I propose would lead to increased litigation, and not cooperation. For reasons stated earlier, the test does not require litigation of as many matters as he suggests. Further, I think it is more likely that the majority position will result in increased litigation. The majority has decided this case on its narrow facts. The majority therefore offers virtually no guidance as to whether different plans in different circumstances would be lawful or unlawful under the Act. Employers wishing to know those answers must look to case by case litigation in the future. By contrast, I have at least provided a framework for analysis and I have listed the factors which should be considered in that analysis.

With respect to the 8(a)(2) question, I apply the four factors set forth above and conclude that the Respondent's conduct was unlawful.

As to the first factor, the evidence recited by my colleagues establishes that the Respondent completely dictated the structure of the committees and controlled their operations. Indeed, the employees had very little, if any, voice in the structural design and operation of the committees.

As to the second factor, the Respondent set up these committees as a mechanism to respond to and address employee complaints and grievances. The Respondent acted because the employees had voiced complaints about employment-related matters. Further, the employees on the committees were perceived as representatives by their fellow employees. In these circumstances, the employees could reasonably view these committees as a substitute for collective bargaining through traditional union representation.

As to the third factor, the employees were never given assurances of their right to choose collective bargaining through traditional union representation.

As to the fourth factor, antiunion motive was not established.

Weighing all of these factors, I believe that the impact of Respondent's conduct on Section 7 rights outweighs the Employer's lawful motives. Accordingly, I would find a violation in this case.

C. DISCRIMINATION

Page 250. Add following the Note:

Problem for Discussion

In February 1989, the Teamsters won an election to represent the Company's trucking workers. A few weeks later the Company announced that it was closing the department (as it had threatened it would) and was contracting out the work. The Regional Director issued a complaint and, with the Board's authorization, sought a section 10(j) injunction. In December 1989, the District Court denied the injunction. It found "reasonable cause" to believe the closing to be retaliatory, but held that interim relief would create such a financial hardship as to "jeopardize the existence of the business." In March of 1990, the ALJ recommended that the status quo ante be restored finding no evidence of "undue hardship." In September 1991, the Board affirmed. In November 1992, the case was heard before the Court of Appeals. How should it rule? See Coronet Foods, Inc. v. NLRB, 981 F.2d 1284 (D.C.Cir.1993).

D. REMEDIES FOR UNFAIR LABOR PRACTICES

Page 261. Add prior to the Note.

In ABF FREIGHT SYSTEM, INC. v. NLRB, ___ U.S. ___, 114 S.Ct. 835, 127 L.Ed.2d 152 (1994), the United States Supreme Court held that the Board is not precluded from ordering the reinstatement with backpay of an employee who had been discharged in violation of § 8(a)(3), where the employee lied under oath in the hearing before the Board's Administrative Law Judge. The Court relied heavily on its decision in Chevron U.S.A., Inc. v. Natural Resources Defense Council, Inc., 467 U.S. 837, 104 S.Ct. 2778, 81 L.Ed.2d 694 (1984), as requiring the "greatest deference" to the Board's remedial authority.

II. SELECTION OF THE REPRESENTATIVE FOR THE PURPOSES OF COLLECTIVE BARGAINING

A. GROUNDS FOR NOT PROCEEDING TO AN INVESTIGATION & CERTIFICATION

Add on page 278:

The National Labor Relations Board has announced that oral argument would be held on July 28, 1994, in two cases which the Board took to present ten enumerated issues. The thrust of these is to determine whether it is statutorily permissible, administratively practicable, and desirable as a matter of policy for the Board to direct an election first and hear disputed questions later. Those questions might include, for example, of unit placement, jurisdiction, and scope of the unit. The Board also asked for argument on whether it could adopt a Show Cause procedure that might obviate the need for a representation-case hearing, or to limit the scope of hearings to cases of materially disputed facts.

B. APPROPRIATE BARGAINING UNIT

2. *Criteria for Unit Determinations*

Page 287. Add before sub-part 3:

AMERICAN HOSPITAL ASS'N v. NLRB
499 U.S. 606, 111 S.Ct. 1539, 113 L.Ed.2d 675 (1991).

JUSTICE STEVENS delivered the opinion of the Court.

For the first time since the National Labor Relations Board was established in 1935, the Board has promulgated a substantive rule defining the employee units appropriate for collective bargaining in a particular line of commerce. The rule is applicable to acute care hospitals and provides, with three exceptions, that eight and only eight units shall be appropriate in any such hospital. The three exceptions are for cases that present extraordinary circumstances, cases in which nonconforming units already exist, and cases in which labor organizations seek to combine two or more of the eight specified units. The extraordinary circumstances exception applies automatically to hospitals in which the eight unit rule will produce a unit of five or fewer employees. See 29 CFR § 103.30 (1990).

Petitioner, American Hospital Association, brought this action challenging the facial validity of the rule on three grounds: First, petitioner argues that § 9(b) of the National Labor Relations Act requires the Board to make a separate bargaining unit determination "in each case" and therefore prohibits the Board from using general rules to define bargaining units; second, petitioner contends that the rule that the Board has formulated violates a congressional admonition to the Board to avoid the undue proliferation of bargaining units in the health care industry; and, finally, petitioner maintains that the rule is arbitrary and capricious.

The United States District Court for the Northern District of Illinois agreed with petitioner's second argument and enjoined enforcement of the rule. 718 F.Supp. 704 (1989). The Court of Appeals found no merit in any of the three arguments and reversed. 899 F.2d 651 (CA7 1990). Because of the importance of the case, we granted certiorari, 498 U.S. ___, 111 S.Ct. 242, 112 L.Ed.2d 201 (1990). We now affirm.

I

Petitioner's first argument is a general challenge to the Board's rulemaking authority in connection with bargaining unit determinations based on the terms of the National Labor Relations Act (NLRA), 49 Stat. 449, 29 U.S.C. § 151 et seq., as originally enacted in 1935. * * *

Sections 3, 4, and 5 of the Act created the Board and generally described its powers. §§ 153–155. Section 6 granted the Board the "authority from time to time to make, amend, and rescind * * * such rules and regulations as may be necessary to carry out the provisions" of the Act. § 156. This grant was unquestionably sufficient to authorize the rule at issue in this case unless limited by some other provision in the Act.

Petitioner argues that § 9(b) provides such a limitation because this section requires the Board to determine the appropriate bargaining unit "in each case." § 159(b). We are not persuaded. Petitioner would have us put more weight on these three words than they can reasonably carry.

Section 9(a) of the Act provides that the representative "designated or selected for the purposes of collective bargaining by the majority of the employees in a unit appropriate for such purposes" shall be the exclusive bargaining representative for all the employees in that unit. § 159(a). This section, read in light of the policy of the Act, implies that the initiative in selecting an appropriate unit resides with the employees. Moreover, the language suggests that employees may seek to organize "a unit" that is "appropriate"—not necessarily the single most appropriate unit. * * * Thus, one union might seek to represent all of the employees in a particular plant, those in a particular craft, or perhaps just a portion thereof.

Given the obvious potential for disagreement concerning the appropriateness of the unit selected by the union seeking recognition by the employer—disagreements that might involve rival unions claiming jurisdiction over contested segments of the work force as well as disagreements between management and labor—§ 9(b) authorizes the Board to decide whether the designated unit is appropriate. * * * Section 9(b) provides:

> "The Board shall decide *in each case* whether, in order to insure to employees the full benefit of their right to self-organization and to collective bargaining, and otherwise to effectuate the policies of this Act, the unit appropriate for the purposes of collective bargaining shall be the employer unit, craft unit, plant unit, or subdivision thereof." (Emphasis added.)

Petitioner reads the emphasized phrase as a limitation on the Board's rulemaking powers. Although the contours of the restriction that petitioner ascribes to the phrase are murky, petitioner's reading of the language would prevent the Board from imposing any industry-wide rule delineating the appropriate bargaining units. We believe petitioner's reading is inconsistent with the natural meaning of the language read in the context of the statute as a whole.

The more natural reading of these three words is simply to indicate that whenever there is a disagreement about the appropriateness of a unit, the Board shall resolve the dispute. Under this reading, the words "in each case" are synonymous with "whenever necessary" or "in any case in which there is a dispute." Congress chose not to enact a general rule that would require plant unions, craft unions or industry-wide unions for every employer in every line of commerce, but also chose not to leave the decision up to employees or employers alone. Instead, the decision "in each case" in which a dispute arises is to be made by the Board.

In resolving such a dispute, the Board's decision is presumably to be guided not simply by the basic policy of the Act but also by the rules that the Board develops to circumscribe and to guide its discretion either in the process of case-by-case adjudication or by the exercise of its rulemaking authority. The requirement that the Board exercise its discretion in every disputed case cannot fairly or logically be read to command the

Board to exercise standardless discretion in each case. As a noted scholar on administrative law has observed: "[T]he mandate to decide 'in each case' does not prevent the Board from supplanting the original discretionary chaos with some degree of order, and the principal instruments for regularizing the system of deciding 'in each case' are classifications, rules, principles, and precedents. Sensible men could not refuse to use such instruments and a sensible Congress would not expect them to." K. Davis, Administrative Law Text 145 (3d ed. 1972). * * *

Even petitioner acknowledges that "the Board could adopt rules establishing general principles to guide the required case-by-case bargaining unit determinations." Brief for Petitioner 19. Petitioner further acknowledges that the Board has created many such rules in the half-century during which it has adjudicated bargaining unit disputes. Reply Brief for Petitioner 8–11. Petitioner contends, however, that a rule delineating the appropriate bargaining unit for an entire industry is qualitatively different from these prior rules, which at most established rebuttable presumptions that certain units would be considered appropriate in certain circumstances.

We simply cannot find in the three words "in each case" any basis for the fine distinction that petitioner would have us draw. Contrary to petitioner's contention, the Board's rule is not an irrebuttable presumption; instead, it contains an exception for "extraordinary circumstances." Even if the rule did establish an irrebuttable presumption, it would not differ significantly from the prior rules adopted by the Board. As with its prior rules, the Board must still apply the rule "in each case." For example, the Board must decide in each case, among a host of other issues, whether a given facility is properly classified as an acute care hospital and whether particular employees are properly placed in particular units.

Our understanding that the ordinary meaning of the statutory language cannot support petitioner's construction is reinforced by the structure and the policy of the NLRA. As a matter of statutory drafting, if Congress had intended to curtail in a particular area the broad rulemaking authority granted in § 6, we would have expected it to do so in language expressly describing an exception from that section or at least referring specifically to the section. And, in regard to the Act's underlying policy, the goal of facilitating the organization and recognition of unions is certainly served by rules that define in advance the portions of the work force in which organizing efforts may properly be conducted. * * *

In sum, we believe that the meaning of § 9(b)'s mandate that the Board decide the appropriate bargaining unit "in each case" is clear and contrary to the meaning advanced by petitioner. Even if we could find any ambiguity in § 9(b) after employing the traditional tools of statutory construction, we would still defer to the Board's reasonable interpretation of the statutory text. Chevron USA Inc. v. Natural Resources Defense Council, Inc., 467 U.S. 837, 842–843, 104 S.Ct. 2778, 2781–2782, 81 L.Ed.2d 694 (1984). We thus conclude that § 9(b) does not limit the Board's rulemaking authority under § 6.

II

Consideration of petitioner's second argument requires a brief historical review of the application of federal labor law to acute care hospitals. Hospitals were "employers" under the terms of the NLRA as enacted in 1935, but in 1947 Congress excepted not-for-profit hospitals from the coverage of the Act. See 29 U.S.C. § 152(2) (1970) (repealed, 1974). In 1960, the Board decided that proprietary hospitals should also be excepted, see *Flatbush General Hospital,* 126 N.L.R.B. 144, 145, but this position was reversed in 1967, see *Butte Medical Properties,* 168 N.L.R.B. 266, 268.

In 1973, Congress addressed the issue and considered bills that would have extended the Act's coverage to all private health care institutions, including not-for-profit hospitals. The proposed legislation was highly controversial, largely because of the concern that labor unrest in the health care industry might be especially harmful to the public. Moreover, the fact that so many specialists are employed in the industry created the potential for a large number of bargaining units, in each of which separate union representation might multiply management's burden in negotiation and might also increase the risk of strikes. Motivated by these concerns, Senator Taft introduced a bill that would have repealed the exemption for hospitals, but also would have placed a limit of five on the number of bargaining units in nonprofit health care institutions. S. 2292, 93d Cong., 1st Sess. (1973). Senator Taft's bill did not pass.

In the second session of the same Congress, however, the National Labor Relations Act Amendments of 1974 were enacted. See 88 Stat. 395. These amendments subjected all acute care hospitals to the coverage of the Act but made no change in the Board's authority to determine the appropriate bargaining unit in each case. See ibid. Both the House and the Senate Committee Reports on the legislation contained this statement:

"EFFECT ON EXISTING LAW
Bargaining Units

Due consideration should be given by the Board to preventing proliferation of bargaining units in the health care industry. In this connection, the Committee notes with approval the recent Board decisions in *Four Seasons Nursing Center,* 208 NLRB No. 50, 85 LRRM 1093 (1974), and *Woodland Park Hospital,* 205 NLRB No. 144, 84 LRRM 1075 (1973), as well as the trend toward broader units enunciated in *Extendicare of West Virginia,* 203 NLRB No. 170, 83 LRRM 1242 (1973)."

Petitioner does not—and obviously could not—contend that this statement in the Committee Reports has the force of law, for the Constitution is quite explicit about the procedure that Congress must follow in legislating. Nor, in view of the fact that Congress refused to enact the Taft bill that would have placed a limit of five on the number of hospital bargaining units, does petitioner argue that eight units necessarily constitute proliferation. Rather, petitioner's primary argument is that the admonition, when coupled with the rejection of a general rule imposing a five-unit limit, evinces Congress' intent to emphasize the importance of the "in each case" requirement in § 9(b).

We find this argument no more persuasive than petitioner's reliance on § 9(b) itself. Assuming that the admonition was designed to emphasize the requirement that the Board determine the appropriate bargaining unit in each case, we have already explained that the Board's rule does not contravene this mandate. See Part I, supra.

Petitioner also suggests that the admonition "is an authoritative statement of what Congress intended when it extended the Act's coverage to include nonproprietary hospitals." Brief for Petitioner 30. Even if we accepted this suggestion, we read the admonition as an expression by the Committees of their desire that the Board give "due consideration" to the special problems that "proliferation" might create in acute care hospitals. Examining the record of the Board's rulemaking proceeding, we find that it gave extensive consideration to this very issue. See App. 20, 78–84, 114, 122, 131, 140, 158–159, 191–194, 246–254.

In any event, we think that the admonition in the Committee Reports is best understood as a form of notice to the Board that if it did not give appropriate consideration to the problem of proliferation in this industry, Congress might respond with a legislative remedy. So read, the remedy for noncompliance with the admonition is in the hands of the body that issued it. * * * If Congress believes that the Board has not given "due consideration" to the issue, Congress may fashion an appropriate response.

III

Petitioner's final argument is that the rule is arbitrary and capricious because "it ignores critical differences among the more than 4,000 acute-care hospitals in the United States, including differences in size, location, operations, and work-force organization." Brief for Petitioner 39. Petitioner supports this argument by noting that in at least one earlier unit determination, the Board had commented that the diverse character of the health care industry precluded generalizations about the appropriateness of any particular bargaining unit. See *St. Francis*

Hospital, 271 N.L.R.B. 948, 953, n. 39 (1984), remanded sub nom. Electrical Workers v. NLRB, 259 U.S.App.D.C. 168, 814 F.2d 697 (1987).

The Board responds to this argument by relying on the extensive record developed during the rulemaking proceedings, as well as its experience in the adjudication of health care cases during the 13–year period between the enactment of the health care amendments and its notice of proposed rulemaking. Based on that experience, the Board formed the "considered judgment" that "acute care hospitals do not differ in substantial, significant ways relating to the appropriateness of units." App. 188–189. Moreover, the Board argues, the exception for "extraordinary circumstances" is adequate to take care of the unusual case in which a particular application of the rule might be arbitrary.

We do not believe that the challenged rule is inconsistent with the Board's earlier comment on diversity in the health care industry. The comment related to the entire industry whereas the rule does not apply to many facilities, such as nursing homes, blood banks, and outpatient clinics. See *St. Francis,* 271 N.L.R.B., at 953, n. 39. Moreover, the Board's earlier discussion "anticipate[d] that after records have been developed and a number of cases decided from these records, certain recurring factual patterns will emerge and illustrate which units are typically appropriate." See ibid.

Given the extensive notice and comment rulemaking conducted by the Board, its careful analysis of the comments that it received, and its well-reasoned justification for the new rule, we would not be troubled even if there were inconsistencies between the current rule and prior NLRB pronouncements. The statutory authorization "from time to time to make, amend, and rescind" rules and regulations expressly contemplates the possibility that the Board will reshape its policies on the basis of more information and experience in the administration of the Act. See 29 U.S.C. § 156. The question whether the Board has changed its view about certain issues or certain industries does not undermine the validity of a rule that is based on substantial evidence and supported by a "reasoned analysis." See Motor Vehicle Mfrs. Assn. v. State Farm Mutual Automobile Ins. Co., 463 U.S. 29, 42, 57, 103 S.Ct. 2856, 2866, 2874, 77 L.Ed.2d 443 (1983).

The Board's conclusion that, absent extraordinary circumstances, "acute care hospitals do not differ in substantial, significant ways relating to the appropriateness of units," App. 189, was based on a "reasoned analysis" of an extensive record. See 463 U.S., at 57, 103 S.Ct., at 2874. The Board explained that diversity among hospitals had not previously affected the results of bargaining unit determinations and that diversification did not make rulemaking inappropriate. See App. 55–59. The Board justified its selection of the individual bargaining units by detailing the factors that supported generalizations as to the appropriateness of those units.   See, e.g., id., at 93–94, 97, 98, 101, 118–120, 123–129, 133–140.   * * *

It is so ordered.

———

In PARK MANOR CARE CENTER, 305 N.L.R.B. 872 (1991), the Board confronted the task of making unit determinations in privately owned nursing homes, which were excluded from the coverage of the rule that was approved by the Supreme Court, which applied only to "acute care hospitals."   The Board stated that the much more varied employment circumstances obtaining in nursing homes warrant the continued making of unit determinations on a case-by-case adjudicatory basis.   Both for this proposition, and for much of the background information that went into its unit determination in this case regarding technical employees at the Park Manor Care Center, the Board relied upon a considerable amount of evidence that had been forthcoming in its earlier rulemaking proceeding.   [If and when a court were to review the Board's unit determination in *Park Manor,* would that review be based on the adjudicatory record in the representation case, or could it also include reference to the legislative-type record that was developed in the rulemaking proceeding?]

———

On March 5, 1992, the National Labor Relations Board published an "Advance notice of proposed rulemaking" soliciting views on whether a labor organization's duties under Communications Workers of America v. Beck, infra at 1110–1111, with respect to the assessment of fees and dues necessary for performing the duties of an exclusive bargaining representative are better defined by the use of rulemaking.

> Responses may be directed to any relevant topic, including but not limited to (1) the substantive issues that should be addressed in an administrative rulemaking proceeding, and (2) the manner in which such a proceeding should be structured.

57 Fed.Reg. 7897 (1992).   At the same time, the Board published for comment a set of proposed rules codifying standardized remedial provisions in Board decisions regarding offers of reinstatement, make-whole remedies, computation of interest, and the posting of notices.   Id.   No final rules have yet been promulgated.

On June 2, 1994, the Board published an "advance notice of proposed rulemaking" inviting all interested parties to comment on (a) the wisdom of promulgating a rule or rules governing the appropriateness of single-location bargaining units in the retail, manufacturing, and trucking industries, and (b) the content of such rule or rules. The notice suggests that a rule or rules might limit the necessity for litigation and suggested some lines the rules might take.

----

4. *Multiemployer and Coordinated Bargaining*

Page 306. Add prior to the Note:

On May 9, 1994, the National Labor Relations Board held oral argument in two cases to reconsider Retail Associates, 120 N.L.R.B. 388 (1958), and its rules governing withdrawal from a multi-employer bargaining unit. Of special concern to the Board was the situation in which negotiations were commenced prior to the date set by the collective agreement and without notice to an employer that such had begun.

III. SECURING BARGAINING RIGHTS THROUGH UNFAIR LABOR PRACTICE PROCEEDINGS

Page 361. Add new Problem:

4. The NLRB's position is that the evidence needed to justify an employer poll is the same as would justify its withdrawal of recognition or the filing of an employer petition for a Board-conducted election. Should the standard to permit polling be less stringent than the standard for withdrawal of recognition? Texas Petrochemicals Corp., 296 N.L.R.B. 1057 (1989), remanded as modified Texas Petrochemicals Corp. v. NLRB, 923 F.2d 398 (5th Cir.1991).

Part Three

NEGOTIATION OF THE COLLECTIVE BARGAINING AGREEMENT

II. THE DUTY TO BARGAIN IN GOOD FAITH

Page 411. Add Problem 5:

5. Two cocktail waitresses at a gambling casino were discharged as a result of complaints by two customers, and the union has challenged the discharge via the grievance procedure in the collective bargaining agreement. It has requested the names, addresses, and telephone numbers of the complaining customers. The casino has offered to contact the customers and to release their names if they so authorize. The union has rejected the offer and filed a charge of a violation of § 8(a)(5). Should a complaint issue? See Resorts Int'l Hotel Casino v. NLRB, 996 F.2d 1553 (3d Cir.1993).

III. SUBJECTS OF COLLECTIVE BARGAINING

Page 470. Substitute for *Arrow Automotive*:

UNITED FOOD & COMMERCIAL WORKERS, LOCAL 150–A v. NLRB (DUBUQUE PACKING CO.)

1 F.3d 24 (D.C.Cir.1993).

Before EDWARDS, RUTH BADER GINSBURG, and BUCKLEY, CIRCUIT JUDGES.

BUCKLEY, CIRCUIT JUDGE:

Dubuque Packing Company petitions for review of a National Labor Relations Board order holding that it committed unfair labor practices by breaching its duty to bargain with its union regarding the relocation of its "hog kill and cut" operations. We hold that the new standard adopted by the Board for evaluating such claims is an acceptable reading of the National Labor Relations Act and Supreme Court precedents; that the Board's finding that Dubuque owed a duty to bargain was supported by substantial evidence; and that the Board properly applied its new test retroactively to the facts of this case. Hence, we deny Dubuque's petition and enforce the Board's remedial order. * * *

I. Background

A. Facts and Procedural History

The facts of this case were set forth at length in our earlier opinion, United Food & Commercial Workers Int'l Union, Local 150–A v. NLRB, 880 F.2d 1422, 1423–27 (D.C.Cir.1989) ("UFCW I"); in relevant part, they are these. Beginning about 1977, the Dubuque Packing Company, a processor and packager of beef and pork, began losing money at its Dubuque, Iowa, home plant. In 1978, Dubuque won an agreement from the plant's workers, who were represented by the United Food and Commercial Workers International Union ("UFCW"), requiring the workers to produce at higher rates in return for a one-time cash payment. In August 1980, Dubuque extracted concessions worth approximately $5 million per annum in return for a pledge that it would not ask for further concessions before the September 1, 1982, expiration of the union contract then in effect. In March 1981, however, it again requested concessions, this time in the form of additional productivity increases in its hog kill department.

On March 30, 1981, the events at issue here began to unfold. On that date, Dubuque gave six-months' notice, as required by its labor contract, of its intention to close its hog kill and cut operations at Dubuque. Various maneuvers between the company and the UFCW ensued, culminating in the union's rejection of a wage freeze aimed at keeping the Dubuque hog kill and cut operation open. The following day, June 10, 1981, the company announced that it was considering relocating—rather than closing—its hog kill and cut department, and that it was also considering relocating up to 900 Dubuque plant pork processing jobs. The UFCW responded by requesting detailed financial information from Dubuque, which the company refused to provide. Dubuque then advised its employees in writing that they could save their jobs by approving its wage freeze proposal. On June 28, 1981, the wage freeze was resubmitted to the workers for a vote, accompanied by the union leadership's recommendation that it be rejected until Dubuque opened its books. The workers voted overwhelmingly with their union and against the company. Three days later, Dubuque informed the union that its decision to close the hog kill and cut department was "irrevocable."

Over the next few months, Dubuque and the UFCW continued to negotiate over Dubuque's proposed relocation of its pork processing operations. On October 1, 1981, Dubuque opened a hog kill and cut operation at its newly acquired Rochelle, Illinois, plant and, two days later, eliminated approximately 530 hog kill and cut jobs at the Dubuque plant. On October 19, 1981, an agreement was signed granting wage concessions for the remaining workers at the Dubuque plant in return for the company's agreement to keep the 900 pork processing jobs in Dubuque and to extend the current labor agreement. By early 1982, however, the company's hope of obtaining new financing had collapsed, taking with it Dubuque's prospects for remaining in business at Dubuque and Rochelle. Both plants were closed and sold on October 15, 1982.

On June 26, 1981, and August 7, 1981, the UFCW filed unfair labor practice complaints with the Board. It claimed that Dubuque had refused to bargain in good faith as to both the consummated relocation and the proposed one, objecting especially to the company's alleged duplicity and its refusal to disclose financial data. On June 17, 1985, an administrative law judge ("ALJ") rendered a decision on these complaints. Dubuque Packing Co., Nos. 33–CA–5524, 33–CA–5588 (ALJ June 15, 1985) ("ALJ Decision"), appended to Dubuque Packing Co., 287 N.L.R.B. 499 (1987). The ALJ suggested that Dubuque's conduct may indeed have fallen below the standards of good-faith bargaining, ALJ Decision, 287 N.L.R.B. at 538, 540 n. 132, but he nevertheless held that Dubuque committed no unfair labor practice, id. at 543, because it was under no duty to negotiate over its decision to relocate. Id. at 540. Over two years later, the NLRB summarily affirmed the ALJ, adopting his findings and opinion. Dubuque Packing Co., 287 N.L.R.B. 499 (1987).

On review of the Board's decision, we remanded the case, declaring that the Board's opinion had been inadequately explained. UFCW I, 880 F.2d at 1439. * * *

On remand, the Board unanimously approved a new test [which it applied] to the relocation of the Dubuque hog kill and cut operation and found that a duty to bargain had existed and had been breached. Id. at 398. As a remedy, it ordered Dubuque to pay back wages to all employees terminated as a result of the relocation, from the date of their termination to October 15, 1982, the date operations ceased at Dubuque and Rochelle. * * *

[Dubuque] petitioned for review of the Board ruling * * * while the NLRB cross-petitioned for the enforcement of its order. * * *

B. Legal Framework

The critical question in this litigation is whether Dubuque's relocation of its hog kill and cut operation constitutes a mandatory subject of bargaining under the National Labor Relations Act ("NLRA" or "Act") * * * [i.e.,] whether a plant relocation such as the one executed by Dubuque constitutes a "term[ ] [or] condition[ ] of employment" under section 8(d) of Act; if it does, then Dubuque's failure to bargain in good faith over the relocation constitutes an unfair labor practice under section 8(a)(5). The two critical Supreme Court decisions interpreting "terms and conditions of employment" for these purposes are First National Maintenance Corp. v. NLRB, 452 U.S. 666, 101 S.Ct. 2573, 69 L.Ed.2d 318 (1981), which held that an employer's decision to close a part of its business is not a mandatory subject of bargaining, and Fibreboard Paper Products Corp. v. NLRB, 379 U.S. 203, 85 S.Ct. 398, 13 L.Ed.2d 233 (1964), which held that the replacement of union labor with subcontracted workers is.

II. Discussion

A. Dubuque's Petition

Dubuque argues that the Board's new test improperly interprets Supreme Court precedent, that it was improperly applied to these facts, and that the Board erred by retroactively applying its new test to this case. We disagree on all counts.

1. The Legality of the Board's New Test

Dubuque claims the Board erred in finding that its relocation involved a "term[ ] [or] condition[ ] of employment" subject to mandatory bargaining under the NLRA. In particular, it argues that the Board's new test represents an impermissible reading of the Supreme Court's decision in *First National Maintenance*. In reviewing such claims, we will respect the Board's "policy choices," so long as "its interpretation of what the Act requires is reasonable, in light of the purposes of the Act and the controlling precedent of the Supreme Court." UFCW I, 880 F.2d at 1429. * * *

In these proceedings, the Board set out to enunciate a new legal test "guided by the principles set forth in *First National Maintenance*." Dubuque Packing, 303 N.L.R.B. at 390. It adopted the following standard for determining whether "a decision to relocate [bargaining] unit work," id., is a mandatory subject of bargaining: Initially, the burden is on the [NLRB] General Counsel to establish that the employer's decision involved a relocation of unit work unaccompanied by a basic change in the nature of the employer's operation. If the General Counsel successfully carries his burden in this regard, he will have established prima facie that the employer's relocation decision is a mandatory subject of bargaining. At this juncture, the employer may produce evidence rebutting the prima facie case by establishing that the work performed at the new location varies significantly from the work performed at the former plant, establishing that the work performed at the former plant is to be discontinued entirely and not moved to the new location, or establishing that the employer's decision involves a change in the scope and direction of the enterprise. Alternatively, the employer may proffer a defense to show by a preponderance of the evidence: (1) that labor costs (direct and/or indirect) were not a factor in the decision, or (2) that even if labor costs were a factor in the decision, the union could not have offered labor cost concessions that could have changed the employer's decision to relocate. Id. at 391. * * *

The Board's test involves three distinct layers of analysis. First, the test recognizes a category of decisions lying "at the core of entrepreneurial control," Fibreboard, 379 U.S. at 223, 85 S.Ct. at 409 (Stewart, J., concurring), in which employers may unilaterally take action. Specifically, the test exempts from the duty to bargain relocations involving (1) "a basic change in the nature of the employer's operation," (2) "a change in the scope and direction of the enterprise," (3) situations in which "the work performed at the new location varies significantly from the work performed at the former plant," or (4) situations in which "the work performed at the former plant is to be discontinued entirely and not moved to the new location." Dubuque Packing, 303 N.L.R.B. at 391.

This language would appear broad enough to cover key entrepreneurial decisions such as setting the scale (e.g., the quantity of product produced) and scope (e.g., the type of product produced) of the employer's operations, and determining the basic method of production. Moreover, as to these issues, the Board's test requires an analysis based on the objective differences between the employer's old and new operations. It asks whether various types of "basic change," "change," "vari[ance]," or "discontinu[ance]" were involved in the relocation. Where such objective differences appear, an entrepreneurial decision is deemed to have been taken, and the employer is permitted to relocate without negotiating.

The second layer of the Board's analysis is a subjective one. Cf. Dubuque Packing, 303 N.L.R.B. at 392 (referring to the employer's "motivation for the relocation decision"). Under this heading, the relevant question is whether "labor costs (direct and/or indirect) were ... a factor" in the employer's relocation decision. Id. at 391. As illustrated by the Board, this analysis will distinguish relocations motivated by labor costs from those motivated by other perceived advantages of the new location. Compare id. at 390 n. 9 (collecting cases in which the relocation was motivated by labor costs) with id. at 390 n. 10 (collecting cases in which the decision was motivated by other factors).

The third layer includes a futility provision. As we shall see below, the Board permits an employer to relocate without negotiating where its union either would not or could not offer sufficient concessions to change its decision. See Dubuque Packing, 303 N.L.R.B. at 391. Also, the Board has pledged to consider circumstances such as the need to implement a relocation "expeditiously" in determining whether bargaining over a relocation has reached "a bona fide impasse," id. at 392; that is, the point at which a party may act unilaterally.

Dubuque objects that the Board's test is inconsistent with *First National Maintenance*. Its argument tends toward the proposition that a *per se* rule exempting relocation decisions from the duty to bargain is implicit in *First National Maintenance's* reasoning, if not its holding. Dubuque's general objection is that the Board's test is insufficiently

protective of management prerogatives, both on its face and because it is
not capable of certainty in application. Dubuque pointedly reminds us
that *First National Maintenance* held that employers "must have some
degree of certainty beforehand" as to which decisions are and are not
subject to a bargaining duty. See First National Maintenance, 452 U.S.
at 679, 101 S.Ct. at 2581. More specifically, Dubuque argues that
relocation decisions must be exempt from the duty to bargain because
they involve the reallocation of capital, observing that allocations of
capital are "core managerial decisions." See Brief for Dubuque at 38.

We pause to emphasize that our analysis of the Board's test is
premised on our resolution of an important ambiguity in the Board's
statement of its second affirmative defense. As stated by the Board,
that defense requires an employer to establish that "the union *could not*
have offered labor cost concessions that could have changed the employer's decision to relocate." Dubuque Packing, 303 N.L.R.B. at 391
(emphasis added). On its face, this language might be read as an
impossibility exception—a provision allowing an employer to eschew
negotiations only if its union could not possibly have changed the
relocation decision no matter how accommodating the union might have
been at the bargaining table. This reading is strengthened by the
Board's illustration of the defense, which involves a case in which an
employer "would not remain at the present plant because ... the costs
for modernization of equipment or environmental controls were greater
than [the value of] any labor cost concessions the union *could* offer." Id.
(emphasis added).

Despite this evidence, we think this defense was intended to cover
situations in which bargaining would be futile, as well as ones in which it
would be impossible for the union to persuade the employer to rescind
its relocation decision. Immediately after setting forth its test and the
above illustration, the Board stated that under the second affirmative
defense, "an employer would have a bargaining obligation *if the union
could and would* offer concessions that approximate, meet, or exceed the
anticipated costs or benefits that prompted the relocation decision."
Dubuque Packing Co., 303 N.L.R.B. at 391 (emphasis added). * * * As
we read it, the Board's test holds that no duty to bargain exists where
bargaining would be futile—either because the union was unable to offer
sufficient concessions, or because it was unwilling to do so.

Viewing the Board's test through the lens of this interpretation, we
find it sufficiently protective of an employer's prerogative to manage its
business. Under *First National Maintenance*, employers may be required to negotiate management decisions where "the benefit, for labor-
management relations and the collective-bargaining process, outweighs
the burden placed on the conduct of the business." First National
Maintenance, 452 U.S. at 679, 101 S.Ct. at 2581. The Board's test
exempts from the duty to negotiate relocations that, viewed objectively,
are entrepreneurial in nature. It exempts decisions that, viewed subjec-

tively, were motivated by something other than labor costs. And it explicitly excuses employers from attempting to negotiate when doing so would be futile or impossible. What is left are relocations that leave the firm occupying much the same entrepreneurial position as previously, that were taken because of the cost of labor, and that offer a realistic hope for a negotiated settlement. The Board's determination that bargaining over such decisions promises benefits outweighing the "burden[s] placed on the conduct of [an employer's] business" was in no way unreasonable.

Similarly, the Board was also justified in finding that its test accords with Supreme Court precedent. A relocation satisfying the three layers of the Board's test will resemble the subcontracting decision held subject to a mandatory bargaining duty in *Fibreboard* in three distinct ways: Because of the new test's objective component, such a relocation will not "alter the Company's basic operation," Fibreboard, 379 U.S. at 213, 85 S.Ct. at 404, in a way that implicates the employer's "core of entrepreneurial control," id. at 223, 85 S.Ct. at 409 (Stewart, J., concurring); because of the new test's subjective component, "a desire to reduce labor costs" will lie "at the base of the employer's decision," see First National Maintenance, 452 U.S. at 680, 101 S.Ct. at 2581 (discussing *Fibreboard*); and because of the new test's exclusion of situations in which bargaining would be futile, there will be some prospect of resolving the relocation dispute "within the collective bargaining framework." Fibreboard, 379 U.S. at 213–14, 85 S.Ct. at 404. Like its balancing of burdens and benefits, the Board's finding that its test accords with precedent is fully defensible.

Dubuque counters that relocation decisions should not be treated the same as the subcontract considered in *Fibreboard* because they will differ from that arrangement on a crucial point—relocations involve the expenditure of capital. Cf. Fibreboard, 379 U.S. at 225, 85 S.Ct. at 410 (Stewart, J., concurring) ("larger entrepreneurial questions [such] as * * * *how capital shall be invested in fixed assets*" not governed by *Fibreboard*'s holding) (emphasis added); id. at 213, 85 S.Ct. at 404 (noting that "[n]o capital investment was contemplated" in connection with the subcontract). Furthermore, as Dubuque points out, key portions of the *First National Maintenance* opinion relied on Justice Stewart's concurrence in *Fibreboard*, which was particularly solicitous of management prerogatives over capital expenditure. See, e.g., First National Maintenance, 452 U.S. at 676–77, 101 S.Ct. at 2579–80 (citing Fibreboard, 379 U.S. at 223, 85 S.Ct. at 409 (Stewart, J., concurring)).

For several reasons, we remain unconvinced. First, the Board's test exempts from the duty to bargain relocations in which "the work performed at the new location varies significantly from the work performed at the former plant." Dubuque Packing, 303 N.L.R.B. at 391. Under this standard, relocations involving a sufficiently altered pattern of fixed-capital use (such as a shift from a labor-intensive production line to a fully automated factory) would appear exempt from the bargaining duty. Cf. Local 777, Democratic Union Org. Comm., Seafarers Int'l Union v. NLRB, 603 F.2d 862, 884 (D.C.Cir.1978) ("*Local 777*") (stating that "major shifts in the capital investment or corporate strategy of a company are not mandatory bargaining subjects"). Second, many "terms and conditions of employment" over which employers are plainly bound to bargain involve the expenditure of "capital." Unless management rights are impermissibly invaded every time a union bargains for a breakroom water-cooler or shop-floor safety equipment, the realm of mandatory bargaining must include at least some decisions involving capital expenditures. Third, while *First National Maintenance* did reflect the influence of Justice Stewart's *Fibreboard* opinion, it did not reiterate that opinion's specific concerns with management's prerogative over the expenditure of capital, or otherwise indicate that a line protecting all decisions to expend capital must be drawn. Given this, and the deference owed the Board's policy choices, see UFCW I, 880 F.2d at 1429, we find that the Board's test does not impermissibly fail to protect management's prerogatives over capital investment. The dicta Dubuque cites are too thin to bear the weight placed on them.

Dubuque's final contention is that the test is so imprecise that employers are denied the degree of certainty or guidance that it believes the Supreme Court mandated in *First National Maintenance*. See 452 U.S. at 679, 101 S.Ct. at 2581. While we can agree that *First National Maintenance* affirms management's need for "*some* degree of certainty" so that it "may proceed to reach decisions without fear of later evaluations labeling its conduct an unfair labor practice," id. (emphasis added), this does not require that the Board establish standards devoid of ambiguity at the margins. The test announced in *Dubuque Packing* provides more than the "some" degree of certainty required by the Supreme Court. It establishes rules on which management may plan with a large degree of confidence; and while the test undoubtedly leaves areas of uncertainty between relocation decisions that are clearly within the exclusive prerogatives of management and those that are equally clearly subject to negotiation, these will in time be narrowed through future adjudications. We therefore conclude that the standard adopted by the Board was a reasonable policy choice and that its decision to proceed by adjudication, not rulemaking, was also within its discretion. See NLRB v. Bell Aerospace Co., 416 U.S. 267, 294, 94 S.Ct. 1757, 1772, 40 L.Ed.2d 134 (1974) (upholding a decision to proceed by adjudication where the relevant facts "vary widely depending on the company or industry"); see also Bechtel v. FCC, 957 F.2d 873, 881 (D.C.Cir.1992) (affirming that an agency may "choose to make new policy through either rulemaking or adjudication").

Finally, we find no fatal uncertainty in the Board's test as it applies to these facts. As we explain below, the Board's ruling easily survives Dubuque's contention that the test's requirements were not met in regard to its particular relocation. Employers should have no trouble understanding that actions such as Dubuque's run afoul of the Board's newly articulated standard.

2. *The Application of the Board's Test to Dubuque*

Dubuque next contends that the Board improperly applied its test to the facts of this case and that under the new standard, properly applied, its actions did not give rise to a bargaining duty. In addressing this contention, we are required by statute to uphold "the findings of the Board with respect to questions of fact if supported by substantial evidence on the record considered as a whole." 29 U.S.C. § 160(f).

Dubuque objects, first, to the Board's finding that its relocation did not constitute a change in the scope and direction of its business. It relies for support on the ALJ's finding that the Rochelle plant was a "smaller, newer, more modern ..., better laid out" facility and his conclusion "that [Dubuque's] relocation of the hog kill and cut to Rochelle clearly turned on a fundamental change in the scope, nature, and direction of [its] business of which labor costs were but a single important factor." ALJ Decision, 287 N.L.R.B. at 538. The Board rejected this conclusion, stating that "[t]here is no evidence that the relocation decision was accompanied by a basic change in the nature of the employer's operation." Dubuque Packing, 303 N.L.R.B. at 393.

The Board's position enjoys ample support in the record. In fact, its rejection of the ALJ's conclusion is specifically supported by the ALJ's findings. The ALJ stated that Dubuque

> used the Rochelle facility to substantially replace the Dubuque facility. As production in Rochelle increased, there was a corresponding reduction at Dubuque until the hog kill and cut processing departments and related operations there were completely phased out. Larry J. Tangeman, general plant superintendent at Dubuque, became superintendent of the Rochelle facility and about 13 members of Dubuque management also were transferred to Rochelle, as was certain production equipment. The purposes of the Rochelle plant, to slaughter hogs, dress carcasses, and to process pork into hams, bacon, and sausage, were the same as at the Dubuque plant.

ALJ Decision, 287 N.L.R.B. at 529. Indeed, in view of these facts, the ALJ felt it necessary to "find" on the record that "the transfer ... did not constitute subcontracting." Id. at 529 n. 82. Aside from the ALJ's conclusory statement, Dubuque points to nothing indicating that the Dubuque and Rochelle operations were objectively dissimilar enough (in scale of operations for example) for the relocation to constitute a "basic change in the nature of the employer's operation" as that phrase is used in the test. See Dubuque Packing, 303 N.L.R.B. at 391. Viewed as a whole, the record offers substantial support for the Board's position.

Dubuque's second contention is that because "the record . . . is very clear that the union 'would not' offer labor concessions," bargaining would have been futile; hence it was not required.   * * *

While we agree that our precedent, like the Board's test, relieves employers from any duty to bargain in the face of a union's adamantine intransigence, that principle has no bearing here. As counsel for the UFCW pointed out at oral argument, the UFCW "could, would, and did" accept concessions—in 1978, in August 1980, and again in October 1981—all in a vain attempt to keep the Dubuque facility open. Indeed, the vote that led to Dubuque's "irrevocable" decision to relocate was not a vote to categorically refuse Dubuque's overtures, but a vote to insist on financial disclosure as a prelude to bargaining. The Board's finding that good-faith bargaining between Dubuque and the UFCW might not have been futile was substantially supported by the record.

3. Retroactivity

Finally, Dubuque argues that the Board erred by "retroactively" employing its new test in this case. Again, we disagree.

Our formulation of the standard for evaluating challenges to the retroactive application of a ruling from an agency adjudication has varied. * * * What has not varied is our consistent willingness to approve the retroactive application of rulings that do not represent an "abrupt break with well-settled policy" but merely "attempt to fill a void in an unsettled area of the law." * * * Indeed, an agency's authority to proceed by adjudication, as opposed to rulemaking, see Bell Aerospace Co., 416 U.S. at 294, 94 S.Ct. at 1772, implies a power to fill interstices in the law by proceeding case by case. * * *

Although our multi-factor tests have been stated in terms of a balancing of co-equal factors, each includes one that, in practice, has been given primary importance; namely, the critical question of whether the challenged decision "creates a new rule, either by overruling past precedents relied upon by the parties or because it was an issue of first impression." * * * As a practical matter, where an agency ruling seeks only to clarify the contours of established doctrine, we will almost per force allow its retroactive application.

In this case, the Board's test merely clarifies the line between relocation decisions that, because they are analogous to subcontracting arrangements, are subject to a duty to bargain and those that, because they are analogous to partial closings, are not. At the time Dubuque announced its "irrevocable" decision to relocate, the question of whether relocation decisions must be negotiated was an old one and the existence of this legal "interstice" was apparent. By that time, July 1, 1981, both Fibreboard and First National Maintenance had been decided. The Court's opinion in the latter had called into question the Board's former practice of "consistently holding that relocation of work from one plant to another was a mandatory subject of bargaining," UFCW I, 880 F.2d at 1429. See id. at 1431. First National Maintenance had also expressly reserved judgment on "management decisions[ ] such as plant relocations." 452 U.S. at 686 n. 22, 101 S.Ct. at 2584 n. 22.

Moreover, the gap in the law that had already been opened when Dubuque acted was not closed until the announcement of the test we approve today. In the intervening years, a Board majority never embraced a standard under which Dubuque's failure to bargain would have been lawful. Thus, the Board's test does not "create[ ] a new rule, either by overruling past precedents relied upon by the parties or because it was an issue of first impression," District Lodge 64, 949 F.2d at 447; rather it "fill[s] a void" in the law. Local 900, 727 F.2d at 1195. We have observed before that

> [c]ircumstances such as these are the stuff that adjudications are made of: the law is unclear; opposing parties mount reasonable arguments on both sides; the adjudicator says what the law is. In such circumstances, the general rule [is] that judicial or administrative precedents apply not only prospectively but to cases pending at the time they are decided.

Atchison, Topeka & Santa Fe Ry. Co. v. ICC, 851 F.2d 1432, 1437 (D.C.Cir.1988) (brackets and quotation marks omitted). Because we find on these facts no special inequity in allowing this interstitial ruling to apply retroactively, we affirm the Board's application of its new test to the present case.

* * *

III. Conclusion

For the foregoing reasons, we deny Dubuque's petition for review [and] enforce the Board's remedial order against Dubuque * * *. So ordered.

Problems for Discussion

1. It was the apparent purpose of the members of the NLRB to: (a) achieve unanimity on this complex issue; (b) to adhere to the teaching of the Supreme Court in *First National Maintenance;* (c) to assure more clearly the rights of employees in major corporate decisions less "drastic" than the closing of part or all of a business; (d) to provide clear guidelines to companies and unions seeking to know their bargaining rights and duties; and (e) to provide clear guidelines for the parties in litigation before the Board. Did the Board achieve these objectives with *Dubuque Packing?*

2. Does the Board give too great weight to employer interests when it holds that there is no duty to bargain about the decision to relocate whenever there is a "basic change in the nature" of the company's business? (What does that mean? Why should that matter?) Does the Board give too great weight to employee interests when it holds that there *is* a duty to bargain about the

decision to relocate whenever labor costs are "a factor" in the decision? (How often will that *not* be the case?)

3. Would it be feasible, and wise, for the NLRB to extrapolate from the guidelines announced in *Dubuque Packing* so as to have them apply to *all* major corporate decisions, such as automation, subcontracting and even partial closings? Would such an extension be consistent with *First National Maintenance* and with *Fibreboard?* See Torrington Indus., 307 NLRB No. 129 (1992).

VI. RECONSIDERING THE LABOR ACT IN THE CONTEMPORARY CONTEXT

A. CHANGE IN EMPLOYER POLICIES

Page 515. Add to the references at the conclusion of section VI(A):

P. Doerenger et al., TURBULENCE IN THE AMERICAN WORKPLACE (1991) (and especially Chap. 7 on "The Two–Tiered Workforce in U.S. Corporations").

D. THE CURRENT AND FUTURE SIGNIFICANCE OF LABOR UNIONS

Page 523. Add at the end of the page:

The Secretaries of Labor and Commerce appointed a Commission on the Future of Worker–Management Relations to investigate and report on three questions:

1. What (if any) new methods or institutions should be encouraged, or required, to enhance work-place productivity through labor-management cooperation and employee participation?

2. What (if any) changes should be made in the present legal framework and practices of collective bargaining to enhance cooperative behavior, improve productivity, and reduce conflict and delay?

3. What (if anything) should be done to increase the extent to which work-place problems are directly resolved by the parties themselves, rather than through recourse to state and federal courts and government regulatory bodies?

On June 2, 1994, the Commission, chaired by John T. Dunlop, a distinguished labor economist from Harvard University and former Secretary of Labor, which has taken the name of its chairman in common usage ("the Dunlop Commission"), issued a 140 page "fact finding report" in which it summarized the broad sweep of its preliminary conclusions and identified areas of particular concern. It anticipates issuing a final report and recommendations in November, 1994. The Commission's General Observations identify themes that transcend the three questions presented—the complexity and diversity of workplaces and of workplace practices, the diversity of the workforce—and the widening disparity in incomes—and the need for greater cooperation, participation, and trust. The Commission discerned what it termed a "mismatch" between policy and practice, especially in American labor law. Commission on the Future of Worker–Management Relations, Fact Finding Report 140–141 (1994).

A good deal of attention was devoted to the contemporary role of § 8(a)(2). On that, the Commission identified a variety of questions respecting future legal policy—including whether or not § 8(a)(2) "should be retained in its present form"—as well as the following propositions:

— Section 8(a)(2) should no longer limit the freedom of nonunion employers to establish procedures by which its employees will "deal with" (as opposed to "collectively bargain" about) conditions of employment.

— Section 8(a)(2) should be relaxed to permit employers to establish such employee participation procedures dealing with conditions of work, if these procedures meet certain standards about employee selection, access to information, protection against reprisals, and the like.

— Section 8(a)(2) should be altered to require employers to offer their employees participation procedures meeting these minimum quality standards.

Id. at 57. With respect to the Labor Act the Commission's "principal findings" included the following:

3. Representation elections as currently constituted are a highly conflictual activity for workers, unions, and firms. This means that many new collective bargaining relationships start off in an environment that is highly adversarial.

4. The probability that a worker will be discharged or otherwise unfairly discriminated against for exercising legal rights under the NLRA has increased over time. Unions as well as firms have engaged in unfair labor practices under the NLRA. The bulk of meritorious charges are for employer unfair practices.

* * *

7. Roughly a third of workplaces that vote to be represented by a union do not obtain a collective bargaining contract with their employer.

Id. at 79. The critical questions this poses for labor law reform were identified as:

— How can the level of conflict and amount of resources devoted to union recognition campaigns be de-escalated?

— What new techniques might produce more effective compliance with prohibitions against discriminatory discharges, bad faith bargaining, and other illegal actions?

— Should the labor law seek to provide workers who want representation but who are a minority at a workplace a greater option for non-exclusive representation?

— Should unions be given greater access to employees on the job during organizational campaigns, and if so how?

— What if anything, should be done to increase the probability that workers who vote for representation and their employers achieve a first contract and on-going collective bargaining relationship?

— How might cooperation in mature bargaining relationships be increased?

Id. at 79–80.

For more on the future of unions (and of the direction of U.S. labor law), see *Symposium: Labor Market Institutions and the Future Role of Unions*, 30 Indus.Rel. 1–228 (1992). For more on the question of representation, by modification of § 8(a)(2), by fostering informal methods of representation, or—as the Commission has drawn attention to—by non-majority non-exclusive representation, see *The Legal Future of Employee Representation* (M. Finkin ed. 1994).

Part Four

STRIKES, PICKETING AND BOYCOTTS

I. RIGHTS OF EMPLOYEE PROTESTERS
UNDER THE NLRA

A. PROTECTED AND UNPROTECTED
CONCERTED ACTIVITY

Page 545. Insert before Problems:

HARRAH'S LAKE TAHOE RESORT CASINO
307 N.L.R.B. 182 (1992)

By CHAIRMAN STEPHENS and MEMBERS DEVANEY and OVIATT.

[Larry George is a baccarat dealer at the casino, owned by the Promus Companies, a publicly traded corporation. The casino has an employee stock ownership plan (ESOP) holding one percent of Promus's stock. George has devoted considerable time to developing an ESOP proposal which would give the employees fifty percent ownership of the company. As the Administrative Law Judge found:

> Some employees told George they would be willing to take a more active role if he prepared a petition to sign. Accordingly, George drafted a three page outline of a modified ESOP proposal and a cover letter addressed to Michael Rose, chairman of the Promus board of directors, from an *ad hoc* organization he called the "Employee Shareholders Association."

> Under George's modified proposal, the ESOP trust would borrow $335,000,000 to purchase 50 percent of the outstanding Promus stock (12,750,000 shares) at $25.25 per share. In addition, Promus would shift 50 percent ($450,000,000) of the current corporate debt to the ESOP trust as a form of equity allocation leaving the trust with a total debt of $785,000,000 which was to be guaranteed by the future operating income of Promus. By this transaction, George believed, both the principal and interest on the total trust debt would become tax deductible and would result in an annual $31,-000,000 tax savings to Promus. This and other benefits flowing from the ESOP ownership would, in his view, be sufficient to

75

implement the proposal "at no cost to either the shareholders or the employees."

He was disciplined for circulating a petition and related literature—a "Money for Nothin' " leaflet—among his co-workers. The ALJ held the terms imposed upon him, requiring him to submit all literature he wished in future to circulate for management's review, violated section 8(a)(1). He held, however, that the particular petition and supporting literature he had circulated were not protected by section 7. The Board, by vote of 2-to-1, agreed.]

Contrary to our dissenting colleague, we agree with the judge that employee Larry George's activities on behalf of his proposal for the employee stock option plan (ESOP) to purchase 50 percent of Promus Corporation, the Respondent's parent corporation, are not protected by Section 7 of the Act. George prepared a petition and a three-page summary of his proposal which he used to solicit employee support. He also distributed a leaflet briefly outlining his plan. The proposal concerned a leveraged buyout of Promus Corporation by the ESOP. Specifically, George proposed that the ESOP borrow $335 million to purchase 50 percent of the outstanding Promus stock and assume $450 million of Promus' corporate debt. George explained that the current employees would benefit from his proposal through increased job stability, pay, and pension funding and from enhanced morale, productivity, and profitability through "participatory management."

There is no question that George's activities were concerted. The sole issue is whether George's activities are protected within the mutual aid or protection provision of Section 7 of the Act, which turns on whether his proposal relates to "employees' interests as employees." *Eastex, Inc. v. NLRB*, 437 U.S. 556, 567 (1978). For the following reasons, we agree with the judge that the relationship of George's proposal to employees' interests as employees is "so attenuated that [the] activity cannot fairly be deemed to come with the 'mutual aid or protection' clause." *Eastex* at 568.

The dissent correctly points out that George's proposal envisioned enhanced benefits for current employees and was not designed solely to produce changes in management. The fact remains, however, that the thrust of the proposal was to cast employees in the role of owners with ultimate corporate control, and thus fundamentally to change how and by whom the corporation would be managed. The current employees would not enjoy any of the envisioned benefits unless and until they, through the ESOP, effectively controlled the corporation.[3] It is not surprising that, other than the implication from the phrase "participatory management" that there would be new additions to management

---

3. Furthermore, while the proposal emphasized benefits to employees, it entailed a substantial entrepreneurial risk—a hefty debt—that current employees would have to assume.

ranks, the proposal did not specify any particular management changes. If the goal of gaining majority stock ownership were achieved, neither the ESOP nor the employees would need to actively run the business in order to exercise effective control. We agree with the judge that any 50–percent shareholder, including an ESOP trust, would as a practical matter exercise effective control over every detail of corporate policy. In sum, although George presented his proposal within the employee-employer relationship, the proposal was designed to change that relationship.

Although the cases cited by the judge are factually distinguishable because they did not involve improved benefits for employees, we find that the underlying rationale of those cases supports our decision in this case. The test of whether an employee's activity is protected within the mutual aid or protection provision is not whether it relates to employees' interests generally but whether it relates to "the interests of employees qua employees." *G & W Electric Speciality Co.,* 154 NLRB 1136, 1137 (1965). Contrary to our dissenting colleague, we do not view the envisioned benefits for current employees as bringing the proposal within the mutual aid or protection provision of Section 7 of the Act. We agree with the judge that the proposal does not advance employees' interests as employees but rather advances employees' interests as entrepreneurs, owners, and managers.[5] Accordingly, we affirm the judge's decision.

MEMBER DEVANEY, dissenting.

* * *

In finding that George's activities on behalf of his ESOP proposal were not protected, the judge relied on the administrative law judge's decision in *Nephi Rubber Products Corp.,* 303 NLRB No. 19, JD slip op. at 11–12 (May 29, 1991), and cases cited therein. In *Nephi,* the employer closed its plant and filed for bankruptcy. Subsequently, the union representing the affected employees initiated the formation of an ESOP group to pursue the possibility of reopening the plant. To this end, the ESOP group, which consisted of former plant management, bargaining unit members, and city government officials, raised money and sought loans and grants in order to purchase the plant. The Board in *Nephi* adopted the judge's finding that employee participants in the ESOP who competed against the respondent as purchasers were not engaged in protected activity because they were acting to improve their lot as entrepreneurs and were trying to substitute themselves as management. In so finding, the judge in *Nephi* cited, inter alia, *Retail Clerks*

---

5. In other contexts the Board has long recognized the difference in interests between employees as employees and employees as owners. For example, employee-stockholders are excluded from bargaining units when they collectively have an effec-tive voice in determining or formulating corporate policy through their authority to select directors. *Side of Hawaii, Inc.,* 191 NLRB 194, 195 (1971); *Red & White Airway Cab Co.,* 123 NLRB 83, 85 (1959).

Local 770, 208 NLRB 356, 357 (1974), for the proposition that employee activity designed solely to influence or produce changes in the management hierarchy is not protected by Section 7 of the Act.[3]

In my view, the following facts demonstrate that George's activities on behalf of his ESOP proposal bear an immediate relationship to employees' interests as employees, and are therefore protected by Section 7 of the Act under Eastex, Inc. v. NLRB, 437 U.S. 556 (1978). First, it is clear that in the instant case, unlike the activity in *Nephi* and *Retail Clerks,* above, George's ESOP proposal was not designed *solely* to produce changes in management. At the time George presented his proposal, the Respondent's employees were able to own Promus stock through the existing ESOP and the 401(k) plan, which had been granted and maintained by the Respondent as economic benefits and were clearly terms and conditions of employment. Further, it is evident from the language of the leaflets that the primary objective behind the ESOP proposal was to increase employee compensation by enhancing the existing benefit programs.

The "Money For Nothin'" leaflet that George prepared for the employees stated in pertinent part:

> Our ESOP Trust borrows money from a commercial bank to buy 50% of Promus stock for the employees.

> Since the employees then own 50% of the stock, we get 50% of the operating income ("profits").

> For the following 10 to 15 years, we use our share of the profits to pay off the bank loan.

> At the end of 10 years, each employee owns stock which could be worth as much as 3 times his annual earnings (salary plus tips). If we leave sooner, we get less. If we stay longer, we get more.

The remainder of the leaflet explained why "the stock costs us nothin'!" and suggests that the employees can promise to the Respondent, in return, "one of the most dynamic and profitable service companies in America." Significantly, this leaflet does not even refer to an increased managerial role by the employees who become part owners of the Respondent, but focuses on the extent of the profits that would accrue to the employees if they were to own 50 percent of the stock and, indeed, the leaflet is bordered by dollar signs. George's written proposal outlines the benefits that would flow to employees if the proposal were implemented. Although the proposal mentions "participatory management" in terms of enhanced "morale, productivity, and profitability," its focus on the monetary benefits that would result makes clear that the proposal, rather than being intended solely to produce changes in management, was aimed at improving the savings and retirement benefits offered to employees. In this regard, the proposal lists as benefits the

---

3. In *Retail Clerks,* the Board found that the respondent employer-union did not violate Sec. 8(a)(1) by discharging certain employees who had engaged in internal union electioneering activities in an effort to effect a change in the union's top management. The Board emphasized that the employees were not engaged in organizing activities to seek a separate representative, and that they were not seeking to redress grievances within the framework of the employer-employee relationship.

estimated value of the ESOP account after 15 years, secondary income from benefits and profit sharing, increased employee compensation as a percentage of gross revenue, sellers of stock receiving market value for their shares, and reinforced stock valuation. Finally, the proposal refers to the "windfall compensation" that employees would receive. The focus of this literature makes it impossible to conclude that the ESOP was designed solely to produce changes in management. See *Retail Clerks,* above.

This case is unlike the precedent relied on by the judge for the further reason that George presented his proposal to the Respondent within the framework of the employer-employee relationship. In fact, George's ESOP activities were prompted by the request of the Respondent's president to employees to contact him with their work-related concerns via a special toll free number. George submitted his proposal at a time when both the Respondent and its parent corporation were promoting the ownership of stock by employees, and the Respondent was considering an employee stock purchase program. By contrast, the ESOP group in *Nephi* was not limited to former employees. The unique facts of that case are not subject to the interpretation that the ESOP was working in the context of an employer-employee relationship to gain improved economic benefits. Rather, the judge found that during the relevant period, the sole purpose of the employee-members was to use the ESOP to become owners of the plant to the exclusion of the respondent.[4] For these reasons, I find that the judge's reliance on *Nephi* in the instant case is misplaced.

Page 546.   Add new Problem:

3. A non-unionized Company's introduction of a random drug testing policy has proved highly controversial among employees. Many of them have joined a local civic organization seeking a city ordinance to ban such employment policies and seeking as well the election of a city council member committed to that effort. Employees have sought to solicit membership and support for the organization, in non-work areas on non-work time, but the Company has prohibited that solicitation. Has any unfair labor practice been committed? See NLRB v. Motorola, Inc., 991 F.2d 278 (5th Cir.1993).

4. This critical relationship between the employees' activities and the improvement of terms or conditions of employment was also absent in the additional cases relied on by the judge in the instant case to find George's activities unprotected. In *Good Samaritan Hospital,* 265 NLRB 618 (1982), and *Lutheran Social Service of Minnesota,* 250 NLRB 35 (1980), the Board found unprotected employee complaints about the competency of management that concerned the quality of care offered by the program, and were therefore efforts to affect the ultimate direction and philosophy of the respondents. Similarly, in *N.Y. Chinatown Senior Citizens Coalition Center,* 239 NLRB 614 (1978), the Board found unprotected employee complaints that focused on the effect of the perceived mismanagement on the community, rather than on the working conditions of employees.

Page 559. Add new Problems:

7. Fibers, Inc., a non-unionized firm, has announced that for two days free ice cream cones would be given to employees in the lunchroom to celebrate a "sole supplier" agreement with a major customer. In response, two employees wrote and posted a letter which provided in part:

> The employees of Fibers, Inc. would like to express their great appreciation of the 52 flavors of left over ice cream from the closed Meadow Gold Plant. It has boosted moral [sic] tremendously. Several employees were heard to say they were going to work harder together, and do better so we could have some more old ice cream.

> We realize what a tremendous sacrifice this has been for the management and will be long remembered. We hope this has not cut into computer expenses.

They were dismissed for action "disruptive to the workforce * * * undermining to management and fellow workers." Has Fibers, Inc. violated the Act? Compare New River Industries, Inc. v. NLRB, 945 F.2d 1290 (4th Cir.1991), with Reef Industries, Inc. v. NLRB, 952 F.2d 830 (5th Cir.1991), reh'g denied, publication granted, 952 F.2d 839 (1992).

8. In the midst of a long and bitter strike, the Beefy Meat Packing Company began to hire permanent replacements and continued to be unyielding in its demands for wage and benefit concessions from its unionized employees. The strike severely divided the community and, indeed, the state and the nation, for it was covered widely in the media, and represented for many a turning point in labor-management relations, given the Company's tough (but lawful) tactics. Company employees, friends in the community, and sympathizers across the nation organized a boycott of Beefy's products, and staged a number of large public rallies in support of the boycott. Beefy employee Gary Gristle, who had initially been on strike but returned to work, attended one of those rallies, and drove his auto in the parade that preceded it; he did not, however, deliver a speech there, or wear one of the tee-shirts or buttons worn by many boycott supporters. When the Company learned of this involvement, it discharged him.

The Board and the court of appeals, interpreting *Jefferson Standard* to render any product disparagement (even when used in the context of a labor dispute) unprotected against discharge, found no unfair labor practice. They also rejected Gristle's contentions that he could, at worst, be discharged only if he had a subjective intention to endorse the boycott, and that he in fact had no such intention. If you were to review this decision, as a member of the Supreme Court, how would you decide these issues? See George A. Hormel & Co. v. NLRB, 962 F.2d 1061 (D.C.Cir.1992).

9. A non-unionized company has a grievance procedure in its personnel handbook. The procedure commits the company to an "open door" for the reception of employee grievances and a right of appeal through the Company's hierarchy. A group of production workers have been distressed about the Company's selection of a lead person and they have sought an explanation under the procedure. After three meetings with one of the group's spokesmen, the group, which worked the third shift, ceased work and demanded to meet with the

Plant Manager. They were told to go back to work, or to clock out and return at 7:30 a.m. when the Plant Manager would be available; it was then around 3:00 a.m. They assembled in the Company dining room and reiterated their demand. About an hour later the order was repeated, upon the instruction of the Plant Manager who had been telephoned; but the employees did neither. The Plant Manager arrived at 6:00 a.m. and suspended the group. They were later discharged. Has the Company violated the Act? See Cambro Mfg. Co., 312 N.L.R.B. No. 111 (1993).

Page 562.　Insert after Problems:

————

On July 17, 1991, the House of Representatives passed H.R. 5, the Workplace Fairness Act, that would amend the National Labor Relations Act and the Railway Labor Act to prohibit the hiring of permanent strike replacements and to prohibit employers from granting preferences at the conclusion of labor disputes. 137 Cong.Rec. H5589–90 (July 17, 1991). The House rejected an amendment that would have prohibited hiring permanent replacements only during the first eight weeks of a strike. But the House accepted an amendment limiting the prohibition to strikes conducted by certified or recognized exclusive representatives—so as to exclude strikes at non-unionized workplaces, save for separate treatment of organizational and recognitional strikes. The final vote in support of the bill was 247 to 182, considerably fewer than necessary to override a Presidential veto. Secretary of Labor Lynn Martin issued a press release, "Martin Claims Victory For American Jobs," following the vote:

> This bill, which started with almost as many co-sponsors as it received final votes was touted by organized labor as a potential great victory. The large veto margin is a setback for that agenda. Martin said, "This is not just a victory for President Bush, but for all working men and women. By this vote, the Congress has denied a narrow vision of the past to concentrate on opportunities for the future."

On July 12, 1994, the Senate—in the face of a threatened filibuster—failed to close debate on S. 55, the companion bill. The vote fell seven short of the sixty required.

Page 599.　Add new Problem:

3. The collective bargaining agreement between Monsieur Pierre Liquors and the General Deliverymen Union was to expire on May 31. It had a provision for the payment of a cost-of-living increase (COLA) effective on that date (to be paid on June 4) applied to hours worked the previous six months. The Company and the Union have been bargaining over the terms of a successor agreement, and on May 29 the Company submitted its final offer which included retroactive abrogation of the COLA under the expiring contract. The union rejected the Company's offer in its entirety, the Company proceeded to implement it, and the

Union struck; filed an unfair labor practice; and filed a grievance under the expired contract demanding payment of the COLA with interest. On July 28 the Company paid the COLA; the check to each employee was accompanied by a letter in which the Company insisted upon the propriety of its actions. That letter also demanded that strikers return to work by August 4 or be replaced permanently. The union membership met on August 3. The members were vocal in demanding amnesty for strikers whom the Company had discharged in the interim for alleged picket line misconduct, and the inclusion of a COLA in the new contract. They voted to continue the strike. By August 11 all the strikers had been permanently replaced. Must they be returned to their jobs upon making an unconditional offer to return to work? See General Indus. Employees Union, Local 42 v. NLRB, 951 F.2d 1308 (D.C.Cir.1991).

III. THE NATIONAL LABOR RELATIONS ACT

B. SECONDARY PRESSURE

1. *Under the Taft–Hartley Act*

Page 665. Add new Problem:

A struck employer has contracted with a labor contractor to supply it with replacement workers. The labor contractor has booked rooms for the replacements at a local motel. The union picketed in the parking lot of the motel at 4:30 a.m. The picket signs stated that the dispute is solely with the labor contractor and the replacement workers. The motel manager approached the strikers, and was asked why he would rent to "scabs." He assured the union they would be gone. Has the union violated § 8(b)(4)(ii)(B)? See District 29, United Mine Workers v. NLRB, 977 F.2d 1470 (D.C.Cir.1992).

E. VIOLENCE AND UNION RESPONSIBILITY

Page 736. Add to Note:

In UNITED MINE WORKERS V. BAGWELL, ___ U.S. ___ (June 30, 1994), the United States Supreme Court was called upon to decide whether fifty-two million dollars in fines levied upon the union for violent activity in contempt of an injunction was civil or criminal in nature. A proceeding in criminal contempt would require a jury trial and proof beyond a reasonable doubt; a civil contempt would not. The Court noted the traditional if often "elusive" distinction between the two: civil contempt is a sanction to coerce obedience (e.g., to pay alimony or to give testimony), while criminal contempt is punitive. And it noted the concern that the contempt power is especially liable to abuse, where the offended judge is solely responsible for identifying, prosecuting, adjudicating, and sanctioning the contumacious conduct. In the instant case, the trial court had laid down an exacting code of behavior to govern the striking union, and had later identified precise dollar amounts it would fine the union for each future violation. Under all the circumstances, the Court concluded the fines imposed were criminal in nature and could not be imposed without a jury trial.

Part Five

ADMINISTRATION OF THE COLLECTIVE AGREEMENT

III. JUDICIAL ENFORCEMENT OF COLLECTIVE AGREEMENTS

Page 785. Insert after Problems:

In GROVES v. RING SCREW WORKS, 498 U.S. 168, 111 S.Ct. 498, 112 L.Ed.2d 508 (1990), the collective bargaining agreement prohibited discharge except for "just cause," and provided a multi-step grievance procedure ending in a joint union-management conference. No provision was made for arbitration; but there was a "no strike" clause prohibiting strikes during the term of the agreement "until all negotiations have failed through the grievance procedure." The discharge of an employee was grieved through the procedure but, upon the company's failure to agree, the union sued under § 301 to secure a judicial determination of whether or not the employee was discharged for cause. The Supreme Court held the suit justiciable under § 301. The Company argued that the contract reserved the strike as the exclusive remedy in the event negotiations over the grievance failed. The Court agreed that the plain language of a collective bargaining contract could reserve the use of force to resolve grievances, but declined to find such to be the case here:

> Of course, the parties may expressly agree to resort to economic warfare rather than to mediation, arbitration, or judicial review, but the statute surely does not favor such an agreement. For in most situations a strike or a lockout, though it may be a method of ending the impasse, is not a method of resolving the merits of the dispute over the application or meaning of the contract. Rather, it is simply a method by which one party imposes its will upon its adversary. Such a method is the antithesis of the peaceful methods of dispute resolution envisaged by Congress when it passed the Taft–Hartley Act.

Problem for Discussion

Assume that the collective agreement did not contain a "just cause" for discharge provision, but did provide that the union might use "all lawful economic recourse" upon deadlock in the grievance procedure. Could the union

84

successfully sue in federal district court to determine whether or not the company had just cause to discharge the employee? See Truck Drivers, Union Local 705 v. Schneider Tank Lines, Inc., 958 F.2d 171 (7th Cir.1992).

Page 799. Insert after Note on Nolde:

LITTON FINANCIAL PRINTING DIV. v. NLRB
501 U.S. 190, 111 S.Ct. 2215, 115 L.Ed.2d 177 (1991).

JUSTICE KENNEDY delivered the opinion of the Court.

This case requires us to determine whether a dispute over layoffs which occurred well after expiration of a collective-bargaining agreement must be said to arise under the agreement despite its expiration. The question arises in the context of charges brought by the National Labor Relations Board (Board) alleging an unfair labor practice in violation of §§ 8(a)(1) and (5) of the National Labor Relations Act (NLRA), 49 Stat. 449, as amended, 29 U.S.C. §§ 158(a)(1) and (5). We interpret our earlier decision in Nolde Bros., Inc. v. Bakery Workers, 430 U.S. 243, 97 S.Ct. 1067, 51 L.Ed.2d 300 (1977).

I

Petitioner Litton operated a check printing plant in Santa Clara, California. The plant utilized both cold-type and hot-type printing processes. Printing Specialties & Paper Products Union No. 777, Affiliated With District Council No. 1 (Union), represented the production employees at the plant. The Union and Litton entered into a collective-bargaining agreement which, with extensions, remained in effect until October 3, 1979. Section 19 of the Agreement is a broad arbitration provision:

> "Differences that may arise between the parties hereto regarding this Agreement and any alleged violations of the Agreement, the construction to be placed on any clause or clauses of the Agreement shall be determined by arbitration in the manner hereinafter set forth." App. 34.

Section 21 of the Agreement sets forth a two-step grievance procedure, at the conclusion of which, if a grievance cannot be resolved, the matter may be submitted for binding arbitration. Id., at 35.

Soon before the Agreement was to expire, an employee sought decertification of the Union. The Board conducted an election on August 17, 1979, in which the Union prevailed by a vote of 28 to 27. On July 2, 1980, after much postelection legal maneuvering, the Board issued a decision to certify the Union. No contract negotiations occurred during this period of uncertainty over the Union's status.

Litton decided to test the Board's certification decision by refusing to bargain with the Union. The Board rejected Litton's position and found its refusal to bargain an unfair labor practice. *Litton Financial Printing Division,* 256 N.L.R.B. 516 (1981). Meanwhile, Litton had decided to eliminate its cold-type operation at the plant, and in late August and early September of 1980, laid off 10 of the 42 persons working in the plant at that time. The laid off employees worked either primarily or exclusively with the cold-type operation, and included six of the eleven most senior employees in the plant. The layoffs occurred without any notice to the Union.

The Union filed identical grievances on behalf of each laid off employee, claiming a violation of the Agreement, which had provided that "in case of layoffs, lengths of continuous service will be the determining factor if other things such as aptitude and ability are equal." App. 30. Litton refused to submit to the grievance and arbitration procedure or to negotiate over the decision to lay off the employees, and took a position later interpreted by the Board as a refusal to arbitrate under any and all circumstances. It offered instead to negotiate concerning the effects of the layoffs.

On November 24, 1980, the General Counsel for the Board issued a complaint alleging that Litton's refusal to process the grievances amounted to an unfair labor practice within the meaning of §§ 8(a)(1) and (5) of the NLRA, 29 U.S.C. §§ 158(a)(1) and (5). App. 15. * * *

[The NLRB found violations of section 8(a)(5). It concluded that Litton had a duty to bargain about the layoffs. It also held that Litton's unilateral abandonment of the contractual grievance procedure, short of arbitration, upon the expiration of the labor agreement violated the Act. And, construing the Supreme Court's decision in Nolde Bros., Inc. v. Local No. 358, Bakery Workers, 430 U.S. 243, 97 S.Ct. 1067, 51 L.Ed.2d 300 (1977), the Board found another section 8(a)(5) violation in Litton's "wholesale repudiation" of any duty to arbitrate after the expiration of the labor contract. (None of these conclusions was later presented to the Supreme Court for review.) In fashioning a remedy, however, the Board concluded that it would not order Litton to arbitrate the layoff grievances, because it interpreted the arbitration clause of the agreement as not covering those grievances because they did not, in *Nolde*'s terms, "arise under" the expired contract. The court of appeals enforced the Board's order that Litton bargain about the layoffs and that it process the grievances through the two-step grievance procedure. It disagreed with the Board, however, about Litton's duty to arbitrate the layoff grievances failing their resolution in the grievance procedure; the court held that the right to layoff in order of seniority if other things such as aptitude and ability are equal *did* arise under the contract, and that Litton had a duty under section 8(a)(5) to arbitrate.]

Litton petitioned for a writ of certiorari. Because of substantial disagreement as to the proper application of our decision in *Nolde Bros.,* we granted review limited to the question of arbitrability of the layoff grievances. ___ U.S. ___, 111 S.Ct. 426, 112 L.Ed.2d 410.

II

A

Sections 8(a)(5) and 8(d) of the NLRA, 29 U.S.C. §§ 158(a)(5) and (d), require an employer to bargain "in good faith with respect to wages, hours, and other terms and conditions of employment." The Board has taken the position that it is difficult to bargain if, during negotiations, an employer is free to alter the very terms and conditions that are the subject of those negotiations. The Board has determined, with our acceptance, that an employer commits an unfair labor practice if, without bargaining to impasse, it effects a unilateral change of an existing term or condition of employment. See NLRB v. Katz, 369 U.S. 736, 82 S.Ct. 1107, 8 L.Ed.2d 230 (1962). In *Katz* the union was newly certified and the parties had yet to reach an initial agreement. The *Katz* doctrine has been extended as well to cases where, as here, an existing agreement has expired and negotiations on a new one have yet to be completed. See, *e.g.*, Laborers Health and Welfare Trust Fund v. Advanced Lightweight Concrete Co., 484 U.S. 539, 544, n. 6, 108 S.Ct. 830, 833, n. 6, 98 L.Ed.2d 936 (1988).

Numerous terms and conditions of employment have been held to be the subject of mandatory bargaining under the NLRA. See generally 1 C. Morris, The Developing Labor Law 772–844 (2d ed. 1983). Litton does not question that arrangements for arbitration of disputes are a term or condition of employment and a mandatory subject of bargaining. See id., at 813 (citing cases); *United States Gypsum Co.*, 94 N.L.R.B. 112, 131 (1951).

The Board has ruled that most mandatory subjects of bargaining are within the *Katz* prohibition on unilateral changes. The Board has identified some terms and conditions of employment, however, which do not survive expiration of an agreement for purposes of this statutory policy. For instance, it is the Board's view that union security and dues check-off provisions are excluded from the unilateral change doctrine because of statutory provisions which permit these obligations only when specified by the express terms of a collective-bargaining agreement. See 29 U.S.C. § 158(a)(3) (union security conditioned upon agreement of the parties); 29 U.S.C. § 186(c)(4) (dues check-off valid only until termination date of agreement); *Indiana & Michigan*, 284 N.L.R.B., at 55 (quoting *Bethlehem Steel*, 136 N.L.R.B., at 1502). Also, in recognition of the statutory right to strike, no-strike clauses are excluded from the unilateral change doctrine, except to the extent other dispute resolution methods survive expiration of the agreement. See 29 U.S.C. §§ 158(d)(4), 163 (union's statutory right to strike); Southwestern Steel & Supply, Inc. v. NLRB, 257 U.S.App.D.C. 19, 23, 806 F.2d 1111, 1114 (1986).

In *Hilton–Davis Chemical Co.,* 185 N.L.R.B. 241 (1970), the Board determined that arbitration clauses are excluded from the prohibition on unilateral changes, reasoning that the commitment to arbitrate is a "voluntary surrender of the right of final decision which Congress * * * reserved to [the] parties * * *. [A]rbitration is, at bottom, a consensual surrender of the economic power which the parties are otherwise free to utilize." Id., at 242. The Board further relied upon our statements acknowledging the basic federal labor policy that "arbitration is a matter of contract and a party cannot be required to submit to arbitration any dispute which he has not agreed so to submit." United Steelworkers of America v. Warrior & Gulf Navigation Co., 363 U.S. 574, 582, 80 S.Ct. 1347, 1353, 4 L.Ed.2d 1409 (1960). See also 29 U.S.C. § 173(d) (phrased in terms of parties' agreed upon method of dispute resolution under an *existing* bargaining agreement). Since *Hilton–Davis* the Board has adhered to the view that an arbitration clause does not, by operation of the NLRA as interpreted in *Katz,* continue in effect after expiration of a collective-bargaining agreement.

B

The Union argues that we should reject the Board's decision in *Hilton–Davis Chemical Co.,* and instead hold that arbitration provisions are within *Katz'* prohibition on unilateral changes. The unilateral change doctrine, and the exclusion of arbitration from the scope of that doctrine, represent the Board's interpretation of the NLRA requirement that parties bargain in good faith. And "[i]f the Board adopts a rule that is rational and consistent with the Act * * * then the rule is entitled to deference from the courts." Fall River Dyeing & Finishing Corp. v. NLRB, 482 U.S. 27, 42, 107 S.Ct. 2225, 2235, 96 L.Ed.2d 22 (1987); see, *e.g.,* NLRB v. Curtin Matheson Scientific, Inc., 494 U.S. ___, ___, 110 S.Ct. 1542, ___, 108 L.Ed.2d 801 (1990).

We think the Board's decision in *Hilton–Davis Chemical Co.* is both rational and consistent with the Act. The rule is grounded in the strong statutory principle, found in both the language of the NLRA and its drafting history, of consensual rather than compulsory arbitration. See *Indiana & Michigan,* supra, at 57–58; *Hilton–Davis Chemical Co.,* supra. The rule conforms with our statement that "[n]o obligation to arbitrate a labor dispute arises solely by operation of law. The law compels a party to submit his grievance to arbitration only if he has contracted to do so." Gateway Coal Co. v. Mine Workers, 414 U.S. 368, 374, 94 S.Ct. 629, 635, 38 L.Ed.2d 583 (1974). We reaffirm today that under the NLRA arbitration is a matter of consent, and that it will not be imposed upon parties beyond the scope of their agreement.

In the absence of a binding method for resolution of postexpiration disputes, a party may be relegated to filing unfair labor practice charges with the Board if it believes that its counterpart has implemented a unilateral change in violation of the NLRA. If, as the Union urges, parties who favor labor arbitration during the term of a contract also desire it to resolve postexpiration disputes, the parties can consent to that arrangement by explicit agreement. Further, a collective-bargaining agreement might be drafted so as to eliminate any hiatus between expiration of the old and execution of the new agreement, or to remain in effect until the parties bargain to impasse.[2] Unlike the Union's suggestion that we impose arbitration of postexpiration disputes upon parties once they agree to arbitrate disputes arising under a contract, these alternatives would reinforce the statutory policy that arbitration is not compulsory.

* * *

IV

The duty not to effect unilateral changes in most terms and conditions of employment, derived from the statutory command to bargain in good faith, is not the sole source of possible constraints upon the employer after the expiration date of a collective-bargaining agreement. A similar duty may arise as well from the express or implied terms of the expired agreement itself. This, not the provisions of the NLRA, was the source of the obligation which controlled our decision in Nolde Bros., Inc. v. Bakery Workers, 430 U.S. 243, 97 S.Ct. 1067, 51 L.Ed.2d 300 (1977). We now discuss that precedent in the context of the case before us.

In *Nolde Bros.,* a union brought suit under § 301 of the Labor Management Relations Act, 29 U.S.C. § 185, to compel arbitration. Four days after termination of a collective-bargaining agreement, the employer decided to cease operations. The employer settled employee wage claims, but refused to pay severance wages called for in the agreement, and declined to arbitrate the resulting dispute. The union argued that these wages

> "were in the nature of 'accrued' or 'vested' rights, earned by employees during the term of the contract on essentially the same basis as vacation pay, but payable only upon termination of employment." *Nolde Bros.,* 430 U.S., at 248, 97 S.Ct. at 1070.

We agreed that

> "whatever the outcome, the resolution of that claim hinges on the interpretation ultimately given the contract clause providing for severance pay. The dispute therefore, although arising *after* the

---

2. See, *e.g.,* NLRB v. New England Newspapers, Inc., 856 F.2d 409, 410 (CA1 1988) (agreement would continue in effect until a new agreement was reached); Montgomery Mailers' Union No. 127 v. The Advertiser Co., 827 F.2d 709, 712, n. 5 (CA11 1987) (agreement to continue in effect "for a reasonable time for negotiation of a new agreement"); Teamsters Local Union 688 v. John J. Meier Co., 718 F.2d 286, 287 (CA8 1983) ("all terms and provisions of the expired agreement shall continue in effect until a new agreement is adopted or negotiations are terminated").

expiration of the collective-bargaining contract, clearly arises *under* that contract." Id., at 249, 97 S.Ct., at 1071 (emphasis in original).

We acknowledged that "the arbitration duty is a creature of the collective-bargaining agreement" and that the matter of arbitrability must be determined by reference to the agreement, rather than by compulsion of law. Id., at 250–251, 97 S.Ct., at 1071–1072. With this understanding, we held that the extensive obligation to arbitrate under the contract in question was not consistent with an interpretation that would eliminate all duty to arbitrate as of the date of expiration. That argument, we noted,

> "would preclude the entry of a post-contract arbitration order even when the dispute arose during the life of the contract but arbitration proceedings had not begun before termination. The same would be true if arbitration processes began but were not completed, during the contract's term." Id., at 251, 97 S.Ct., at 1072.

We found "strong reasons to conclude that the parties did not intend their arbitration duties to terminate automatically with the contract," id., at 253, 97 S.Ct., at 1073, and noted that "the parties' failure to exclude from arbitrability contract disputes arising after termination * * * affords a basis for concluding that they intended to arbitrate all grievances arising out of the contractual relationship," id., at 255, 97 S.Ct., at 1074. We found a presumption in favor of postexpiration arbitration of matters unless "negated expressly or by clear implication," ibid, but that conclusion was limited by the vital qualification that arbitration was of matters and disputes arising out of the relation governed by contract.

A

Litton argues that provisions contained in the Agreement rebut the *Nolde Bros.* presumption that the duty to arbitrate disputes arising under an agreement outlasts the date of expiration. The Agreement provides that its stipulations "shall be in effect for the time hereinafter specified," in other words, until the date of expiration and no longer. The Agreement's no-strike clause, which Litton characterizes as a *quid pro quo* for arbitration, applies only "during the term of this [a]greement," id., at 34. Finally, the Agreement provides for "interest arbitration" in case the parties are unable to conclude a successor agreement, id., at 53–55, proving that where the parties wished for arbitration other than to resolve disputes as to contract interpretation, they knew how to draft such a clause. These arguments cannot prevail. The Agreement's unlimited arbitration clause, by which the parties agreed to arbitrate all "[d]ifferences that may arise between the parties" regarding the Agreement, violations thereof, or "the construction to be placed on any clause or clauses of the Agreement," id., at 34, places it within the precise rationale of *Nolde Bros.* It follows that if a dispute arises under the contract here in question, it is subject to arbitration even in the post-contract period.

B

With these matters resolved, we come to the crux of our inquiry. We agree with the approach of the Board and those courts which have interpreted *Nolde Bros.* to apply only where a dispute has its real source in the contract. The object of an arbitration clause is to implement a contract, not to transcend it. *Nolde Bros.* does not announce a rule that postexpiration grievances concerning terms and conditions of employment remain arbitrable. A rule of that sweep in fact would contradict the rationale of *Nolde Bros.* The *Nolde Bros.* presumption is limited to disputes arising under the contract. A postexpiration grievance can be said to arise under the contract only where it involves facts and occurrences that arose before expiration, where an action taken after expiration infringes a right that accrued or vested under the agreement, or where, under normal principles of contract interpretation, the disputed contractual right survives expiration of the remainder of the agreement.

Any other reading of *Nolde Bros.* seems to assume that postexpiration terms and conditions of employment which coincide with the contractual terms can be said to arise under an expired contract, merely because the contract would have applied to those matters had it not expired. But that interpretation fails to recognize that an expired contract has by its own terms released all its parties from their respective contractual obligations, except obligations already fixed under the contract but as yet unsatisfied. Although after expiration most terms and conditions of employment are not subject to unilateral change, in order to protect the statutory right to bargain, those terms and conditions no longer have force by virtue of the contract. See Office and Professional Employees Ins. Trust Fund v. Laborers Funds Administrative Office of Northern California, Inc., 783 F.2d 919, 922 (CA9 1986) ("An expired [collective bargaining agreement] * * * is no longer a 'legally enforceable document.'" (citation omitted)); cf. Derrico v. Sheehan Emergency Hosp., 844 F.2d 22, 25–27 (CA2 1988) (Section 301 of the LMRA, 29 U.S.C. § 185, does not provide a federal court jurisdiction where a bargaining agreement has expired, although rights and duties under the expired agreement "retain legal significance because they define the *status quo* " for purposes of the prohibition on unilateral changes).

The difference is as elemental as that between *Nolde Bros.* and *Katz.* Under *Katz,* terms and conditions continue in effect by operation of the NLRA. They are no longer agreed-upon terms; they are terms imposed by law, at least so far as there is no unilateral right to change them. As the Union acknowledges, the obligation not to make unilateral changes is "rooted not in the contract but in preservation of existing terms and conditions of employment and applies before any contract has been negotiated." Brief for Respondents 34, n. 21. *Katz* illustrates this point with utter clarity, for in *Katz* the employer was barred from imposing unilateral changes even though the parties had yet to execute their first collective-bargaining agreement.

* * *

* * * [C]ontractual obligations will cease, in the ordinary course, upon termination of the bargaining agreement. Exceptions are determined by contract interpretation. Rights which accrued or vested under the agreement will, as a general rule, survive termination of the agreement. And of course, if a collective-bargaining agreement provides in explicit terms that certain benefits continue after the agreement's expiration, disputes as to such continuing benefits may be found to arise under the agreement, and so become subject to the contract's arbitration provisions. See United Steelworkers of America v. Fort Pitt Steel Casting, Division of Conval–Penn, Inc., 598 F.2d 1273 (CA3 1979) (agreement provided for continuing medical benefits in the event of postexpiration labor dispute).

Finally, as we found in *Nolde Bros.*, structural provisions relating to remedies and dispute resolution—for example, an arbitration provision—may in some cases survive in order to enforce duties arising under the contract. *Nolde Bros.'* statement to that effect under § 301 of the LMRA is similar to the rule of contract interpretation which might apply to arbitration provisions of other commercial contracts.[3] We presume as a matter of contract interpretation that the parties did not intend a pivotal dispute resolution provision to terminate for all purposes upon the expiration of the agreement.

C

The Union, and Justice Stevens' dissent, argue that we err in reaching the merits of the issue whether the post-termination grievances arise under the expired agreement because, it is said, that is an issue of contract interpretation to be submitted to an arbitrator in the first instance. Whether or not a company is bound to arbitrate, as well as what issues it must arbitrate, is a matter to be determined by the court, and a party cannot be forced to "arbitrate the arbitrability issue." AT & T Technologies, Inc. v. Communication Workers of America, 475 U.S. 643, 651, 106 S.Ct. 1415, 1419–20, 89 L.Ed.2d 648. We acknowledge

---

3. See, e.g., West Virginia ex rel. Ranger Fuel Corp. v. Lilly, 165 W.Va. 98, 100–101, 267 S.E.2d 435, 437–438 (1980) (duty to arbitrate survives termination of lease); Warren Brothers Co. v. Cardi Corp., 471 F.2d 1304 (CA1 1973) (arbitration clause survives completion of work under construction contract); Mendez v. Trustees of Boston University, 362 Mass. 353, 356, 285 N.E.2d 446, 448 (1972) (termination of em- ployment contract "does not necessarily terminate a provision for arbitration or other agreed procedure for the resolution of disputes"); The Batter Building Materials Co. v. Kirschner, 142 Conn. 1, 10–11, 110 A.2d 464, 469–470 (1954) (arbitration clause in building contract not affected by a party's repudiation or total breach of contract).

that where an effective bargaining agreement exists between the parties, and the agreement contains a broad arbitration clause, "there is a presumption of arbitrability in the sense that '[a]n order to arbitrate the particular grievance should not be denied unless it may be said with positive assurance that the arbitration clause is not susceptible of an interpretation that covers the asserted dispute.' " Id., at 650, 106 S.Ct., at 1419 (quoting Steelworkers v. Warrior & Gulf Navigation Co., 363 U.S. 564, 582–583, 80 S.Ct. 1343, 1352–1353, 4 L.Ed.2d 1403 (1960)). But we refuse to apply that presumption wholesale in the context of an expired bargaining agreement, for to do so would make limitless the contractual obligation to arbitrate. Although "[d]oubts should be resolved in favor of coverage," *AT & T Technologies,* supra, 475 U.S., at 650, 106 S.Ct., at 1419, we must determine whether the parties agreed to arbitrate this dispute, and we cannot avoid that duty because it requires us to interpret a provision of a bargaining agreement.

We apply these principles to the layoff grievances in the present case. The layoffs took place almost one year after the Agreement had expired. It follows that the grievances are arbitrable only if they involve rights which accrued or vested under the Agreement, or rights which carried over after expiration of the Agreement, not as legally imposed terms and conditions of employment but as continuing obligations under the contract.

The contractual right at issue, that "in case of layoffs, lengths of continuous service will be the determining factor if other things such as aptitude and ability are equal," App. 30, involves a residual element of seniority. Seniority provisions, the Union argues, "create a form of earned advantage, accumulated over time, that can be understood as a special form of deferred compensation for time already worked." Brief for Respondents 23–25, n. 14. Leaving aside the question whether a provision requiring all layoffs to proceed in inverse order of seniority would support an analogy to the severance pay at issue in *Nolde Bros.,* which was viewed as a form of deferred compensation, the layoff provision here cannot be so construed, and cannot be said to create a right that vested or accrued during the term of the Agreement, or a contractual obligation that carries over after expiration.

The order of layoffs under the Agreement was to be determined primarily with reference to "other factors such as aptitude and ability." Only where all such factors were equal was the employer required to look to seniority. Here, any arbitration proceeding would of necessity focus upon whether aptitude and ability—and any unenumerated "other factors"—were equal long after the Agreement had expired, as of the date of the decision to lay employees off and in light of Litton's decision to close down its cold-type printing operation.

The important point is that factors such as aptitude and ability do not remain constant, but change over time. They cannot be said to vest or accrue or be understood as a form of deferred compensation. Specific aptitudes and abilities can either improve or atrophy. And the importance of any particular skill in this equation varies with the requirements of the employer's business at any given time. Aptitude and ability cannot be measured on some universal scale, but only by matching an employee to the requirements of an employer's business at that time. We cannot infer an intent on the part of the contracting parties to freeze any particular order of layoff or vest any contractual right as of the Agreement's expiration.[4]

V

For the reasons stated, we reverse the judgment of the Court of Appeals to the extent that the Court of Appeals refused to enforce the Board's order in its entirety and remanded the cause for further proceedings.

It is so ordered.

JUSTICE MARSHALL, with whom JUSTICE BLACKMUN and JUSTICE SCALIA join, dissenting.

Although I agree with JUSTICE STEVENS' dissent, *post,* I write separately to emphasize the majority's mischaracterization of our decision in Nolde Bros., Inc. v. Bakery Workers, 430 U.S. 243, 97 S.Ct. 1067, 51 L.Ed.2d 300 (1977). *Nolde* states a broad, rebuttable presumption of arbitrability which applies to *all* post-termination disputes arising under the expired agreement; it leaves the merits of the underlying dispute to be determined by the arbitrator. Today the majority turns *Nolde* on its head, announcing a rule that requires courts to reach the merits of the underlying posttermination dispute in order to determine whether it should be submitted to arbitration. This result is not only unfaithful to precedent but also it is inconsistent with sound labor-law policy.

I

The dispute in *Nolde* concerned whether employees terminated after the expiration of a collective-bargaining agreement were entitled to severance pay under a severance-pay clause of the expired agreement. See id., at 248–249, 97 S.Ct., at 1070–1071. The Court stated that the severance-pay dispute "hinge[d] on the interpretation [of] the contract clause providing for severance pay" but that "the merits of the underlying claim" were not implicated "in determining the arbitrability of the dispute." Id., at 249, 97 S.Ct., at 1071. To determine whether the

---

4. Although our decision that the dispute does not arise under the Agreement does, of necessity, determine that as of August 1980 the employees lacked any vested contractual right to a particular order of layoff, the Union would remain able to argue that the failure to lay off in inverse order of seniority if "other things such as aptitude and ability" were equal amounted to an unfair labor practice, as a unilateral change of a term or condition of employment. We do not decide whether, in fact, the layoffs were out of order.

dispute was arbitrable, the Court looked solely to the expired agreement's *arbitration* clause. It found the severance-pay dispute arbitrable because "[t]he parties agreed to resolve *all* disputes by resort to the mandatory grievance-arbitration machinery" and "nothing in the arbitration clause * * * expressly exclude[d] from its operation a dispute which arises under the contract, but which is based on events that occur after its termination." Id., at 252–253, 97 S.Ct., at 1072–1073.[1] Thus, under *Nolde*, the key questions for determining arbitrability are whether (1) the dispute is "based on * * * differing perceptions of a provision of the expired collective-bargaining agreement" or otherwise "arises under that contract," id., at 249, 97 S.Ct., at 1071 (emphasis omitted), and, if so, (2) whether the "presumptions favoring" arbitrability have been "negated expressly or by clear implication," id., at 255, 97 S.Ct., at 1074.

The majority grossly distorts *Nolde's* test for arbitrability by transforming the first requirement that posttermination disputes "arise under" the expired contract. The *Nolde* Court defined "arises under" by reference to the *allegations* in the grievance. In other words, a dispute "arises under" the agreement where "the resolution of [the Union's] claim hinges on the interpretation ultimately given the contract." Id., at 249, 97 S.Ct., at 1071.

By contrast, the majority today holds that a postexpiration grievance can be said to "arise under" the agreement only where the court satisfies itself (1) that the challenged action "infringes a right that accrued or vested under the agreement," or (2) that "under normal principles of contract interpretation, the disputed contractual right survives expiration of the remainder of the agreement." Ante, at 2225. Because they involve inquiry into the substantive effect of the terms of the agreement, these determinations require passing upon the merits of the underlying dispute. Yet the *Nolde* Court expressly stated that "in determining the arbitrability of the dispute, the merits of the underlying claim * * * are not before us." 430 U.S., at 249, 97 S.Ct. at 1071.

Since the proper question under *Nolde* is whether the dispute in this case "arises under" the agreement in the sense that it is "based on * * * differing perceptions of a provision in the expired collective bargaining agreement," ibid., I have no difficulty concluding that this test is met here. The Union's grievance "claim[ed] a violation of the Agreement," ante, at 2219, by petitioner's layoffs. And, as even the majority concedes, "[t]he Agreement's unlimited arbitration clause" encompasses any dispute that "arises under the contract here in question." Ante, at 2225. Thus, the dispute is arbitrable because the "presumptions favoring" arbitrability have not been "negated expressly or by clear implication." 430 U.S., at 255, 97 S.Ct., at 1074.

---

1. I agree with the majority that the National Labor Relations Board's (Board) determination as to arbitrability under the contract is not entitled to deference.

* * * Consequently, the issue here, as it was in *Nolde,* is not whether a substantive provision of the expired collective-bargaining agreement (in this case the provision covering layoffs) remains enforceable but whether the expired agreement reflects the parties' intent to *arbitrate* the Union's contention that this provision remains enforceable. The majority itself acknowledges a general rule of contract construction by which arbitration or other dispute resolution provisions may survive the termination of a contract. Ante, at 2226, and n. 3. That is all *Nolde* stands for. * * *

II

The majority's resolution of the merits of the contract dispute here reinforces my conviction that arbitrators should be the preferred resolvers of such questions. * * *

As the majority appears to concede, ante, at 2227, and as the Board has held, an unconditional seniority provision can confer a seniority right that is "capable of accruing or vesting to some degree during the life of the contract." *United Chrome Products, Inc.,* 288 N.L.R.B. 1176, 1177 (1988). * * *

In my view, a provision granting only "qualified" seniority may vest in the same way. (Here, the provision guaranteeing seniority is "qualified" by the requirement that the employee claiming seniority possess "aptitude and ability" that is equal to that of less senior employees who seek to avoid being laid off.) As with an employee's seniority rank, a given worker's "aptitude and ability" relative to other employees may change over time, yet the right to have layoffs made according to the *standard* of qualified seniority could vest under the contract. Under this view, a laid off employee would have the opportunity to prove to the arbitrator that he should not have been laid off under the terms of the contract because other factors such as aptitude and ability *were* equal at the time he was laid off.

Indeed, I think this is the more plausible reading of the parties' intent in this case, particularly given related contract provisions involving *loss* of seniority. * * * In the present case, the expired agreement enumerates six specific ways an employee could lose seniority, and these do not include termination of the agreement. See App. 31. Thus, the qualified seniority at issue in this case would seem as likely to accrue as did the unconditional seniority in *Uppco.*

In any event, the conclusion that the contracting parties in this case did *not* intend qualified seniority rights to vest is sufficiently implausible as to raise serious questions about the majority's assignment of the task of deciding this interpretive issue to itself. Had the majority left this issue to the arbitrator to decide, as *Nolde* requires, the arbitrator would have had the benefit of an evidentiary hearing on the contractual question and the opportunity to explore petitioner's actual postexpiration seniority practices. The contractual text, alone, may not be the only relevant information in determining the parties' intent. * * * In sum, the majority's problematic reasoning regarding the substance of the layoff grievance only underscores the soundness of the *Nolde* presumption of arbitrability which the majority today displaces. Accordingly, I dissent.[4]

JUSTICE STEVENS, with whom JUSTICE BLACKMUN and JUSTICE SCALIA join, dissenting.

As the Court today recognizes, an employer's obligation to arbitrate postcontract termination grievances may arise by operation of labor law or by operation of the expired collective-bargaining agreement. I think the Court is correct in deferring to the National Labor Relations Board's line of cases and holding that a *statutory* duty to arbitrate grievances does not automatically continue after contract termination by operation of labor law, see ante, at 2221–2224. I also agree with the Court's recognition that notwithstanding the absence of an employer's statutory duty to arbitrate posttermination grievances, a *contractual* duty to arbitrate such grievances may nevertheless exist, see ante, at 2224–2226. I part company with the Court, however, at Part IV–C of its opinion, where it applies its analysis to the case at hand. Because I am persuaded that the issue whether the posttermination grievances in this case "arise under" the expired agreement is ultimately an issue of contract interpretation, I think that the Court errs in reaching the merits of this issue rather than submitting it to an arbitrator in the first instance, pursuant to the broad agreement of the parties to submit for arbitration any dispute regarding contract construction. * * *

In my opinion, the question whether the seniority clause in fact continues to provide employees with any rights after the contract's expiration date is a separate issue concerning the merits of the dispute, not its arbitrability. Whatever the merits of the Union's contention that the seniority-rights provision survives the contract's termination date, I think that the merits should be resolved by the arbitrator, pursuant to the parties' broad contractual commitment to arbitrate all disputes concerning construction of the agreement, rather than by this Court.

---

4. Although I believe the parties have a contractual duty to arbitrate in this case, I agree with the majority's conclusion that the Board articulated rational grounds for not imposing a statutory duty under the National Labor Relations Act, 29 U.S.C. § 151 et seq., to arbitrate grievances arising after the termination of a collective-bargaining agreement. See Ante, at 2222–2223. In *Indiana and Michigan Electric Co.*, 284 N.L.R.B. 53 (1987), the Board noted that "an agreement to arbitrate is a product of the parties' mutual consent to relinquish economic weapons, such as strikes or lockouts" and therefore the con-

tractual obligation to arbitrate could be distinguished from other "terms and conditions of employment routinely perpetuated [after termination of a collective-bargaining agreement] by the [statutory] constraints of [the unilateral change doctrine]." Id., at 58. Under § 13 of the Act, 29 U.S.C. § 163, the Act may not be construed to interfere with a union's right to strike. Therefore, the Board rationally concluded that employers should not, as a matter of statutory policy, be compelled to arbitrate and thus forbear from using their economic weapons, when no concomitant statutory obligation can be imposed on a union.

I respectfully dissent.

Page 806. Add the following Problems:

4. Acme Company has a labor agreement with the Machinists Union containing, among other things, a no-strike clause and a standard arbitration clause. During the term of the agreement, a strike was under way on the part of another union, the Laborers, in another Acme bargaining unit at the same plant; 150 employees in the Machinists unit honored the Laborers' picket line, and Acme acted promptly (and lawfully, under the NLRA) to replace 60 of them. When the Laborers ended their strike and withdrew their picket line, the Machinists requested reinstatement on behalf of all in their unit, but the Company declined to reinstate the 60 who had been replaced.

Rather than challenge this action before the NLRB (which would probably have been fruitless), the Machinists Union took the replacement issue through the grievance procedure and to arbitration. The arbitrator held that "elementary due process" requires that Acme, prior to permanently replacing its employees honoring a picket line of a fellow union, must warn those employees of the consequences of their action and of the Company's otherwise lawful intention to replace them. Acme having failed to do so, the arbitrator ordered the 60 grievants reinstated with backpay from the date of the Machinists' request to return to work.

Acme has asked a federal court to vacate the award. How should the court rule? (Reconsider this question again after studying the *Misco* decision, immediately below.) Would your analysis be different if the labor agreement had contained a provision barring "discipline or discharge without just cause," and had the arbitrator purported to construe that provision in reaching her decision? See Harry Hoffman Printing, Inc. v. Graphic Communications Intern. Union, Local 261, 950 F.2d 95 (2d Cir.1991).

5. The labor agreement between the Hotel Workers Union and Harlowe Hotels requires the payment of time-and-one-half the usual wage rate for "employees who, at the request of the employer, work less than five full days per work." In a dispute about Harlowe's pay for a part-time bellman at one of its hotels, Arbitrator Axelrod held that the quoted clause did not apply; he stated that "it stretches language too far to apply this provision to a part-time employee, as opposed to a full-time employee who works less than a full week for the company's convenience." Two months later, when Harlowe paid straight-time wages to a food-service employee at a different hotel location, the Union once again took the case to arbitration, this time before Arbitrator Beta; Harlowe relied on the Axelrod decision. Arbitrator Beta refused to be bound by the Axelrod decision. He stated, "I must make my own decision, one that I believe reflects a just interpretation of the contract. I am free to disagree with an earlier decision, involving a different grievant, that I believe to have been clearly incorrect. That is so here." Beta decided that the disputed clause applied, and he ordered Harlowe to pay time-and-one-half for the hours worked by the part-time food-service employee.

Harlowe has brought an action in the federal court, seeking to have the Beta award vacated. It makes the following arguments: (1) Arbitrator Beta was bound by the doctrine of res judicata to apply the Axelrod decision; (2) the labor agreement provides that arbitration decisions "shall be final and binding," and that makes the Axelrod decision binding on the parties and on Beta; (3) the interpretation by Arbitrator Axelrod became the definitive interpretation of the disputed clause, as if it were agreed to by the parties and incorporated in the writing, and it could thus not be subsequently altered except by mutual agreement in negotiation; and (4) national labor policy favors the final resolution of disputes through arbitration, and that policy is undermined by Beta's relitigation of the same issue.

How would you dispose of the Company's arguments, if you were the federal judge? See Hotel Association of Washington, D.C. v. Hotel Employees Union, Local 25, 963 F.2d 388 (D.C.Cir.1992).

Page 816. Add at the close of Problem 2(d).

Compare Exxon Shipping Co. v. Exxon Seamen's Union, 993 F.2d 357 (3d Cir.1993) (marijuana use), and Gulf Coast Indus. Workers Union v. Exxon Co., 991 F.2d 244 (5th Cir.1993) (cocaine use), *with* Monroe Auto Equip. Co. v. UAW, 981 F.2d 261 (6th Cir.1992) (marijuana use).

Page 816. Add after Problem 2(e):

(f) Chrysler Company discharged one of its male employees, who stealthily approached a woman co-worker from behind, while she was at her work station, and placed his arms around her and grabbed her breasts. The union, claiming that the employee's conduct was intolerable but that discharge was too severe, and was in violation of the contractual "just cause" provision, took the case through the grievance procedure and demanded arbitration. In preparing for the arbitration, Chrysler learned that the grievant had molested four other women employees on earlier occasions.

At the arbitration hearing, the arbitrator refused to permit the Company to introduce the evidence of the earlier molestations. In light of the grievant's long service and his unblemished work record, without even a prior oral warning for misconduct, the arbitrator concluded that discipline should be regarded as corrective rather than punitive (as was the Company's practice) and that the grievant was capable of rehabilitation. He ordered Chrysler to reinstate the grievant and, because of the seriousness of the grievant's conduct, the arbitrator reduced the discipline to a thirty-day suspension; backpay was calculated accordingly.

Chrysler seeks to have the award vacated. It cites, in particular, federal law barring discrimination on the basis of sex, and regulations of the EEOC that interpret this to embrace physical sexual harassment and that make an employer liable for condoning such employee behavior. (See 29 C.F.R. § 1604.11.) It also claims that the arbitrator abused his discretion by refusing to hear evidence about the other instances of similar misbehavior. How should the court decide the case? See Chrysler Motors Corp. v. International Union, Allied Industrial Workers, 959 F.2d 685 (7th Cir.), cert. denied, ___ U.S. ___, 113 S.Ct. 304, 121 L.Ed.2d 227 (1992).

[If you had been counsel to the Union, would you have felt obliged to decline pursuing the grievance when initially presented, by virtue of the Union's duty of fair representation? If instead you were counsel to Chrysler, would you have recommended that the Company save time and expense by not bringing an action to vacate the arbitrator's award, but rather—after losing in arbitration—simply by discharging the grievant for the earlier four molestations?]

IV.　THE ROLE OF THE NATIONAL LABOR RELATIONS BOARD AND THE ARBITRATOR DURING THE TERM OF A COLLECTIVE AGREEMENT

A.　CONDUCT WHICH ALLEGEDLY VIOLATES BOTH THE CONTRACT AND THE LABOR ACT

Page 848.　Insert after *Olin Corp.*:

Problem for Discussion

Union officers who participated in a strike and picketing in violation of a collective bargaining agreement were suspended pending a discharge. They were, however, reinstated pursuant to a "last chance agreement" that prohibited them from holding any union office for the duration of the collective agreement nor any office involving direct dealing with the Company. This provision was challenged before and sustained by an arbitrator as reasonable in light of their conduct. But the General Counsel has issued a complaint that the conditions imposed violate sections 8(a)(1) and (3) of the Act. What should the Board hold? See Bethenergy Mines, Inc., 308 N.L.R.B. 1242 (1992).

PLUMBERS & PIPEFITTERS LOCAL UNION 520 v. NLRB (C–CATALYTIC INC.)

955 F.2d 744 (D.C.Cir.), cert. denied, ___ U.S. ___, 113 S.Ct. 61, 121 L.Ed.2d 29 (1992).

HARRY T. EDWARDS, CIRCUIT JUDGE:

The simple question in this case is whether the National Labor Relations Board ("NLRB" or "Board") may give deference to a pre-arbitration settlement reached by an employer and a union disposing of an employee's contract grievance with respect to a matter covered by the parties' collective bargaining agreement. The simple answer is yes.

In this case, the applicable collective bargaining agreement between UE & C–Catalytic, Inc. ("Catalytic") and fourteen International building trades unions—the General Presidents' Project Maintenance Agreement ("GPPMA")—prohibits work stoppages and provides that an employer may discharge or discipline employees for "proper cause." In 1985, Catalytic fired Garland Berry, a union steward with the petitioner, Plumbers and Pipefitters Local Union No. 520 ("Local 520"), for insubordination in connection with a threatened work stoppage. In protest against Berry's dismissal, Local 520 filed a grievance under the collective bargaining agreement and an unfair labor practice ("ulp") charge with the NLRB; the factual circumstances underlying the grievance and the ulp were exactly the same. The contract grievance dispute was thereafter settled in lieu of arbitration, with an agreement between representatives from Catalytic and the International Union providing for Berry's reinstatement without backpay. Subsequently, during proceedings at the NLRB, an Administrative Law Judge ("ALJ") refused to grant deference to the settlement agreement and found for Berry on the merits, ordering his reinstatement *with* backpay. The Board reversed the ALJ and held that deference was appropriate. *Catalytic, Inc.,* 301 N.L.R.B. No. 44 (Jan. 28, 1991), reprinted in Deferred Appendix ("App.") 11.

We uphold the Board's decision and deny the petition for review. We find that the Board's policy of granting deference to pre-arbitration settlement agreements is consistent with the National Labor Relations Act ("NLRA"), 29 U.S.C. §§ 151–169 (1988), and that the Board did not abuse its discretion by applying the policy in this case. In denying the petition for review in this case, however, we do not mean to suggest that the Board's opinion is without flaws. Indeed, as indicated during the oral argument before this panel, the Board's present policy on "deference"[1] is vacuous in significant respects, because it lacks any coherent theoretical basis. Although remand is unnecessary in this case because deference to the settlement agreement was clearly permissible on the record before us, the Board will be well-advised to reconsider the basis for its deference policy in order to avoid the need for remand in future cases.

I. Background

[Catalytic and several other engineering contractors have a nationwide collective bargaining agreement, the GPPMA, with fourteen International unions representing employees in the building trades. Although the Internationals are the signatories to the agreement as the bargaining representatives for the various local units, local unions affiliated with the Internationals monitor the agreements on a day-to-day basis, and also negotiate the wage and benefit provisions. The local

---

1. The Board historically has followed two separate policies of adjudicatory restraint, both of which have been referred to as "deferral" policies: one is the so-called "post-arbitral deferral" or "*Spielberg*" policy, pursuant to which the Board *grants* deference to arbitration decisions rendered through the grievance processes of collective bargaining agreements if certain conditions are met, see *Spielberg Mfg. Co.,* 112 N.L.R.B. 1080 (1955); the other is the "pre-arbitral deferral" or "*Collyer*" policy, under which the Board *defers* (delays) consideration of unfair labor practice charges in certain circumstances until remedies under the applicable collective bargaining agreement have been exhausted by the complaining party, see *Collyer Insulated Wire,* 192 N.L.R.B. 837 (1971). *See also* Hammontree v. NLRB, 925 F.2d 1486, 1490–91 (D.C.Cir. 1991) (en banc) (describing Board's "deferral" policies); part I.C., infra (describing *Spielberg* policy). The Board policy at issue in this case—the granting of deference to pre-arbitration grievance settlements—is an outgrowth of the older *Spielberg* policy.

In *Hammontree,* we distinguished between the Board's "deferral" policies by referring to the *Spielberg* doctrine as a "*deference policy*" and to the *Collyer* doctrine as a "*deferment policy.*" See 925 F.2d at 1490–91. For purposes of clarity, we will follow *Hammontree's* terminology in this opinion. Thus, we will refer to the policy at issue in this case as a policy of *deference.*

union involved in this case, Local 520, is affiliated with the United Association of Journeymen and Apprentices of the Plumbing and Pipe Fitting Industry, the International union referred to as the "United Association."

In the summer of 1985, Catalytic was awarded a contract to remove the "snubbers" (large shock absorbers) at a Pennsylvania nuclear power plant owned by the Philadelphia Electric Company (PECO). (PECO awarded certain related work to another contractor, which displeased the pipefitters in Local 520, who thought they were capable of doing it.) Catalytic decided to do the work on the snubbers on "split shifts" and directed its eight pipefitters, who normally all worked on the day shift, to work four on the day shift and four on the second shift. When Berry, the union steward, so informed Hartinger, the Local's Business Manager, of this directive, Hartinger—citing safety concerns, but apparently motivated by his displeasure over the award of related work to another contractor—told Berry to inform the eight pipefitters that they ought to ignore the "shift splitting" directive and should all report instead for the day shift; Berry did so. This led to discussions between Greeley, the Labor Relations Manager for Catalytic, and a representative of the United Association named DeLuca, and these discussions resulted in compliance with the foreman's directive without any work stoppage. Soon after, company representatives voiced their dissatisfaction with Berry, saying that he was "too much of a trouble maker." He was in fact then informed by McCauley, Catalytic's manager at the site, that Berry was being terminated for gross insubordination, based upon his instruction to the snubber workers to ignore management's directions as to the shift split.

Local 520 filed a grievance under the GPPMA management rights provision authorizing discharge or discipline only "for proper cause." The Local also filed an unfair labor practice charge with the NLRB under section 8(a)(3); the General Counsel did not, however, issue a complaint until January 1987, roughly a year and a half later.

In the meantime, the discharge grievance was being processed under the GPPMA grievance procedure, which had three pre-arbitration steps. The first two steps contemplate discussions between union representatives and, first, the immediate supervisor and then a labor relations manager. At step three, the grievance is presented by the company and the international union to the General Presidents' Committee (GPC), which includes a representative of each of the signatory international unions (but no employer representative); if the GPC and the employer cannot agree on the disposition of the grievance, it can be taken to arbitration.

When the Berry grievance reached the third step in January 1986, oral and written presentations to the GPC were made by Greeley (labor relations manager) for Catalytic and one Coyne for the United Association, the international union. The written decision of the GPC stated, simply, "After hearing statements from both parties and carefully examining all of the evidence submitted, it was the position of the Committee that Garland Berry should be made eligible for immediate rehire without any back pay." Both Catalytic and the United Association accepted the determination; despite the objection of Hartinger of Local 520, the United Association informed him that the grievance had been satisfactorily resolved at step three and arbitration was therefore inappropriate under the labor agreement.

More than a year later, in April 1987, an ALJ hearing was held on Local 520's unfair labor practice charge. The ALJ refused to defer to the grievance resolution because Berry and Local 520 had objected to the GPC's resolution; he found that Berry had been discharged because of his union activity and that the charge of gross insubordination was a pretext, and he ordered that Berry be reinstated with backpay. The NLRB, however, reversed the ALJ on the deference issue and dismissed the complaint. The Board relied on its decisions in Alpha Beta Co., 273 N.L.R.B. 1546 (1985), and United States Postal Service, 300 N.L.R.B. No. 23 (1990), which articulated the Board's reasons for granting deference to a pre-arbitration grievance settlement. Those cases had gone beyond the Board precedents—*Spielberg* and *Olin Corp.* in particular—providing for deference in certain circumstances to arbitration awards. The Board held that the acquiescence of Catalytic and United Association in the GPC's resolution was "tantamount to a settlement agreement," and that the four deference criteria developed in *Alpha Beta* and *U.S. Postal Service* (and discussed at length infra by the court of appeals in the instant case) had been satisfied.]

II. DISCUSSION

The scope of our review of the Board's decision and order in this case is relatively narrow. The Board's formulation of its deference policy must be upheld so long as it is rational and consistent with the NLRA. See NLRB v. United Food & Commercial Workers Union, Local 23, 484 U.S. 112, 123, 108 S.Ct. 413, 420–21, 98 L.Ed.2d 429 (1987); Hammontree v. NLRB, 925 F.2d 1486, 1491 (D.C.Cir.1991) (en banc). The Board's decision to grant deference in a particular case may be reversed only for an abuse of discretion. Bakery, Confectionery & Tobacco Workers Int'l Union 25 v. NLRB, 730 F.2d 812, 813 (D.C.Cir. 1984). We find that the Board's deference policy constitutes a permissible interpretation of the NLRA and that the Board did not abuse its discretion by applying the policy in this case; accordingly, we deny the petition for review.

A. *The Board's* Alpha Beta *Deference Policy*

The first issue that we must address is whether the Board's policy of granting deference to pre-arbitration grievance settlements constitutes a permissible construction of the NLRA. Local 520 does not strenuously contest the propriety of the policy, reserving its fire for the contention that the Board abused its discretion in applying the policy on the facts of this case. Nonetheless, we must address the policy's facial validity as a threshold matter because, if the policy is invalid, the Board necessarily abused its discretion in giving deference to the pre-arbitration settlement of the Berry grievance.

We begin our analysis by clarifying what is not in dispute in this case. * * *

Local 520 * * * concedes, as it must, that the statutory right asserted by Berry in this case is within the category of rights that are subject to waiver by a union through the collective bargaining process. In Metropolitan Edison Co. v. NLRB, 460 U.S. 693, 103 S.Ct. 1467, 75 L.Ed.2d 387 (1983), the Supreme Court made clear that many of the rights guaranteed to employees by the NLRA may be altered or waived by a union in collective bargaining, so long as the union fulfills its duty of fair representation and takes no action that would impair the employees' choice of their bargaining representative. See id. at 705–07, 103 S.Ct. at 1475–75; American Freight Sys., Inc. v. NLRB, 722 F.2d 828, 832 (D.C.Cir.1983) ("*American Freight* ") ("It is well settled that a union may lawfully waive statutory rights of represented employees in a collective bargaining agreement.").[5] Among the rights that may be modified or waived is the right to strike. * * * Local 520 admits that in this case, as in *Metropolitan Edison Co.,* the statutory right at issue— Berry's purported privilege to counsel unit employees to engage in a work stoppage by ignoring Catalytic's instructions regarding the shift split—is a right which the United Association could waive, either through contract negotiations or the grievance/arbitration process.[6] Thus, Local 520 concedes that the statutory right allegedly infringed in this case is one with respect to which it was permissible for Catalytic and the United Association to bargain.

Finally, Local 520 raises no challenge to the legal regime established by *Alpha Beta,* 273 N.L.R.B. 1546, and *Postal Service,* 300 N.L.R.B. No. 23. Under those cases, the Board will give deference to a pre-arbitration grievance settlement when: (1) the settlement is reached through a

---

5. See also Edwards, Deferral to Arbitration and Waiver of the Duty to Bargain: A Possible Way Out of Everlasting Confusion at the NLRB, 46 Ohio St.L.J. 23, 27–32, 36–40 (1985).

Certain statutory rights may not be waived through collective bargaining. These include, *inter alia,* the free choice of a bargaining representative, the Act's prohibitions on "hot cargo" agreements and secondary boycotts, the statutory bar against "closed shops," and hiring hall practices that give preferences to union members. See id. at 30–31; Charles J. Morris, The Developing Labor Law 865 (2d ed. 1983).

6. Because "the grievance-arbitration procedure forms an integral part of the collective-bargaining process," *Metropolitan Edison Co.,* 460 U.S. at 708, 103 S.Ct. at 1477, a union's power to waive statutory rights during the grievance process is commensurate with its power to waive such rights during negotiation of a collective bargaining agreement.

collective bargaining process which is "fair and regular"; (2) the parties agreed to be bound by the terms of the settlement agreement; (3) the outcome reached is not "palpably wrong," meaning that both sides have compromised to some degree; and (4) the unfair labor practice issue was "considered" in the settlement process, in that the contractual and unfair labor practice issues are factually parallel and both parties were generally aware of the relevant facts. * * *

The concessions made by Local 520 are hardly surprising, for a Board policy of granting deference to grievance settlements seems plainly consistent with the NLRA. We have long recognized that the Board "does not abdicate its responsibilities to implement the National Labor Relations Act by respecting peaceful resolution of disputes through voluntarily agreed upon administrative techniques." * * * On this basis, we have expressed approval of the Board's *Spielberg* deference policy in several cases. See, *e.g.*, *Bakery, Confectionery & Tobacco Workers Int'l Union 25*, 730 F.2d at 814–15; *American Freight*, 722 F.2d at 832–33; Bloom v. NLRB, 603 F.2d 1015, 1019–20 (D.C.Cir.1979); *Associated Press*, 492 F.2d at 666–67. Most recently, in Hammontree v. NLRB, 925 F.2d 1486 (D.C.Cir.1991) (en banc), we upheld the Board's *Collyer* "deferment" policy, pursuant to which the Board requires a complaining party, under specified circumstances, to exhaust available grievance procedures before pursuing an unfair labor practice charge. In *Hammontree,* the court held that the Board's policy furthered the NLRA's policy of encouraging private dispute resolution and did not otherwise contravene the federal labor laws. See id. at 1494, 1496.

* * * Pre-arbitration grievance settlements, like the arbitration awards at issue in *Bloom* and *American Freight,* represent a consensual resolution of labor-management disputes through the collective bargaining process. By recognizing the validity and finality of settlements, the Board promotes the integrity of the collective bargaining process, thereby effectuating a primary goal of the national labor policy. * * * At least where a grievance implicates only "waiveable" rights, we find nothing in the NLRA that prevents the Board from showing deference to a pre-arbitration grievance settlement. Thus, we have no trouble in finding that a policy of deference is rational and consistent with the NLRA, and, therefore the Board is entitled to deference from this court with respect to the adoption of such a policy. See *United Food & Commercial Workers Union, Local 23,* 484 U.S. at 123, 108 S.Ct. at 420–21.

B. *Application of the Deference Policy in this Case*

Having determined that the Board's *general policy* of granting deference to pre-arbitration settlements is permissible, we now turn to the question of whether the Board abused its discretion in applying the policy in the instant case. As discussed above, the Board gives deference to grievance settlements under *Alpha Beta* and *Postal Service* where the grievance procedure through which the settlement is reached is "fair and regular," all parties agree to be bound, the result reached is not "palpably wrong" under the NLRA and the unfair labor practice issue was "considered" by the parties, i.e., the statutory and contractual issues are factually parallel and the parties were generally aware of the relevant facts. *Postal Service,* slip op. at 5–7; *Alpha Beta,* 273 N.L.R.B. at 1547–48. Local 520 argues that none of these four deference criteria is satisfied in the instant case. Contrary to Local 520's assertions, we find that the record contains substantial evidence to support the Board's conclusion that each criterion has been met.

First, Local 520 argues against deference on the ground that the GPC process was not "fair and regular" because, among other things, Berry was not permitted to be present at the GPC meeting, the presentation made by Mr. Coyne on his behalf was inadequate and no written opinion was issued by the GPC. We reject Local 520's contentions. The record demonstrates that Berry's case was fully discussed by representatives of the United Association and Catalytic prior to the GPC meeting. It is true that Berry was not present at the GPC meeting; but this is hardly a fatal flaw in the process. The *parties* to the agreement—not individual employees in the unit—are the ones who must create and administer the grievance procedure under the collective bargaining contract. Thus, within the bounds of the duty of fair representation, individual employees in the bargaining unit are properly subject to the judgment of their union agents in the processing of grievance claims. This is neither surprising nor unfair, for the union is the signatory to the agreement and thus is responsible for enforcing it. In other words, the employer is bound to bargain only with the employees' agent, not with each and every employee in the unit.

Even if either the Board or this court had the authority to second-guess the union's processing of the grievance in this case, there is nothing suspect on this record. Mr. Coyne was briefed on Berry's case by Mr. DeLuca and apparently received summaries of the two prior meetings at the United Association headquarters in Washington (the initial interview with Berry and the "Step Two" meeting). There is no evidence that Coyne's presentation to the GPC was inadequate or that it somehow unfairly characterized Berry's claim. Nor is the lack of a written opinion by the GPC dispositive. Cf. United Steelworkers v. Enterprise Wheel & Car Corp., 363 U.S. 593, 598, 80 S.Ct. 1358, 1361, 4 L.Ed.2d 1424 (1960) ("Arbitrators have no obligation to the court to give their reasons for an award."); *Bloom,* 603 F.2d at 1020–21 (deference appropriate despite fact that arbitration panel's decision not set out in detailed written form). The crucial fact here is that the grievance procedure agreed to by the parties was lawful and was followed in this case; the Board was not required to decline to show deference merely because the petitioner would have preferred a different grievance process.

Next, Local 520 argues that all parties did not agree to be bound by the settlement agreement because both it and Berry objected to the terms of the settlement. This argument is unavailing. The United Association, and not Local 520, is Berry's recognized bargaining representative. * * * No claim is made here that the United Association breached its duty of fair representation in handling Berry's grievance, see Tr. at 51–53 (testimony of Mr. Hartinger); thus, the Board did not err in finding that the *relevant parties,* the United Association and Catalytic, properly agreed to be bound by the terms of the grievance settlement.

Third, and most strenuously, Local 520 claims that the Board erred in granting deference because the result reached by the settlement—Berry's reinstatement without backpay—is repugnant to the NLRA. Local 520 argues that because Berry was discharged for engaging in allegedly protected activity, Board precedent requires that he be given "make whole" relief. Since Berry received less than full relief, Local 520 contends, the settlement agreement was "palpably wrong" under the NLRA and the Board should not have given deference.

We reject this contention on several grounds. First, Local 520's "palpably wrong" argument presumes that this case presents an unfair labor practice issue apart from the contractual issue of whether Catalytic had "proper cause" for discharging Berry. This view has been categorically rejected by this court in *American Freight,* 722 F.2d at 831–32, where we found that *there was no separate statutory issue.* In *American Freight,* we held that where a provision in a collective bargaining agreement relating to the refusal of work assignments differed from an analogous NLRA provision, the parties' agreement constituted a waiver of the employee's statutory right; to have held otherwise, we noted, would have been to embrace

> [t]he obvious fallacy * * * that there is a statutory issue apart from the contractual issue * * *. In other words, assuming, *arguendo,* that an individual employee has a right under the NLRA to refuse to work [in circumstances different from those prescribed in the agreement] * * *, that alleged right was waived by the collective bargaining agreement in this case.

Id. at 832; see also Edwards, supra, at 28 ("The parties' agreement, in essence, supplants the statute as the source of many employee rights in the context of collective bargaining."). In this case, then, the statutory right allegedly infringed—Berry's purported privilege to counsel unit employees to take action tantamount to a work stoppage—was merged into the "no-strike" and "proper cause" provisions of the GPPMA. As such, the result reached through the grievance procedure was, by definition, not "palpably wrong" under the NLRA because there was no separate statutory issue.

Furthermore, the Board granted deference to settlements providing less than make-whole relief in *Alpha Beta* and *Postal Service,* and Local 520 does not challenge the validity of those cases. See *Postal Service,* slip op. at 4, 7; *Alpha Beta,* 273 N.L.R.B. at 1546–47. Additionally, it is well-established that the NLRB's General Counsel may settle unfair labor practice charges prior to a hearing, even over the charging party's objection that the relief obtained is insufficient. See, *e.g., United Food & Commercial Workers Union, Local 23,* 484 U.S. at 118–21, 108 S.Ct. at 418–20; see also 29 C.F.R. §§ 101.7, 101.9 (1991) (regulations governing settlements). We see no significant difference between that accepted practice and the consequence of the deference policy applied in this case.

Lastly, Local 520 contends that the fourth *Alpha Beta/Postal Service* criterion is not met in this case because the unfair labor practice issue was not "considered" by the parties in reaching the settlement agreement. The short answer to this contention is that, because the GPPMA provided rules for evaluating the propriety of Berry's termination (the "proper cause" provision), there was no surviving unfair labor practice issue. Whatever rights Berry may have had under the NLRA were waived by the United Association in the collective bargaining agreement—and again at the settlement table—such that there was no separate statutory issue for the parties or the GPC to "consider." *See American Freight,* 722 F.2d at 832–33.

In any event, using the Board's most recent test for the "considered" criterion, it is clear that the Board properly applied its deference policy in this case. In *Postal Service,* the NLRB held that the requirement that the parties to a settlement "consider" the unfair labor practice issue is satisfied where "the contractual issue and the unfair labor practice issue are factually parallel, and the parties were generally aware of the facts relevant to resolving the unfair labor practice [issue]." Id., slip op. at 7. In this case, the issue under both the GPPMA and the NLRA was whether Catalytic was justified in terminating Berry based upon his alleged insubordination. Berry's defense on his contract claim was the same as his position on the unfair labor practice issue—that he was just following the instructions of Hartinger, the union Business Manager. As such, the same operative facts underlay both issues and the "considered" leg of the deference inquiry is satisfied. Cf. *Bloom,* 603 F.2d at 1020–21 (contract and unfair labor practice issues factually parallel where both turned on whether employee's action was justified).

* * *

In sum, we find substantial evidence in the record to support the Board's conclusion that the four *Alpha Beta/Postal Service* deference criteria are satisfied in this case. The first two criteria clearly are met because the GPPMA grievance procedure was "fair and regular" and the *relevant* parties—the United Association and Catalytic—agreed to be bound by the terms of the settlement. To the extent that the third and fourth criteria are relevant, see *American Freight,* 722 F.2d at 832–33, the record supports the conclusion that they also are satisfied. We therefore conclude that the Board did not abuse its discretion by granting deference to the settlement agreement; accordingly, the petition for review must be denied.

C. *The Theoretical Underpinnings of the Board's Deference Policy*

Although we deny Local 520's petition for review, we are compelled to express concern over the Board's apparent lack of a coherent theory for its *Alpha Beta/Postal Service* deference policy. * * *

Of special concern in this case is the so-called "palpably wrong" criterion for deference. In *Alpha Beta* and *Postal Service,* the Board stated that, in the settlement context, the "palpably wrong" criterion is satisfied so long as both parties to the settlement make concessions. *See Postal Service,* slip op. at 7; *Alpha Beta,* 273 N.L.R.B. at 1547–48. At oral argument, counsel for the Board was unable to give a persuasive rationale for the "concessions" test.

The "concessions" test under the "palpably wrong" criterion makes no sense if the underlying theory of the Board's deference policy is the contractual waiver doctrine, as appears to be the case. See *Postal Service,* slip op. at 5–6 (appearing to apply waiver theory); cf. *Darr,* 801 F.2d at 1408 (noting that Board's *Spielberg* deference policy "seems to partake" of waiver theory). Under the contractual waiver doctrine, the Board could *never* give deference to a settlement with respect to a "non-waiveable" statutory right—such as the employees' choice of a bargaining representative, the NLRA's prohibitions against "closed shops" and secondary boycotts, and the like. Because a union and an employer may not legally bargain about non-waiveable matters, the Board could not, consistent with the NLRA, give deference to a settlement which implicated such rights.

On the other hand, where the statutory right implicated by a grievance settlement is within the category of "waiveable" rights—*e.g.,* economic issues, the right to strike, matters of selective discipline and the like—then it is unclear why the Board *would ever have any choice but to give deference,* at least so long as the grievance procedures through which the settlement is reached are fair and regular and the union has not breached its duty of fair representation. In other words, since a union has broad discretion to alter or modify employees' "waiveable" rights through collective bargaining, see *Metropolitan Edison Co.,* 460 U.S. at 705–07, 103 S.Ct. at 1475–77, we see no basis upon which the Board legitimately could intervene merely because the settlement reached by the union and the employer was not to the Board's liking. As the courts have recognized in the refusal to bargain context, the Board has no generalized authority to command settlements or force parties to agree to contractual terms that meet with the Board's approval. * * *

In short, we are at a loss to discern either the theoretical underpinnings of the "palpably wrong" criterion, or the standards that the Board purports to follow in applying it. Indeed, the current formulation of the criterion seems designed to permit the Board to give deference when it approves of the result of a settlement, but to intervene when it does not, with no apparent standards for judgment. Such an approach gives the parties no clear indication as to what kinds of settlements will be found to be "palpably wrong" in a given case. A cynical observer might be inclined to view this approach as a veritable recipe for arbitrary action.

In this case, we need go no further than to highlight the logical inconsistencies in the current formulation of the Board's deference policy. Local 520 does not contest the validity of the policy, and its application here was clearly permissible because, as Local 520 concedes, the statutory right at issue in Berry's case was within the category of "waiveable" rights. However, we urge the Board to give serious consideration to the logical flaws in its current policy and to attempt to develop a comprehensible theory of deference. * * * [O]ur patience with the Board's failure to develop a coherent theory of deference is not limitless, and the Board's continued recalcitrance may well result in reversal in future cases less clear-cut than the one before us today.

III. CONCLUSION

For the reasons stated above, we deny Local 520's petition for review of the Board's decision and order. However, because the decision under review demonstrates the Board's continued failure to articulate a coherent theory for its deference policy, we urge the Board to clarify its position in future cases.

So Ordered.

Problems for Discussion

1. When Berry was discharged, Local 520 contended that the company's claim of insubordination was a pretext and that in fact he was terminated because of his union activity, apparently for his assertiveness as a shop steward. Does the record in this case permit a determination whether the GPC, at step three of the grievance procedure, gave consideration to this issue of anti-union animus? If no such determination can confidently be made, should the Board and the court of appeals have deferred to the grievance settlement?

2. Are the reasons for deferring to an arbitration award, fully elaborated in *Olin Corp.*, roughly as compelling when deference is sought to a negotiated grievance settlement? Consider, at the least, the nature of the factual record presented to the arbitrator, the airing of arguments and counter-arguments, the usual explication of reasons in the arbitrator's award. Although some of these were present in the instant case in the proceeding before the GPC at step three, some were not—and most are not in the typical pre-arbitration settlements

regularly worked out by management and union representatives. Should the Board therefore defer to such settlements only after giving them some form of "heightened scrutiny"? Should the Board therefore not defer to them at all?

3. If the General Counsel had acted promptly in the instant case, had processed Local 520's charge, and had approved a settlement whereby Catalytic would have reinstated Berry without backpay or with partial backpay, that decision not to issue a complaint would not have been subject to review by the members of the NLRB or by any court. Is it consistent, when the General Counsel *does* issue a complaint in the belief that statutory purposes have *not* been served by a contractual settlement, for the Board and the court of appeals to review and reverse that determination?

4. Does the court of appeals too quickly sustain the parties' contractual definition of Berry's rights as a shop steward as a substitute for the rights that he is entitled to under the NLRA? What if a union's relinquishment of certain claims on his behalf was based upon a misunderstanding of the NLRA, and an inadequate appreciation of the extent of the rights afforded union representatives? What if the union's understanding of Berry's demeanor in dealing with his foreman over the "split shift" issue, at the time the union decided to settle his grievance, is different from that of the General Counsel when issuing a complaint? What if the union's assessment of a fair remedy (i.e., reinstatement without backpay) falls far short of what the Board would order to vindicate the policies of section 8(a)(3)?

Page 859. Substitute for the Note on *Hammontree* :

HAMMONTREE v. NLRB
925 F.2d 1486 (D.C.Cir.1991).

WALD, CIRCUIT JUDGE:

Paul Hammontree challenges a National Labor Relations Board ("NLRB" or "Board") order that requires him to exhaust grievance remedies established by a collective bargaining agreement before the Board considers his unfair labor practice complaint. Hammontree contends that such an exhaustion requirement is both inconsistent with the Board's authority under the National Labor Relations Act ("NLRA") and the Labor Management Relations Act ("LMRA"), and a departure from the Board's past policy. We find that the NLRA and the LMRA permit the Board to require an individual employee to exhaust his grievance remedies prior to the filing of an unfair labor practice charge and that the Board's order was both reasonable and consistent with its established practices. Accordingly, we deny Hammontree's petition for review.

I. BACKGROUND

A. *Factual Background*

Hammontree is employed as a truck driver by intervenor Consolidated Freightways ("CF"); he drives "peddle" runs—short roundtrips of less than 200 miles.[1] In 1982, when CF first offered peddle runs out of its Memphis, Tennessee terminal, it established a "choice of runs" policy under which available runs were posted and drivers chose runs in order of seniority. Although under this system senior drivers could choose longer (and thus more lucrative) runs, no driver knew the departure time of his or her run; as a result, drivers often "babysat the telephone." Later that year, CF and Hammontree's union local reached an oral agreement: CF would post departure times for peddle runs, but would eliminate the seniority-based "choice of runs." As part of this *quid pro quo,* the union also agreed to withdraw any grievances that might be filed by drivers claiming choice of runs.

In February 1985, as the union's collective bargaining agreement ("CBA") with CF was expiring, Jimmy Carrington, the local's newly-elected president, wrote a letter to CF which stated that "any agreements [between the union and CF] become null and void [on] March 31, 1985." The new CBA, which became effective in April 1985, included a maintenance of standards provision[2] and required that any local standards not already included in the CBA be "reduce[d] to writing." The new contract failed to specify procedures for the assignment of peddle runs and the *quid pro quo* agreement exchanging departure times for seniority rights was not reduced to writing.

In late 1985, Hammontree filed a grievance ("Grievance 180") claiming that his seniority rights had been violated by peddle-run assignment practices. Pursuant to the CBA, Hammontree's grievance was heard by a "Multi–State Grievance Committee" composed of an equal number of union and management representatives. This committee failed to resolve the grievance, which Hammontree then pursued to the next level, the Southern Area Grievance Committee. That committee sustained Hammontree's claim and awarded him damages.

Thereafter, CF stopped posting run departure times. Hammontree then filed a second grievance ("Grievance 101") claiming, *inter alia,* that the removal of run times violated the maintenance of standards provision. The first-level grievance committee denied the claim. Hammontree then filed an unfair labor practice ("ULP") charge, and the NLRB's General Counsel issued a complaint, alleging that by removing departure times in response to Hammontree's exercise of his grievance rights (in

---

1. Throughout the dissent, Hammontree is characterized as a "dissident member of the union," Dissent ("Diss.") at 1505, and as "at odds with his union's leadership," id. at 1516. These characterizations, if true, are atmospherics only; the record contains absolutely no evidence of any hostility between Hammontree and the union in regard to this dispute. As discussed below, infra Part II. B. 1, this lack of hostility is indeed significant to our analysis.

2. Article 6 of the CBA provides, in relevant part:

The Employer agrees, subject to the following provisions, that all conditions of employment in his individual operation relating to * * * working conditions shall be maintained at not less than the highest standards in effect at the time of the signing of this Agreement * * *.

Grievance 180) and by assigning Hammontree less desirable runs, CF had violated §§ 8(a)(1) and 8(a)(3) of the NLRA.[3]

Before the Administrative Law Judge ("ALJ"), CF maintained that the grievance committee had adequately considered Hammontree's discrimination complaint and that the Board should defer to the committee's decision and thus need not consider anew the § 8(a) allegations. In the alternative, CF contended, the Board should refer the claim to the grievance procedures established under the CBA,[4] because the contract, like § 8(a), bars discrimination against union members. The ALJ ruled that the § 8(a) claims raised a sufficiently different question from that heard by the grievance committee so that deference to the committee's decision did not bar consideration of the complaint. She also ruled that because the individual rights of an employee (as opposed to the group interests of the union) were at stake, it would be improper to require Hammontree to exhaust his grievance remedies. Upon review, the Board affirmed the first and reversed the second of these holdings. The Board held that under its policy set forth in *United Technologies Corp.*, 268 N.L.R.B. 557 (1984), Hammontree was required to exhaust the grievance procedures established by the CBA. *Consolidated Freightways Corp.*, 288 N.L.R.B. 1252 (1988). Hammontree seeks review of the Board's order.

B. *The NLRB's "Deferral" Policies*

This case concerns one of the Board's two "deferral" policies, its so-called "pre-arbitral deferral" policy. Under this policy, the Board refers complaints filed by the General Counsel to arbitration procedures established in the governing CBA; in doing so, the Board *defers* or delays its consideration of the complaint. Under a separate, so-called "post-arbitral deferral" policy, not directly implicated in this case,[6] the Board shows limited *deference* to decisions made through grievance and arbitration processes pursuant to collective bargaining provisions.[7]

---

3. Section 8(a) of the NLRA provides, in relevant part:

(a) It shall be an unfair labor practice for an employer—

(1) to interfere with, restrain, or coerce employees in the exercise of the rights guaranteed in section 7;

* * *

(3) by discrimination in regard to hire or tenure of employment or any term or condition of employment to encourage or discourage membership in any labor organization * * *.

29 U.S.C. § 158(a).

4. Article 8 of the CBA outlines grievance procedures and provides that "[a]ll grievances or questions of interpretations

[sic] arising under this * * * Agreement * * * shall be processed" according to those procedures.

6. In this case, CF raised both deference and deferment issues before the ALJ. The Board affirmed the ALJ's deference decision, but ordered deferment of Hammontree's claim. It is this latter aspect of the Board's order that Hammontree now challenges.

7. The CBA in this case provides for multiple levels of grievance proceedings, but does not provide for final and binding arbitration by a neutral arbitrator. Nonetheless, in this court and others, "bipartite committee grievance resolution procedures and decisions have been upheld as equivalent to arbitration." American Freight Sys-

As this discussion suggests, the Board's two "deferral" policies operate in different ways and serve different purposes.[8] Pre-arbitral deferral (what we will, for clarity's sake, call "*deferment*") resembles the exhaustion requirements often found in administrative regimes and the abstention doctrines employed by federal courts. Post-arbitral deferral (what we will call "*deference*") resembles appellate judicial deference.

1. *The Board's Deferment Policy*

In *Collyer Insulated Wire,* 192 N.L.R.B. 837 (1971), the Board considered a § 8(a)(5) claim arising out of an alleged unilateral change of working conditions by an employer. The Board ruled that it would require exhaustion of CBA-provided arbitration remedies before it considered a § 8(a)(5) claim, if certain conditions are met. Such deferment is appropriate, the Board ruled, if

> (i) there is a long-standing bargaining relationship between the parties;

> (ii) there is no enmity by the employer toward the employee's exercise of rights;

> (iii) the employer manifests a willingness to arbitrate;

> (iv) the CBA's arbitration clause covers the dispute at issue; and

> (v) the contract and its meaning lie at the center of the dispute.

192 N.L.R.B. at 842; see also Local Union No. 2188 v. NLRB, 494 F.2d 1087, 1090–91 (D.C.Cir.) (affirming *Collyer* deferment), cert. denied, 419 U.S. 835, 95 S.Ct. 61, 42 L.Ed.2d 61 (1974).

The Board extended this deferment policy to § 8(a)(1) and § 8(a)(3) complaints in *National Radio Co.,* 198 N.L.R.B. 527 (1972). After a temporary contraction of the policy, the Board reaffirmed the *National Radio* policy in its 1984 decision in *United Technologies Corp.,* 268 N.L.R.B. 557 (1984). In that case, the Board recognized that the alleged violations of § 8(a) were also "clearly cognizable under the broad grievance-arbitration provision of * * * the [CBA]," *id.* at 560, and ruled that "[w]here an employer and a union have voluntarily elected to create dispute resolution machinery * * *, it is contrary to the basic principles of the Act for the Board to jump into the fray prior to an honest attempt by the parties to resolve their disputes through that machinery." *Id.* at 559.

tem, Inc. v. NLRB, 722 F.2d 828, 830 n. 4 (D.C.Cir.1983) (collecting authorities). Therefore, references to "arbitration" in this opinion should be read to include grievance proceedings such as those at issue in this case.

8. Thus, "deferral policy" is an unfortunate misnomer. "Post-arbitral deferral" is not deferral at all, but deference, a limitation on the scope of the Board's review of arbitration awards. More importantly, pre- and post-arbitral deferral differ substantially in justification and in practice.

2. *The Board's Deference Policy*

The critical NLRB decision involving the Board's policy of deference to arbitration awards is *Spielberg Manufacturing Co.*, 112 N.L.R.B. 1080 (1955). In *Spielberg*, the Board ruled that it would give deference to an arbitrator's resolution of an unfair labor practice claim if certain conditions are met. As refined in subsequent cases, the Board's policy is to defer if:

(i) the ULP issue was presented to and considered by the arbitrator;

(ii) the arbitration proceedings were fair and regular;

(iii) the parties agreed to be bound by the arbitration award; and

(iv) the arbitration award was not clearly repugnant to the purposes and policies of the NLRA.

112 N.L.R.B. at 1082; see also *Raytheon Co.*, 140 N.L.R.B. 883 (1963). Although the policy has undergone several subsequent revisions, see Darr v. NLRB, 801 F.2d 1404, 1408 (D.C.Cir.1986) (discussing the "various twists and turns" of deference policy), *Spielberg* remains the seminal statement of the Board's deference policy.

II. Analysis

The central issue in this case, whether the Board may require an individual employee to exhaust grievance procedures prior to filing a ULP charge, is governed by the now-familiar two-step analysis set forth in Chevron U.S.A., Inc. v. Natural Resources Defense Council, 467 U.S. 837, 104 S.Ct. 2778, 81 L.Ed.2d 694 (1984). Under *Chevron,* we first determine "whether Congress has directly spoken to the precise question at issue"; if it has, then "that intention is the law and must be given effect." *Chevron,* 467 U.S. at 842–43 & n. 9, 104 S.Ct. at 2781–82 & n. 9. If the statute is "silent or ambiguous with respect to the specific issue," and if "the agency's answer is based on a permissible construction of the statute," we must defer. Id. at 843, 104 S.Ct. at 2782. Part A reviews the petitioner's *"Chevron I"* contentions that the NLRA and the LMRA affirmatively prohibit Board deferment in this case. Part B considers the petitioner's *"Chevron II"* arguments that the Board's decision was an impermissible exercise of its discretion and a departure from established Board policy.

A. Chevron I *Analysis*

1. *Section 10(a) of the NLRA*

Section 10(a) of the NLRA provides that the Board's power to "prevent * * * unfair labor practice[s]" "shall not be affected by any other means of adjustment or prevention that has been or may be established by agreement, law, or otherwise * * *." 29 U.S.C. § 160(a).

Relying on his reading of the plain meaning and legislative history of § 10(a), Hammontree argues that this section prohibits Board deferment of his claim. We disagree and find that § 10(a) does not reflect any express congressional intention to preclude the Board's imposition of exhaustion requirements in cases such as Hammontree's.

Hammontree first contends that the plain language of § 10(a) prohibits Board deferment of his claim; he reads that section as providing that no one (not even the Board itself) may diminish the Board's authority to resolve and prevent ULPs in the first instance. Although read literally and in isolation, § 10(a) might permit such an interpretation, a far more natural reading is that § 10(a) is an affirmative grant of authority to the Board, not an express limitation on the Board's authority. In other words, a more plausible reading of § 10(a) is that no one *other than* the Board shall diminish the Board's authority over ULP claims.

This latter interpretation is supported by a contemporary congressional analysis which explained that the contested sentence "is intended to make it clear that although *other* agencies may be established by code, agreement, or law to handle labor disputes, such *other* agencies can never divest the National Labor Relations Board of jurisdiction which it would otherwise have." Staff of Senate Comm. on Education and Labor, 74th Cong., 1st Sess., Comparison of S. 2926 (73d Congress) and S. 1958 (74th Congress) at 3 (Comm. Print 1935) (emphasis supplied) [hereinafter "Comparison"] reprinted in NLRB, 1 Legislative History of the National Labor Relations Act 1319, 1323 (1949) [hereinafter "Leg.Hist. of the NLRS"]. As that analysis indicates, Congress was concerned about other entities—such as states or industrial boards—infringing upon the Board's jurisdiction; Congress was not concerned about the Board itself deferring the exercise of its own jurisdiction. Thus, contrary to Hammontree's contention, § 10(a) is most logically read as an affirmative grant of power, firmly establishing the Board as the "Supreme Court of Labor." Comparison at 30, reprinted in 1 Leg.Hist. of the NLRA at 1357.

Hammontree also maintains that the legislative history of § 10 indicates Congress' express intention to preclude Board deferment. In particular, Hammontree relies on Congress' elimination of a provision (in earlier bills and earlier drafts of the Act) which expressly stated that the "Board may, in its discretion, defer its exercise of jurisdiction over any such unfair labor practice in any case where there is another means of prevention provided for by agreement * * *." S. 1958, Original Senate Print, 74th Cong., 1st Sess. § 10(b) (1935); reprinted in 1 Leg.Hist. of the NLRA 1295, 1301. Citing hearing testimony that Board deferment authority would result in insufficient protection of individual employee rights, Hammontree argues that Congress, reacting to that testimony, eliminated the proposed language in order to preclude Board deferment.

An equally plausible reading of Congress' deletion of the proposed language, however, is that Congress deemed it superfluous in light of the sweeping language of § 10(a) itself. Again contemporary congressional analysis supports this interpretation of the legislative history, characterizing the deleted language as "carr[ying] out the same thought as the second sentence of § 10(a)" and as "carr[ying] out more explicitly the purpose to establish the Board as the paramount body in labor relations." Comparison at 3, 32, reprinted in 1 Leg.Hist. of the NLRA at 1323, 1358. In sum, there is strong evidence that Congress deleted the proposed section on grounds of redundancy. Certainly, we cannot say that the legislative history of § 10 reflects a specific congressional intention to foreclose Board deferment; at best, we can only say that Congress' intention in deleting the proposed section is ambiguous.

For these reasons, we must disagree with the petitioner's contention that § 10(a) evidences a clear intent to preclude the Board from deferring consideration of a ULP claim until the claimant has exhausted grievance remedies under the CBA.

2. *Section 203(d) of the LMRA*

Hammontree also argues that the Board's deferment authority is limited by § 203(d) of the LMRA, which provides that "[f]inal adjustment by a method agreed upon by the parties is declared to be the desirable method for settlement of grievance disputes *arising over the application or interpretation* of an existing collective-bargaining agreement." 29 U.S.C. § 173(d) (emphasis supplied). Hammontree contends that his claim does not "arise over" the interpretation of the CBA and thus that deferment of his claim is not authorized by § 203(d)'s mandate. We conclude, however, that Hammontree's claim falls squarely within the scope of § 203(d) and accordingly that that section in no way precludes the Board's deferment of Hammontree's claim.

Hammontree, as we have noted, contends that § 10(a) generally bars deferment, and interprets § 203(d) as authorizing deferment only in cases "arising over" interpretation of the CBA. He then goes on to argue that his discrimination claim under the NLRA does not "arise over" contract interpretation even though the CBA contains an anti-discrimination provision parallel to the section of the NLRA upon which his statutory claim is based.

Initially, we observe that § 203(d) reads most naturally as a general policy statement in favor of private dispute resolution, not as any kind of limitation on Board authority. But even if we were to assume *arguendo* that § 203(d) does in some way limit the Board's deferment authority, Hammontree's argument fails on its own terms, for his § 8(a)(3) claim *does* "aris[e] over [contract] application or interpretation." Hammontree's discrimination claim, although raised under §§ 8(a)(1) and 8(a)(3), is also actionable under the contract. Article 21 of the CBA prohibits "discrimination against any employee because of Union membership or activities" and Article 37 of the CBA bars "discriminatory acts prohibited by law." These provisions led the Board to conclude that the alleged discrimination "is clearly prohibited by the contract." 288 N.L.R.B. at 1255. * * *

Hammontree cannot nullify his contractual claim simply by choosing to pursue his statutory claim. Such an interpretation of the law would severely undermine Congress' "decided preference for private settlement of labor disputes without the intervention of government" as reflected in § 203(d). United Paperworkers International Union v. Misco, Inc., 484 U.S. 29, 37, 108 S.Ct. 364, 370, 98 L.Ed.2d 286 (1987). If a party could unilaterally release itself from a contractual pledge to submit complaints to arbitration simply because it had a parallel claim under the statute, then the pro-private dispute resolution policies of § 203(d) would be substantially abrogated.[15]

Hammontree's complaint, therefore, clearly arises under Articles 21 and 37 of the CBA. As such, any limitations on the Board's deferment authority arguably created by § 203(d) do not affect Hammontree's claim, and § 203(d) does not preclude Board deferment of that claim.

3. *Section 10(m) of the NLRA*

Hammontree also argues that § 10(m) prohibits deferment of his claim, because that section requires that § 8(a)(3) and § 8(b)(2) discrimination claims be "given priority" over most other claims. Again, we find the petitioner's reading of the statute cramped; and we reject his contention that § 10(m) prohibits the Board from requiring the exhaustion of grievance remedies in § 8(a)(3) and § 8(b)(2) cases.

* * *

B. Chevron II *Analysis*

1. *Limitations on the Board's Deferment Authority*

Hammontree argues under the second prong of *Chevron* that, even if Congress did not expressly limit the Board's deferment authority in the NLRA and the LMRA, its action in his case is based on an impermissible construction of the Board's authority under those statutes. Hammon-

---

15. The dissent's suggestion that § 203(d)'s preference for private dispute resolution is only involved when "the [individual] employee has [ ] *voluntarily* submitted his [ ] claim to arbitration," Diss. at 1510 (emphasis supplied), is similarly infirm. To contend that Congress' "decided preference"—and a collectively bargained arbitration clause—can be automatically defeated at the option of an aggrieved employee is not only contrary to congressional intent, but also inconsistent with the fundamental tenet of labor law that a sound collective-bargaining agreement binds all employees. Moreover, as the Board noted, the dissent's view "would mean * * * that a union could circumvent the contractual grievance procedure by the simple expedient of having the individual employee, instead of the union, file the charge with the Board." *Consolidated Freightways Corp.,* 288 N.L.R.B. 1252, 1255 (1988).

tree contends that Board deferment in cases in which individual employee rights are at stake is inconsistent with a series of Supreme Court decisions beginning with Alexander v. Gardner–Denver Co., 415 U.S. 36, 94 S.Ct. 1011, 39 L.Ed.2d 147 (1974). We find the alleged conflict illusory.

In *Alexander,* the Supreme Court held that Title VII creates individual statutory rights that supplement, rather than supplant, contractual rights under a CBA. Accordingly, the Court held that an employee's use of arbitration procedures did not bar a subsequent action, based on the same facts, brought in federal court under Title VII. The Court reached a similar conclusion in Barrentine v. Arkansas–Best Freight System, Inc., 450 U.S. 728, 101 S.Ct. 1437, 67 L.Ed.2d 641 (1981) (considering an analogous claim brought under the Fair Labor Standards Act ("FLSA")) and in McDonald v. West Branch, 466 U.S. 284, 104 S.Ct. 1799, 80 L.Ed.2d 302 (1984) (considering a first amendment claim brought under 42 U.S.C. § 1983). In each of these cases, the Court ruled that Congress (in Title VII, the FLSA, and § 1983) provided a public forum for individual-rights claims and that participation in private arbitration must not diminish one's right to such a forum. Hammontree reads these cases broadly, for the proposition that "individual statutory rights cannot be sacrificed on the altar of arbitration." Thus, Hammontree maintains that these cases limit the Board's discretion to defer claims in which an individual seeks to vindicate personal rights under the NLRA.

We disagree. In *Alexander, Barrentine,* and *McDonald,* the Supreme Court held that, when individual statutory rights are at stake, arbitration of a contractual claim does not preclude a subsequent statutory claim. In this case, however, we consider not the preclusive effect of arbitration awards but rather the Board's authority to require the exhaustion of arbitration remedies. These issues are analytically distinct. To give an arbitration award preclusive effect would destroy an individual's right to a public forum for the protection of her statutory rights; Board deferment does not similarly nullify an employee's rights under the Act.[23] As the Board has stated:

> [D]eferral is not akin to abdication. It is merely the prudent exercise of restraint, a postponement of the use of the Board's processes to give the parties' own dispute resolution machinery a chance to succeed.

United Technologies, 268 N.L.R.B. at 560. Deferment does not diminish

---

23. A different question would be raised if the Board's deferment policy were grounded on a waiver theory, rather than on exhaustion grounds. See generally Edwards, Deferral to Arbitration and Waiver of the Duty to Bargain: A Possible Way Out of Everlasting Confusion at the NLRB, 46 Ohio St.L.J. 23 (1985). However, as we noted in *Darr,* "[s]ince the Board has not explicitly adopted that theory, it would be premature to express our view on the issue." 801 F.2d at 1409 n. 8.

Hammontree's right to a public forum; it merely delays it.[25]

Moreover, cases following *Alexander* and suggesting that an exhaustion requirement would be inconsistent with Title VII are also not dispositive, for Title VII and the NLRA differ in several critical ways. First, under Title VII, Congress has expressly recognized that private dispute resolution and statutory relief are distinct and independent remedies; in contrast, under the NLRA, Congress has expressly legislated a preference for the use of private remedies, whenever feasible, before the resort to public remedies. * * *

We, like the Board, recognize that in some circumstances justice deferred could be justice denied. As we emphasized in approving the Board's *Collyer* policy, deferment is a "balancing rule which requires deferral to arbitration only where a balance of * * * policies favors deferral." *Local Union No. 2188,* 494 F.2d at 1090. Thus, if deferment posed "an undue financial burden upon one of the parties," or "prevent[ed] an orderly exposition of the law," or if "anti-union animus [indicated] that deferral * * * would be a futile gesture," or if arbitration would render a subsequent statutory claim untimely, then deferment might be impermissible. See *Local Union No. 2188,* 494 F.2d at 1091. As evidenced by the multi-factor analysis in its *Collyer* and *United Technologies* doctrines, the Board has also long recognized these limitations. However, in this case there is no indication that Board deferment taken along [sic] will prejudice Hammontree's right to a public forum should his claim be denied at grievance proceedings.

We also recognize that Board deferment may be impermissible if charges are filed by an individual employee and the interests of the charging party are so inimical to those of the union as to render arbitration an empty exercise. Like our dissenting colleague, we are sensitive to the "possibility that [in some cases] the interests of the union may diverge from those of the employee." Diss. at 1516. Board abstention in such cases might indeed "constitute[] not deference, but abdication." *Local Union No. 2188,* 494 F.2d at 1091. Thus, the Board only defers if it holds a " 'reasonable belief that arbitration procedures would resolve the dispute' " and has " 'refused to defer where the interests of the union * * * are adverse to those of the employee.' "

25. Only if Hammontree had exhausted his arbitration remedies and filed a charge, and only if the Board had then deferred to the arbitration award in deciding his complaint, would we need to determine the applicability of *Alexander* to claims arising under the NLRA. Notwithstanding the passionate protests of our dissenting colleague, Diss. at 1516, that is not this case and we need not now make such a determination.

We do note, however, that the Supreme Court has indicated that employee rights under the FLSA and the NLRA may differ. Compare *Barrentine,* 450 U.S. at 740, 101 S.Ct. at 1444 (holding that a union cannot waive FLSA rights) with Metropolitan Edison Co. v. NLRB, 460 U.S. 693, 707–10, 103 S.Ct. 1467, 1476–78, 75 L.Ed.2d 387 (1983) (holding that a union may, under certain circumstances, waive members' NLRA rights). Whether any such differences exist in the area of post-arbitral deference is not now before us.

United Technologies, 268 N.L.R.B. at 560 (citation omitted); see also NLRB General Counsel, Guideline Memorandum Concerning *United Technologies Corporation* (March 6, 1984), reprinted in 1984 *Lab.Rel. Y.B.* 344. In this case, however, the record contains no suggestion of such hostility between the union and Hammontree and, as a result, the grievance procedures offer some hope of resolving Hammontree's discrimination claim.[32]

More broadly, we find that the Board's policy of deferment represents a reasonable construction of the Board's statutory duties and authority under the NLRA and the LMRA. Courts have long recognized a "principle of deference" in reviewing agency actions " 'involv[ing] reconciling [potentially] conflicting policies.' " *Chevron,* 467 U.S. at 844, 104 S.Ct. at 2782 (citations omitted). In this case, as discussed above, Congress has established the Board as "the paramount body" in labor relations law in § 10(a), called for the expeditious resolution of discrimination claims in § 10(m), and expressed its "decided preference for private settlement of labor disputes" in § 203(d). As the NLRB itself has observed, it is the Board's " 'duty to serve the objectives of Congress [by seeking] a rational accommodation' " among these policies. *United Technologies,* 268 N.L.R.B. at 559 (quoting *National Radio,* 198 N.L.R.B. at 531). The Board's deferment policy simultaneously recognizes the need for the prompt resolution of ULP claims, the importance of individual statutory rights, the limitations on Board resources, and the salutary effects of arbitration and minimal governmental intervention in labor disputes. Accordingly, the Board's deferment policy constitutes a reasonable accommodation of its multiple statutory obligations.

For these reasons, we find that the Supreme Court's decisions in *Alexander* and its progeny are not controlling and that the Board's deferment policy constitutes a permissible and reasonable construction of the NLRA and the LMRA. * * *

III. Conclusion

In summary, we find that the NLRA and the LMRA do not preclude the Board from requiring a claimant to exhaust contractual grievance remedies before the Board hears a § 8(a)(3) discrimination claim. We also find that the Board's deferment policy is reasonable and is informed by a permissible construction of the Board's various statutory obligations, and that the Board's order in this case was wholly consistent with that policy. Accordingly, we deny the petition for review.

---

32. There is absolutely no evidence in the record to support the dissent's assertion that the dispute-resolution mechanism in this case is "a sham grievance proceeding," Diss. at 1515, or a meaningless "drumhead proceeding," id. at 1516. Empirically, it seems most unlikely, for, as noted above, Hammontree's first grievance was, in fact, *successfully* resolved in his favor.

EDWARDS, CIRCUIT JUDGE, concurring.

I do not view the issue posed in this case as raising a difficult question. Indeed, in light of well established legal precedent (including the case law commanding deference to the judgment of the Board on the issue at hand), I think that no serious challenge can be raised to the Board's policy of deferment with respect to arbitral issues. I write separately, however, to indicate why, in my view, this is not a difficult issue, and also to underscore certain points that I believe to be critical to our disposition of this case.

I.

I agree with the majority that the Supreme Court's decisions in *Alexander, Barrentine* and *McDonald,* denying deference or preclusive effect to arbitral awards, do not control the disposition of this case.
* * *

[In those cases, the Court] viewed an exhaustion requirement as simply inconsistent with the notion of distinct and independent remedies.
* * *

II.

Although it seems clear that there can be no requirement of arbitral deferment under *Alexander* and its progeny, it is equally clear that the *Alexander* line of authority is easily distinguishable from the case at hand. The distinction rests on the fundamental differences between the National Labor Relations Act, as amended, 29 U.S.C. §§ 151–69 (1988) ("NLRA"), and the Labor Management Relations Act of 1947, as amended, 29 U.S.C. §§ 141–67, 171–87 (1988) ("LMRA"), and the statutes at issue in *Alexander, Barrentine, McDonald, et al.*

Under Title VII, the FLSA and section 1983, Congress emphasized that private dispute resolution mechanisms and statutory claims are separate and independent remedies; under the collective bargaining statutes, however, as manifested in section 203(d) of the LMRA, 29 U.S.C. § 173(d) (1988), Congress expressed a strong preference for the use of private remedies. And while rights protected by Title VII, the FLSA and section 1983 are individual in nature, the NLRA and the LMRA are designed to protect both individual and collective rights, and have as their paramount goal the promotion of labor peace through the collective efforts of labor and management. Thus, while courts have the undivided responsibility to adjudicate claims of individual discrimination under Title VII and section 1983, the Board is charged with fostering the overall well-being of labor-management relations, which may be best accomplished by requiring the parties to seek to resolve their disputes through contractual dispute resolution mechanisms.

Most tellingly, in the *Alexander* line of cases, the Supreme Court has flatly rejected arguments suggesting that statutory rights may be waived by an agreement to arbitrate disputes arising under a collective bargaining agreement. See *Alexander,* 415 U.S. at 51, 94 S.Ct. at 1021 ("rights conferred [by Title VII] can form no part of the collective-bargaining process since waiver of those rights would defeat the paramount congressional purpose behind Title VII"); *Barrentine,* 450 U.S. at 740, 101 S.Ct. at 1444–45 (FLSA rights are "nonwaivable" and "cannot be abridged by contract"); *McDonald,* 466 U.S. at 292 n. 12, 104 S.Ct. at 1804 (relying upon *Alexander* and *Barrentine* in rejecting waiver argument with regard to § 1983 rights).

In stark contrast, the Court has explicitly recognized that, because a union represents collective interests, it may waive certain NLRA rights of its members. In Metropolitan Edison Co. v. NLRB, 460 U.S. 693, 103 S.Ct. 1467, 75 L.Ed.2d 387 (1983), the Court stated that it had long "recognized that a union may waive a member's statutorily protected rights * * *. Such waivers are valid because they rest on the premise of fair representation and presuppose that the selection of the bargaining representative remains free * * *. Thus a union may bargain away its members' economic rights, but it may not surrender rights that impair the employees' choice of their bargaining representative." Id. at 705–06, 103 S.Ct. at 1476 (quotation marks omitted). The Court rejected the argument that only collective, as opposed to individual, NLRA rights are subject to union waiver, expressly distinguishing its holding in *Alexander* that a union cannot waive its employees' individual Title VII rights. The Court indicated that the possibility of waiver of statutory rights depends upon the "purposes of the statute at issue," and stated that, unlike Title VII, the NLRA "contemplates that individual rights may be waived by the union so long as the union does not breach its duty of good-faith representation." Id. at 706–07 n. 11, 103 S.Ct. at 1476 n. 11.

This court as well has acknowledged that a union may properly waive an employee's individual NLRA rights. * * *

Consistent with these cases, I believe that, in light of the parties' agreement prohibiting discrimination and requiring arbitration, Hammontree was properly required by the Board to arbitrate his grievance pursuant to the terms of the collective bargaining contract. The parties to the collective agreement chose to supplant statutory rights with analogous rights created under the contract, and they provided that disputes concerning those rights would be resolved pursuant to an agreed-upon grievance procedure. Giving legal effect to that agreement respects the private ordering of rights and responsibilities established through collective bargaining, and fosters the strong labor policy of promoting industrial peace through arbitration. Consequently, Board deferment in the case is clearly permissible.

Furthermore, even if it might be argued that there was no "clear and unmistakable" waiver of statutory rights in this case, see *Metropolitan Edison,* 460 U.S. at 708, 103 S.Ct. at 1477, the Board could still require deferment. This is so because the Supreme Court has said in other contexts that, even when parties do not forgo substantive rights afforded by statute, they still may be required to adhere to an agreement to arbitrate a statutory claim. See Mitsubishi Motors Corp. v. Soler Chrysler–Plymouth, Inc., 473 U.S. 614, 636–40, 105 S.Ct. 3346, 3358–61, 87 L.Ed.2d 444 (1985); Shearson/American Express, Inc. v. McMahon, 482 U.S. 220, 229–34, 107 S.Ct. 2332, 2339–42, 96 L.Ed.2d 185 (1987). In such a situation, the parties simply submit the resolution of their dispute "in an arbitral, rather than a judicial, forum." *Mitsubishi,* 473 U.S. at 628, 105 S.Ct. at 3354. And, as the Court noted, "[h]aving made the bargain to arbitrate, the party should be held to it unless Congress itself has evinced an intention to preclude a waiver of judicial remedies for the statutory rights at issue." Id. Thus, absent a finding of the sort underlying *Alexander,* i.e., that statutory and contractual rights are "distinctly separate" and that arbitration cannot adequately substitute for adjudication as a means of enforcing statutory rights, deferment is clearly appropriate. If a union has the acknowledged power to "bargain away" its employees' "statutorily protected rights" under the NLRA, the Board can certainly decline to exercise its jurisdiction when the union takes the lesser step of simply agreeing to have its members' rights vindicated in an arbitral, rather than Board, forum. Accordingly, Board deferment in this case is hardly problematic.[5] * * *

SILBERMAN, CIRCUIT JUDGE, concurring:

Although I find Judge Edwards' logic unassailable, I join the majority opinion because the Board did not articulate (either in its opinion or its brief) Judge Edwards' position.

MIKVA, CHIEF JUDGE, dissenting:

Paul Hammontree works as a truck driver for Consolidated Freightways. The Teamsters Union is the bargaining representative for Consolidated's employees. Hammontree is a dissident member of the union, having disagreed with Teamster officials on numerous occasions. The Teamsters had an understanding with Consolidated whereby the union promised not to press any employee grievances based on certain seniority rights if Consolidated would post departure times for available trucking assignments called peddle runs. Hammontree nevertheless filed a grievance based on his seniority rights and won, but Consolidated then discontinued its practice of posting times and, after Hammontree unsuccessfully challenged that action at a second grievance proceeding, the company retaliated by assigning him several undesirable runs.

The court today tells Mr. Hammontree that he must take his complaints for alleged violations of his rights under the national labor

---

5. Although the *Mitsubishi/McMahon* rationale and contractual waiver theory lead to the same result in this case, i.e., affirmance of the Board's decision to defer, the two approaches are analytically distinct. Under waiver theory, the contractual rights *supplant* the statutory rights, and thus the arbitrator's sole responsibility is to enforce the rights created by the contract. Under *Mitsubishi* and *McMahon,* statutory rights are still being enforced, only in an arbitral, rather than court, forum. As I indicate above, I believe that contractual waiver theory is the correct approach in this case, as it respects the freedom of the parties to replace *waivable* NLRA rights with rights negotiated through collective bargaining.

laws to a grievance committee composed of members half from the union's hierarchy and half from the employer. (It is as if a new kid at school was told to try and work things out with the two bullies who beat him up rather than have the principal intervene and discipline the ruffians.) Inexplicably, the court repeatedly suggests that the "parties" consented to such arbitration in this case, when in fact the "party" most concerned with and affected by the unlawful discrimination against him never consented to such arbitration and instead expressly chose to pursue a complaint arising solely under the National Labor Relations Act. * * *

The court reaches its result by finding equivocal some plain language of the statute, reading the legislative history in a most selective manner, and altogether ignoring the clear directive from subsequent Congresses to pay special and prompt attention to the rights of the individual employees. Brushing aside cogent explanations for the statute's enumerated procedures, the court gives deference to the National Labor Relation Board's clear abdication of its statutory obligations. Mr. Hammontree is consigned to a never-never land of partisan proceedings where his rights under the law may *never* be adjudicated before the Board. If he works long enough, and is persistent enough, the Board might someday review (without the benefit of any explanation or record) a decision of the grievance committee. The sponsors and champions of the Landrum–Griffin Act would be dismayed to see such short shrift made of their efforts to build statutory protections against this very kind of abuse.

I think my colleagues are wrong.

DISCUSSION

This case involves the intersection of two congressional policies: preventing unfair labor practices and fostering the collective bargaining process. Because the collective bargaining agreement between the Teamsters Union and Consolidated contains two provisions forbidding unlawful company discrimination against employees for exercising union rights, the court holds that deferring Hammontree's discrimination charges to arbitration was proper. However, since Hammontree did not pursue his claims under the non-discrimination clauses in the contract, and never consented to arbitration of his statutory claims, this is a straightforward example of the Board abdicating its responsibility to protect rank-and-file workers from their own unions as well as their employers.

A. *Congressional Enactments*

1. The Wagner Act.

There can be no dispute that the Wagner Act gave the Board exclusive power to prevent unfair labor practices. Section 10(a) of the Act, 29 U.S.C. § 160(a) (1988), provides in pertinent part:

The Board is empowered to prevent * * * any person from engaging in any unfair labor practice (listed in Section 8) affecting commerce. This power shall not be affected by any other means of adjustment or prevention that has been or may be established by agreement, law, or otherwise * * *.

The court contends that the section merely "empowers" the Board and in no way constrains its discretion to defer disputes to private arbitration. If this is correct, it is hard to understand why the proviso in the second sentence was even necessary. In fact, a review of the Act's legislative history demonstrates an alternative motivation, namely a clear directive *not* to let private parties interfere with the Board's congressionally mandated function. Furthermore, contrary to the majority's suggestion, the legislative history of the Act and its subsequent amendments confirms that there is no generalized preference for arbitration that would trump an individual employee's right under § 10(a) to have the Board consider his discrimination charges.

In debating the Wagner Act, Congress considered but failed to pass several bills containing the very same deferral authority that the court today discovers. * * *

The court points to the fact that the Senate Committee Report never explicitly disclosed the reasons for the changes. But the result had clear antecedents: Congress made a conscious decision not to adopt language that would broadly allow deferral of claims to arbitration, in response to the concerns expressed by witnesses about the risk of collusion between unions and employers. Instead, Congress opted for the empowering language of § 10(a). Contrary to the court's emphasis on a passage suggesting that the specific arbitration language was deleted only because of a perceived redundancy, see Maj.Op. at 1492, the fact remains that the precise deferral authority the Board now seeks was spelled out in the House and Senate bills but subsequently deleted without any suggestion in the Senate Committee Report that the final language of § 10(a) already gave the Board that authority. The Court restores the very procedure that Congress deleted.

Even the Board's explanation for why Congress settled for the language in § 10(a), namely as a reaction to the excessive power then vested in quasi-private industrial boards, underscores the hazard of deferring to "bipartisan" committees that operate "in an atmosphere of conciliation and compromise that may be admirably suited to the settlement of wage and hour disputes" but are ill-suited to ensuring that all employees were protected against discrimination. See S.Rep. No. 573, at 4–5 (the Act must be "enforced * * * rather than broken by compromise; and its enforcement must reside with governmental rather than quasi-private agencies"), reprinted in History of the Wagner Act, at 2304. As explained below, the Teamster Joint Grievance Committees operate in an identical, and equally objectionable, fashion. Even Senator

Wagner recognized that "[t]he practical effect of letting each industry bargain and haggle about what section 7(a) means is that the weakest groups who need its basic protection most receive the least." Hrgs. on S.1958, at 50–51, reprinted in History of the Wagner Act, at 1426–27.

It is clear, then, that even before the Landrum–Griffin Act was passed in 1959, the substantive sections of the Wagner Act already demonstrated the centrality of safeguarding workers from unfair labor practices such as discrimination. Congress consistently expressed its desire to protect the individual worker against discrimination by his employer *or* his union. * * * While the majority-rule provision of the Wagner Act was designed to ensure that the union with the greatest employee support would be the exclusive bargaining representative for all employees, Congress maintained that the non-discrimination provisions of the Act would protect individual employees even without their union's help. See S.Rep. No. 573, at 13, reprinted in History of the Wagner Act, at 2312–13. As Senator Wagner stated during floor debates, "the prohibition of certain unfair labor practices * * * [is] intended to make the worker a free man." 79 Cong.Rec. 7574 (1935), reprinted in History of the Wagner Act, at 2343.

2. The Taft–Hartley Act.

The preference for arbitration of disputes involving the application or interpretation of a collective bargaining agreement was added by § 203(d) of the Labor–Management Relations ("Taft–Hartley") Act in 1947. After initially charging the Board with preventing unfair labor practices through the Wagner Act, Congress subsequently carved out a limited preference for allowing parties to a collective bargaining agreement to resolve any disputes over that agreement in a manner agreed upon by them. Accordingly, section 203(d) of the Act, 29 U.S.C. § 173(d), provides in pertinent part:

> Final adjustment by a method agreed upon by the parties is hereby declared to be the desirable method for settlement of grievance disputes arising over the application or interpretation of an existing collective bargaining agreement.

The majority contends that § 10(a) is ambiguous in light of this competing congressional directive to promote collective bargaining. Indeed, one of the concurring judges finds this an easy case because the "parties to the collective agreement chose to supplant statutory rights with analogous rights created under the contract * * *."

But this case does not require any application or interpretation of the collective bargaining agreement, and Hammontree never agreed to give up his statutory protections against discrimination by the very parties to the collective bargaining agreement. There is nothing that would dilute the unambiguous command of § 10(a). In fact, § 203(d) is not the generalized preference for private dispute resolution that the court suggests. * * *

The majority suggests that, since Hammontree's statutory claims *could* also have been brought under the parallel non-discrimination clauses in the collective bargaining agreement, these statutory claims necessarily involve the application or interpretation of the contract so as to trigger § 203(d)'s preference for arbitration. See Maj.Op. at 1493–1494. This argument is disingenuous. * * *

The preference for arbitration is simply not involved in a case where the employee has not voluntarily submitted his discrimination claim to arbitration. The court's reasoning may well encourage the routine inclusion of contract provisions that merely incorporate the National Labor Relations Act by reference. If this does not wipe out the statutory rights guaranteed to rank-and-file workers, it certainly assures that their vindication will be substantially diminished and unnecessarily delayed. Hammontree has not "nullified" his rights under the collective bargaining agreement; he has consciously decided not to invoke them. The court's fear that unions might circumvent arbitration provisions by filing charges through individual employees, see Maj.Op. at 1494 n. 15, is unfounded (since the Board can police for good faith) and clearly not the situation here.

3. The Landrum–Griffin Act.

Perhaps nowhere is congressional concern for the well-being of the individual employee vis-a-vis the powerful union more manifest than in the Landrum–Griffin Act (the Labor–Management Reporting and Disclosure Act of 1959). The Act was passed at a time when union corruption was perceived to be widespread and individual employees were powerless to prevent abusive union tactics. In response, title I of Landrum–Griffin created a bill of rights for union members guaranteeing equal rights for all employees, including freedom of speech and the right to sue. See 29 U.S.C. § 411 (1988). It is clear from the legislative history of Landrum–Griffin that Congress no longer was willing to assume that the rights of individual employees would be adequately protected by the unions. * * *

Speaking in support of Landrum–Griffin, Congressman Bosch noted that most cases of discrimination brought before the Board are filed by individual employees, not unions. Many of such cases involved "so-called sweetheart agreements between union leaders and employers and similar activities in which workers are denied their rights." 105 Cong. Rec. 1430 (1959) (remarks of Rep. Bosch), reprinted in History of Landrum–Griffin, at 1616. As Congressman Bosch recognized, without government protection, an individual employee is powerless against his employer and union bosses. Thus, the Board's current policy of deferring individual unfair labor practice claims to grievance committees composed of company and union representatives interdicts its primary statutory responsibility to protect the rights of individual employees.

In addition to codifying the rights of union members and regulating the internal affairs of unions in order to stamp out racketeering and corruption, Landrum–Griffin also added § 10(m) to the National Labor Relations Act, providing that the Board should give discriminatory unfair labor practice claims arising under § 8(a)(3) priority over all other cases except secondary boycotts. See 29 U.S.C. § 160(m). According to Senator Mundt, who introduced this amendment, § 10(m) was intended to redress the problem of the individual employee who loses his job or wages as a result of discriminatory behavior; he explained that the Board often delays hearing such cases: "At present, a vast majority of these cases are left hanging on the vine for a period, sometimes amounting to years." 105 Cong.Rec. 6044 (1959) (remarks of Sen. Mundt), reprinted in History of Landrum–Griffin, at 1253. By introducing this measure, Senator Mundt sought to extend to the individual the same priority treatment that the Board accorded companies faced with secondary boycotts. See id. * * *

* * * The circumstances of this delay, to an individual at odds with both his union and his employer, is particularly egregious.

B. *Statutory Interpretation and Agency Practice*

The court has to overcome all of the plain language and legislative history hurdles described above to even reach the question of whether the Board's interpretation of the statute was reasonable and entitled to deference. * * * When the language of § 10(a) is viewed in tandem with legislative intent and with other parts of the Act (especially in light of the Landrum–Griffin amendments), the statutory question can be settled under step one of *Chevron* rather than shunted into the lazy deference of step two. I believe that the Board violated Congress' clear intent when it deferred Hammontree's statutory claims. Even if we must proceed to step two, however, the court errs in ignoring *Chevron's* requirement that a court gauge the reasonableness of an agency's interpretation by looking at the statute as a whole.

There are cases where the tension created by the twin policies expressed in the Act can best be resolved by deferring to a grievance proceeding. This court has allowed the Board to defer unfair labor practice claims that require contract interpretation. See Associated Press v. NLRB, 492 F.2d 662 (D.C.Cir.1974); Local Union No. 188, IBEW v. NLRB, 494 F.2d 1087 (D.C.Cir.), cert. denied, 419 U.S. 835, 95 S.Ct. 61, 2 L.Ed.2d 61 (1974). Likewise, other circuits have permitted the Board to defer where the *employee* has requested arbitration on the very issue before it, and the employee has not withdrawn that request. See Lewis v. NLRB, 800 F.2d 818 (8th Cir.1986). But until this case, no court has ever sanctioned deferral where the employee did *not* request arbitration and no portion of the claims rested upon a contractual matter. The Board's *own* preference for arbitration cannot implicate § 203(d)'s policy that encourages adjustment through procedures contained in collective bargaining agreements. We have never before allowed the Board to defer *individual, non-contractual* unfair labor practice claims to arbitration.

The lead case establishing the Board's pre-arbitration deferral doctrine is *Collyer Insulated Wire,* 192 N.L.R.B. 837 (1971). * * * The unfair labor practice issue was whether the company violated § 8(a)(5) of the Act by unilaterally altering the terms and conditions of employment when it changed the pay rates for certain job classifications. The Board recognized that adjudicating this statutory claim essentially required an interpretation and application of the terms of the collective bargaining agreement, a task within the special expertise of an arbitrator.

We expressly approved an application of the *Collyer* deferral rule in two cases where resolution of the unfair labor practice claim *required* interpretation of the collective bargaining agreement. * * *

The Board announced an extension of the *Collyer* doctrine, after a series of shifts, in *United Technologies Corp.,* 268 N.L.R.B. 557 (1984). In *United Technologies,* the Board deferred to arbitration even though the unfair labor practice charge filed by the union was for unlawful coercion under § 8(a)(1) of the National Labor Relations Act and did not necessarily implicate any construction of the collective bargaining agreement. Deferral of such claims cannot be squared with the Board's mandatory obligation to remedy unfair labor practices * * *

* * * The Administrative Law Judge in this case appreciated the difference as well: "an individual, as opposed to a labor organization, should not have to resort to the contractual grievance machinery for possible resolution of issues raised in an unfair labor practice charge." *Hammontree,* 288 N.L.R.B. at 1267. In this case, Hammontree did *not* agree to arbitration of his discrimination claims and those claims are wholly separate from any questions of contract interpretation. The union merely created an additional procedure whereby it could arbitrate statutory claims. Absent a conscious waiver by the employee of those statutory rights or a decision to effectuate those rights under the parallel non-discrimination provisions of the collective bargaining agreement, Board deferral was inappropriate. * * *

C. *The Waiver Doctrine*

No one disputes the fact that Hammontree's unfair labor practice charges properly arise under the substantive prohibitions contained in sections 7 and 8(a) of the Act, 29 U.S.C. §§ 157, 158(a)(1) & (3), although counsel for the Board now suggests that the inclusion of parallel non-discrimination provisions in the parties' collective bargaining agreement may have waived Hammontree's statutory right to be free from discrimination for engaging in protected activity. A waiver of an employee's statutory rights may not be found unless it is "established clearly and unmistakably." Metropolitan Edison Co. v. NLRB, 460 U.S. 693, 708–09, 103 S.Ct. 1467, 1477–78, 75 L.Ed.2d 387 (1983) (Courts "will not infer from a general contractual provision that the parties intend to waive a statutorily protected right unless the undertaking is 'explicitly stated.' "). Nor does the arbitration provision by itself waive the statutory rights that might be settled in a grievance proceeding. See id. at 708 n. 12, 103 S.Ct. at 1477 n. 12; Barton Brands, 298 N.L.R.B. No. 139, 135 L.R.R.M. 1022, 1025–26 (1990) ("[A]n agreement to arbitrate a specific discharge, without more, does not meet the exacting standards we require of a waiver of an employee's statutory rights."). As this court has previously observed, "[a]n employee does not waive his statutory right to be free from unfair labor practices by virtue of his being a party to a collective bargaining agreement; he is entitled to a forum in which his complaint is fully and fairly aired." Bloom v. NLRB, 603 F.2d 1015, 1020 (D.C.Cir.1979).

The Board evidently takes a position that is more nuanced than an actual waiver theory, merely suggesting that it will only defer in cases where the statutory right at issue is waivable. A similar theory is proposed in Edwards, Deferral to Arbitration and Waiver of the Duty to Bargain: A Possible Way Out of Everlasting Confusion at the NLRB, 46 Ohio St.L.J. 23 (1985). This distinction between waivable and non-waivable statutory rights, expressed for the first time by counsel at oral argument, appears nowhere in past Board deferral cases and was not made clear in the decision to defer Hammontree's charge. * * * [T]he same concerns about deferring an employee's retaliation charge to a sham grievance proceeding arise whether or not he could waive his § 8(a)(3) rights. The Board did not take the position that deferral was appropriate because Hammontree had or could have waived his statutory rights, and this would be an entirely different case had it done so. Indeed, if there was waiver, the Board would not even have the discretion not to defer, see Concurring Opinion at 1503, a dubious proposition in light of the clear command in § 10(a) that the Board's authority to prevent unfair labor practices cannot be affected by agreement.

The majority maintains that because Articles 21 and 37 in the collective bargaining agreement parallel the nondiscrimination guarantees in the Act, Hammontree's claims of retaliation can properly be submitted to arbitration. However, the fact that the union claims to have bolstered employees' protection against discrimination by negotiating the inclusion of these provisions in the contract would not deprive Hammontree of his preexisting statutory right to bring a claim under section 8(a)(1) and (3) before the Board. An individual's right to freely engage in union activities without fear of retaliation exists independently of any contract and cannot be diminished or diffused by its reiteration in a collective bargaining agreement. Cf. Local 900, Internat'l Union of

Elec., etc. v. NLRB, 727 F.2d 1184, 1190 (D.C.Cir.1984) (non-economic rights of employees under the Act are not waivable to the same extent as economic rights affecting union officials).

In analogous contexts, the Supreme Court has repeatedly made it clear that the statutory rights of individual employees to present their grievances before a public forum could not be denied by the existence of a private dispute resolution mechanism. [Judge Mikva discussed *Gardner–Denver, Barrentine,* and McDonald.] The majority distinguishes these decisions as based on other statutes, but the court thereby ignores the Supreme Court's clear teachings on the general question of deferring employees' claims to arbitration. * * *

One of the reasons for not deferring to arbitration in these cases was the possibility that the union would not fully pursue an employee's statutory rights. In *Barrentine,* the Court recognized that the interests of rank-and-file employees may well diverge from the union. A union might legitimately sacrifice the individual claims of certain employees for what it believes is the greater good of the work force. *See* 450 U.S. at 742, 101 S.Ct. at 1445; *Vaca v. Sipes,* 386 U.S. 171, 190–91, 87 S.Ct. 903, 916–17, 17 L.Ed.2d 842 (1967). Certainly, the joint labor-management arbitration committees at issue here might well choose to address a particular employee's grievances through a generalized give-and-take of union/employee interests, instead of by conscientiously enforcing the terms of the statute. The majority fails to fully appreciate the possibility that the interests of the union may diverge from those of the employee. Indeed, Hammontree was at odds with his union's leadership; restricting him to a drumhead proceeding where his antagonists are viewed as his protectors frustrates the goals of the Act.

D. *Exhaustion of Remedies*

The court contends that this is solely an exhaustion of remedies question and does not foreclose subsequent judicial review in case the grievance committee rejects Hammontree's unfair labor practice claim and the Board summarily affirms that decision. While that characterization may ease the court's conscience, it ignores reality. The Board's precedents amply suggest what will happen if Hammontree's grievance proceeding is ever concluded: it will no doubt defer yet again, according significant deference to the arbitrator's decision. A challenger to an arbitration decision bears the burden of showing that it was repugnant to the Act or that the statutory issues were not fairly decided. See *Olin Corp.,* 268 N.L.R.B. 573 (1984). An individual's right to have the Board review an arbitrator's decision under *Olin* 's highly deferential standard is fundamentally unlike the right to *de novo* consideration of an unfair labor practice claim by the Board. * * *

There are other deficiencies in the Teamsters' grievance mechanism that may well hamper effective review after exhaustion. This is not arbitration in the traditional sense where parties submit their dispute to a neutral third party. After hearing the individual's claim, the joint committee meets in private and either grants or denies the claim without a word of explanation for its decision. Since no record is kept, there is simply no way of knowing that the individual's claim has been fairly decided, let alone the grounds for the curt decision. Such a scenario is particularly unacceptable if the individual employee is, as in this case, at odds with his union leadership. "[T]he Teamster system does not adequately protect the individual from management or union discrimination. In effect, it mandates negotiation over whether the statute has been violated and places the alleged violators in the position of deciding the outcomes of the grievance." Comment, The Teamster Joint Grievance Committee and the NLRB Deferral Policy: A Failure to Protect the Individual Employee's Statutory Rights, 133 U.Pa.L.Rev. 1453, 1457 (1985). * * *

In effect, the court's holding subjects Hammontree to compulsory arbitration, a regime that is anathema to the clear intent of Congress and contrary to this country's general disdain for such a system of dispute resolution. "Congress has expressly rejected compulsory arbitration as a means of resolving collective-bargaining disputes," NLRB v. Amax Coal Co., 453 U.S. 322, 337, 101 S.Ct. 2789, 2798, 69 L.Ed.2d 672 (1981) * * *

The court concludes that the "Board's deferment policy simultaneously recognizes the need for prompt resolution of ULP claims, the importance of individual statutory rights, the limitations on Board resources, and the salutary effects of arbitration * * *." Maj.Op. at 1499. If only the Board's approach were so balanced and enlightened. Deferral to arbitration is perfectly legitimate when the issues submitted to the arbitrator require interpretation of a contract, or when the employee consents to arbitration of his unfair labor practice claim. However, when an unfair labor practice against an employee is involved, and the employee brings the charge before the Board, we ought not allow Board deferral to a potentially hostile or indifferent agent for enforcement of the employee's statutory rights. Although the Board assures Mr. Hammontree that it retains ultimate jurisdiction to ensure that the result reached is not repugnant to the Act, the deferential standard of review makes it extremely unlikely that an arbitration decision will be overturned or thoroughly reviewed, to say nothing of the extensive delay that Congress specifically legislated against in the Landrum–Griffin Act. Indeed, under the Teamsters' grievance system, the goal of expediting employees' discrimination claims is turned on its head.

CONCLUSION

The court today restructures the congressional scheme for protecting workers from unfair labor practices, telling the National Labor Relations Board that it may entrust the statutory rights of individual employees to a grievance system of most dubious dimensions. Congressmen Landrum, Griffin, Senator Dirksen and the other sponsors of the Landrum–Griffin Act would be saddened to know that their valiant efforts in the 86th Congress came to so little avail for Mr. Hammontree and similarly situated dissident union members.

———

In GILMER v. INTERSTATE/JOHNSON LANE CORP., 500 U.S. 20, 111 S.Ct. 1647, 114 L.Ed.2d 26 (1991), the Court held that the rules of the New York Stock Exchange, requiring registered representatives to arbitrate "any controversy ... arising out of employment or termination of employment," were enforceable under the Federal Arbitration Act (FAA), 9 U.S.C. § 1 et seq. The Court also held that an employee's claim that his termination was in violation of the Age Discrimination in Employment Act was subject to the arbitration rule, incorporated as part of his employment agreement. The majority opinion, written by Justice White, distinguished the *Gardner–Denver* line of cases:

> First, those cases did not involve the issue of the enforceability of an agreement to arbitrate statutory claims. Rather, they involved the quite different issue whether arbitration of contract-based claims precluded subsequent judicial resolution of statutory claims. Since the employees there had not agreed to arbitrate their statutory claims, and the labor arbitrators were not authorized to resolve such claims, the arbitration in those cases understandably was held not to preclude subsequent statutory actions. Second, because the arbitration in those cases occurred in the context of a collective-bargaining agreement, the claimants there were represented by their unions in the arbitration proceedings. An important concern therefore was the tension between collective representation and individual statutory rights, a concern not applicable to the present case. Finally, those cases were not decided under the FAA, which, as discussed above, reflects a "liberal federal policy favoring arbitration agreements." ... Therefore, those cases provide no basis for refusing to enforce Gilmer's agreement to arbitrate his ADEA claim.

B. THE DUTY TO BARGAIN DURING THE TERM OF AN EXISTING AGREEMENT

Page 882. Add new Problem 5:

    5. A current collective bargaining agreement has an article on "Management Rights" that provides, among other things, that the Company has the "exclusive right" to "assign employees," to "determine the method, means and personnel" of its operations, and to "maintain the efficiency" of its operations. The collective agreement provides for three categories: a regular work force, which is guaranteed a fixed number of hours of work per week; a "part-time

regular" workforce, who work a fixed schedule of fewer hours; and a "part-time flexible" workforce, who work as needed. The agreement on the latter provides that in the event of a staff reduction, the Company "shall, to the extent possible, minimize the impact on full-time positions by reducing part-time flexible hours." In the face of a serious budgetary reduction, the Company reduced its service hours. No layoff resulted nor were the hours guaranteed to full-time and regular part-time workers reduced, in contrast to the flexible part-timers. But work schedules for the full timers were unilaterally changed. Was the Company's right to alter work hours "contained in" (or "covered by") the collective bargaining agreement? Or did the collective agreement's management rights clause "waive" the union's right to bargain about the change? What is the difference? See NLRB v. U.S. Postal Service, 8 F.3d 832 (D.C.Cir.1993); cf. Chicago Tribune Co. v. NLRB, 974 F.2d 933 (7th Cir.1992).

Part Six

SUCCESSORSHIP

Page 905.   Add new Problems:

5.   Outboard Motors, Inc. (Outboard) has agreed to purchase a plant owned by Marine Engines, Inc. (Marine).   The workforce of Marine Engines is represented by the Motor Workers Union.   On January 13, the sale was completed and the union made a demand upon Outboard for recognition and acceptance of its contract with Marine.   Outboard announced on January 16 that it will neither accept the union contract (which included a variety of work rules the company claimed were inefficient) nor recognize the union, but will hire on a non-discriminatory basis and on its own terms the 396 employees it expected to need by June.   By January 30, Outboard had hired 261 employees, of whom 223 had worked for Marine.   On January 31, the company modified its projection of the workforce required by June to 460 and thereafter hired no more applicants who had been Marine employees.   The 460 figure was never reached and Outboard proceeded to commit a variety of unfair labor practices.   The NLRB has found that Outboard violated § 8(a)(3) by refusing to hire applicants who had been employed at Marine, and § 8(a)(5) by refusing to recognize the union; the Board found that the unrealistic 460 figure, coupled with the refusals to hire, were designed to preclude the union from claiming a majority of Outboard's workforce.   What remedies should be ordered?   Could the Board order Outboard to restore the terms of the Marine–Motor Workers contract?   See U.S. Marine Corp. v. NLRB, 944 F.2d 1305 (7th Cir.1991), cert. denied, ___ U.S. ___, 112 S.Ct. 1474, 117 L.Ed.2d 618 (1992).

6.   If a successor employer wrongfully refuses to bargain with the union, but a majority of employees subsequently petition the employer that they no longer wish to be represented by the union, which petition was not coerced or solicited by the employer, may the Board issue a bargaining order?   See Sullivan Industries v. NLRB, 957 F.2d 890 (D.C.Cir.1992).

Part Eight

FEDERALISM AND LABOR RELATIONS

II. SPECIFIC APPLICATIONS: REPRESENTATION, BARGAINING AND CONCERTED ACTIVITIES

B. COLLECTIVE BARGAINING

Page 1004. Add to Problem 5:

Assume that because of a strike by cemetery workers a number of decedents remained unburied, several of whom were of religions that require immediate or swift burial. Could the state legislate a "religiously required interment" law, requiring interment in those cases by workers from a labor pool to be negotiated by the cemetery authority and the union? See Cannon v. Edgar, 825 F.Supp. 1349 (N.D.Ill.1993).

Page 1025. Add Problem 7:

7. Assume that a state were to enact a Striker Replacement Act that would make it an unlawful labor practice for an employer:

> To grant or offer to grant the status of permanent replacement employee to a person for performing bargaining unit work for an employer during a lockout of employees in a labor organization or during a strike of employees in a labor organization authorized by a representative of employees.

Would such a statute be enforceable, consistent with *Belknap, Inc. v. Hale*? See Midwest Motor Express, Inc. v. Teamsters, Local 120, 494 N.W.2d 895 (Minn. App.1993).

C. ENFORCEMENT OF COLLECTIVE AGREEMENTS

Page 1032. Add immediately after *Lingle:*

LIVADAS v. BRADSHAW
___ U.S. ___, 114 S.Ct. 2068, ___ L.Ed.2d ___ (1994).

JUSTICE SOUTER delivered the opinion of the Court.

California law requires employers to pay all wages due immediately upon an employee's discharge, imposes a penalty for refusal to pay promptly, precludes any private contractual waiver of these minimum labor standards, and places responsibility for enforcing these provisions on the State Commissioner of Labor (Commissioner or Labor Commissioner), ostensibly for the benefit of all employees. Respondent, the Labor Commissioner, has construed a further provision of state law as barring enforcement of these wage and penalty claims on behalf of individuals like petitioner, whose terms and conditions of employment are governed by a collective-bargaining agreement containing an arbitration clause. We hold that federal law pre-empts this policy, as abridging the exercise of such employees' rights under the National Labor Relations Act (NLRA or Act), 29 U.S.C. § 151 et seq., and that redress for this unlawful refusal to enforce may be had under 42 U.S.C. § 1983.

I

Until her discharge on January 2, 1990, petitioner Karen Livadas worked as a grocery clerk in a Vallejo, California, Safeway supermarket. The terms and conditions of her employment were subject to a collective-bargaining agreement between Safeway and Livadas's union, Local 373 of the United Food and Commercial Workers, AFL–CIO. Unexceptionally, the agreement provided that "(d)isputes as to the interpretation or application of the agreement," including grievances arising from allegedly unjust discharge or suspension, would be subject to binding arbitration. See Food Store Contract, United Food & Commercial Workers Union, Local 373, AFL–CIO, Solano and Napa Counties §§ 18.2, 18.3 (Mar. 1, 1989–Feb. 29, 1992) (Food Store Contract).[2] When notified of her discharge, Livadas demanded immediate payment of wages owed her, as guaranteed to all California workers by state law, see Cal.Lab.Code Ann. § 201 (West 1989),[3] but her store manager refused, referring to the company practice of making such payments by check mailed from a central corporate payroll office. On January 5, 1990, Livadas received a

---

2. Section 18.1 of the collective-bargaining agreement defines a "grievance" as a "dispute . . . involving or arising out of the meaning, interpretation, application or alleged violation" of the agreement. Section 18.8 provides that "(i)n the case of a direct wage claim . . . which does not involve an interpretation of any of the provisions of this Agreement, either party may submit such claim for settlement to either the grievance procedure provided for herein or to any other tribunal which is authorized and empowered to effect such a settlement."

3. California Labor Code § 201 provides in pertinent part: "If an employer discharges an employee, the wages earned and unpaid at the time of discharge are due and payable immediately." It draws no distinction between union-represented employees and others. Under another provision of California law, Labor Code § 219, the protections of § 201 (and of other rules governing the frequency and form of wage payments), "can (not) in any way be contravened or set aside by private agreement, whether written, oral, or implied," although employers are free to pay wages more frequently, in greater amounts, or at an earlier date than ordained by these state rules; cf. § 204.2 (executive, administrative, and professional employees may negotiate through collective bargaining for pay periods different from those required by state law).

check from Safeway, in the full amount owed for her work through January 2. On January 9, 1990, Livadas filed a claim against Safeway with the California Division of Labor Standards Enforcement (DLSE or Division), asserting that under § 203 of the Labor Code the company was liable to her for a sum equal to three days' wages, as a penalty for the delay between discharge and the date when payment was in fact received.[4] Livadas requested the Commissioner to enforce the claim.

By an apparently standard form letter dated February 7, 1990, the Division notified Livadas that it would take no action on her complaint:

"It is our understanding that the employees working for Safeway are covered by a collective bargaining agreement which contains an arbitration clause. The provisions of Labor Code Section 229 preclude this Division from adjudicating any dispute concerning the interpretation or application of any collective bargaining agreement containing an arbitration clause.

"Labor Code Section 203 requires that the wages continue at the "same rate" until paid. In order to establish what the "same rate" was, it is necessary to look to the collective bargaining agreement and 'apply' that agreement. The courts have pointed out that such an application is exactly what the provisions of Labor Code § 229 prohibit.[6] App. 16.

4. That section provides that when an employer "willfully fails" to comply with the strictures of § 201 and fails to pay "any wages" owed discharged employees, "the wages of such employees shall continue as a penalty from the due date thereof at the same rate until paid or until an action therefor is commenced; but such wages shall not continue for more than 30 days." Cal.Lab.Code Ann. § 203 (West 1989). In her DLSE claim form, Livadas made plain that she did not dispute Safeway's calculation of the wages owed, but sought only the penalty for the employer's late tender. App. 18.

6. Labor Code § 229 provides: "Actions to enforce the provisions of this article (Labor Code §§ 200–243) for the collection of due and unpaid wages claimed by an individual may be maintained without regard to the existence of any private agreement to arbitrate. This section shall not apply to claims involving any dispute concerning the interpretation or application of any collective bargaining agreement containing such an arbitration agreement." Cf. Perry v. Thomas, 482 U.S. 483, 107 S.Ct. 2520, 96 L.Ed.2d 426 (1987) (§ 229 bar to waiver defeated by Federal Arbitration Act policy).

All concerned identify the allusion to what "courts" have said to be a reference to a 1975 decision of the California Court of Appeal, Plumbing, Heating and Piping Employers Council v. Howard, 53 Cal.App.3d 828, 126 Cal.Rptr. 406 (1975), where the Commissioner was held barred by the statute from enforcing an "unpaid" wage claim arising from an employee's assertion that he was entitled under collective-bargaining agreements then in force, to receive a foreman's rate of pay and not a journeyman's.

The letter made no reference to any particular aspect of Livadas's claim making it unfit for enforcement, and the Commissioner's position is fairly taken to be that DLSE enforcement of § 203 claims, as well as other claims for which relief is pegged to an employee's wage rate, is generally unavailable to employees covered by collective-bargaining agreements.[7]

* * *

II

A

A state rule predicating benefits on refraining from conduct protected by federal labor law poses special dangers of interference with congressional purpose. In Nash v. Florida Industrial Comm'n, 389 U.S. 235, 88 S.Ct. 362, 19 L.Ed.2d 438 (1967), a unanimous Court held that a state policy of withholding unemployment benefits solely because an employee had filed an unfair labor practice charge with the National Labor Relations Board had a "direct tendency to frustrate the purpose of Congress" and, if not pre-empted, would "defeat or handicap a valid national objective by ... withdraw(ing) state benefits ... simply because" an employee engages in conduct protected and encouraged by the NLRA. Id., at 239, 88 S.Ct. at 366; see also Golden State I, supra, 475 U.S., at 618, 106 S.Ct., at 1400–1401 (city may not condition franchise renewal on settlement of labor dispute). This case is fundamentally no different from *Nash*.[11] Just as the respondent State Commission in that

---

7. The Commissioner notes that a small minority of collective-bargaining agreements lack provisions either setting wage rates or mandating arbitration (and therefore might potentially be enforced under the challenged policy). But see n. 14 infra; Lingle v. Norge Division of Magic Chef, Inc., 486 U.S. 399, 411, n. 11, 108 S.Ct. 1877, 1884, n. 11, 100 L.Ed.2d 410 (1988) (noting that 99% of sampled collective-bargaining agreements include arbitration clauses).

11. While the NLRA does not expressly recognize a right to be covered by a collective-bargaining agreement, in that no duty is imposed on an employer actually to reach agreement with represented employees, see 29 U.S.C. § 158(d), a State's penalty on those who complete the collective-bargaining process works an interference with the operation of the Act, much as does a penalty on those who participate in the process. Cf. Hill v. Florida ex rel. Watson, 325 U.S.

538, 65 S.Ct. 1373, 89 L.Ed. 1782 (1945) (State may not enforce licensing requirement on collective-bargaining agents).

We understand the difference between the position of petitioner (who would place this case within our "Machinists" line of labor pre-emption cases, see Machinists v. Wisconsin Employment Relations Comm'n, 427 U.S. 132, 96 S.Ct. 2548, 49 L.Ed.2d 396 (1976)) and that of her amicus, the Solicitor General (who describes it as a case of "conflict" pre-emption, see Brief for United States as Amicus Curiae 14–15 and n. 4) to be entirely semantic, depending on whether Livadas's right is characterized as implicit in the structure of the Act (as was the right to self-help upheld in Machinists) or as rooted in the text of § 7. See generally Golden State II, 493 U.S. 103, 110–112, 110 S.Ct. 444, 450–452, 107 L.Ed.2d 420 (1989) (emphasizing fundamental similarity between enumerated NLRA rights and "Machinists" rights). Neither party here arcase offered an employee the choice of pursuing her unfair labor practice claim or receiving unemployment compensation, the Commissioner has presented Livadas and others like her with the choice of having state-law rights under §§ 201 and 203 enforced or exercising the right to enter into a collective-bargaining agreement with an arbitration clause. This unappetizing choice, we conclude, was not intended by Congress, see infra, and cannot ultimately be reconciled with a statutory scheme premised on the centrality of the right to bargain collectively and the desirability of resolving contract disputes through arbitration. Cf. Metropolitan Life Ins. Co. v. Massachusetts, 471 U.S. 724, 755, 105 S.Ct. 2380, 2397, 85 L.Ed.2d 728 (1985) (state law held not pre-empted because it "neither encourage(s) nor discourage(s) the collective bargaining processes.[12]

B

1

The Commissioner's answers to this pre-emption conclusion flow from two significant misunderstandings of law. First, the Commissioner conflates the policy that Livadas challenges with the state law on which it purports to rest, Labor Code § 229, assuming that if the statutory provision is consistent with federal law, her policy must be also. But on this logic, a policy of issuing general search warrants would be justified if it were adopted to implement a state statute codifying word-for-word the

gues for application of the rule of San Diego Building Trades Council v. Garmon, 359 U.S. 236, 79 S.Ct. 773, 3 L.Ed.2d 775 (1959), which safeguards the primary jurisdiction of the National Labor Relations Board to pass judgment on certain conduct, such as labor picketing, which might be held protected by § 7 of the Act but which might also be prohibited by § 8 of the Act.

12. Despite certain similarities, the question whether federal labor law permits a State to grant or withhold unemployment insurance benefits from striking workers requires consideration of the policies underlying a distinct federal statute, Title IX of the Social Security Act, see 26 U.S.C. § 3301 (1988 ed. and Supp. IV); 42 U.S.C. § 501 et seq.; 42 U.S.C. § 1101 et seq. Thus, straightforward NLRA pre-emption analysis has been held inappropriate. See New York Telephone Co. v. New York Dept. of Labor, 440 U.S. 519, 536–540, 99 S.Ct. 1328, 1339–1341, 59 L.Ed.2d 553 (1979) (plurality opinion); see also id., at 549, 99 S.Ct., at 1345–1346 (BLACKMUN, J., concurring in judgment).

Noting that Nash v. Florida Industrial Comm'n, 389 U.S. 235, 88 S.Ct. 362, 19 L.Ed.2d 438 (1967), held state action pre-

empted that was "like the coercive actions which employers and unions are forbidden to engage in," see id., at 239, 88 S.Ct., at 366, it is argued here, see Brief for Employers Group as Amicus Curiae 7–12, that the NLRA prohibits only state action closely analogous to conduct that would support an unfair labor practice charge if engaged in by a private employer. Our cases, however, teach that parallelism is not dispositive and that the Act sometimes demands a more scrupulous evenhandedness from the States. See generally Wisconsin Dept. of Industry, Labor and Human Relations v. Gould, Inc., 475 U.S. 282, 290, 106 S.Ct. 1057, 1063, 89 L.Ed.2d 223 (1986) (state may not debar employers with multiple NLRA violations from government contracting); compare Golden State I, 475 U.S. 608, 106 S.Ct. 1395 (1986), with NLRB v. Servette, Inc., 377 U.S. 46, 49–54, 84 S.Ct. 1098, 1101–1104, 12 L.Ed.2d 121 (1964) (private actor may refuse to deal with employer based on impending strike); but cf. Building and Constr. Trades Council of Metro Dist. v. Associated Builders & Contractors of Mass./R.I., Inc., 507 U.S. ___, 113 S.Ct. 1190, 122 L.Ed.2d 565 (1993) (the Act does not always preclude a State, functioning as an employer or a purchaser of "good faith" exception to the valid warrant requirement recognized in United States v. Leon, 468 U.S. 897, 104 S.Ct. 3405, 82 L.Ed.2d 677 (1984). The relationship between policy and state statute and between the statute and federal law is, in any event, irrelevant. The question presented by this case is not whether Labor Code § 229 is valid under the Federal Constitution or whether the Commissioner's policy is, as a matter of state law, a proper interpretation of § 229. Pre-emption analysis, rather, turns on the actual content of respondent's policy and its real effect on federal rights. See Nash v. Florida Industrial Comm'n, 389 U.S. 235, 88 S.Ct. 362, 19 L.Ed.2d 438 (1967) (holding pre-empted an administrative policy interpreting presumably valid state unemployment insurance law exception for "labor disputes" to include proceedings under NLRB complaints); see also 987 F.2d, at 561 (Kozinski, J., dissenting).

Having sought to lead us to the wrong question, the Commissioner proposes the wrong approach for answering it, defending the distinction drawn in the challenged statutory interpretation, between employees represented by unions and those who are not, as supported by a "rational basis," see, e.g., Brief for Respondent 17. But such reasoning mistakes a standard for validity under the Equal Protection and Due Process Clauses for what the Supremacy Clause requires. The power to tax is no less the power to destroy, McCulloch v. Maryland, 4 Wheat. 316, 4 L.Ed. 579 (1819), merely because a state legislature has an undoubtedly rational and "legitimate" interest in raising revenue. In labor pre-emption cases, as in others under the Supremacy Clause, our office is not to pass judgment on the reasonableness of state policy, see, e.g., Golden State I, 475 U.S. 608, 106 S.Ct. 1395, 89 L.Ed.2d 616 (1986) (city's desire to remain "neutral" in labor dispute does not determine pre-emption). It is instead to decide if a state rule conflicts with or otherwise "stands as an obstacle to the accomplishment and execution of the full purposes and objectives" of the federal law. Brown v. Hotel Employees, 468 U.S. 491, 501, 104 S.Ct. 3179, 3185, 82 L.Ed.2d 373 (1984) (internal quotation marks and citation omitted).

That is not to say, of course, that the several rationales for the policy urged on the Court by the Commissioner and amici are beside the point here. If, most obviously, the Commissioner's policy were actually compelled by federal law, as she argues it is, we could hardly say that it

labor services, from behaving as a private
employer would be entitled to do).

was, simultaneously, pre-empted; at the least, our task would then be one of harmonizing statutory law. But we entertain this and other justifications claimed, not because constitutional analysis under the Supremacy Clause is an open-ended balancing act, simply weighing the federal interest against the intensity of local feeling, see id., at 503, 104 S.Ct., at 3186, but because claims of justification can sometimes help us to discern congressional purpose, the "ultimate touchstone" of our enquiry. Malone v. White Motor Corp., 435 U.S. 497, 504, 98 S.Ct. 1185, 1189–1190, 55 L.Ed.2d 443 (1978) (internal quotation marks and citation omitted); see also New York Telephone Co. v. New York Dept. of Labor, 440 U.S. 519, 533, 99 S.Ct. 1328, 1337, 59 L.Ed.2d 553 (1979) (plurality opinion).

2

We begin with the most complete of the defenses mounted by the Commissioner, one that seems (or seemed until recently, at least) to be at the heart of her position: that the challenged policy, far from being pre-empted by federal law, is positively compelled by it, and that even if the Commissioner had been so inclined, the LMRA § 301 would have precluded enforcement of Livadas's penalty claim. The nonenforcement policy, she suggests, is a necessary emanation from this Court's § 301 pre-emption jurisprudence, marked as it has been by repeated admonitions that courts should steer clear of collective-bargaining disputes between parties who have provided for arbitration. See, e.g., Allis–Chalmers Corp. v. Lueck, 471 U.S. 202, 105 S.Ct. 1904, 85 L.Ed.2d 206 (1985). Because, this argument runs (and Livadas was told in the DLSE no-action letter), disposition of a union-represented employee's penalty claim entails the "interpretation or application" of a collective-bargaining agreement (since determining the amount owed turns on the contractual rate of pay agreed) resort to a state tribunal would lead it into territory that Congress, in enacting § 301, meant to be covered exclusively by arbitrators.

This reasoning, however, mistakes both the functions § 301 serves in our national labor law and our prior decisions according that provision pre-emptive effect. To be sure, we have read the text of § 301 [15] not only to grant federal courts jurisdiction over claims asserting breach of

---

15. Section 301 states that "(s)uits for violation of contracts between an employer and a labor organization representing employees ... may be brought in any district court of the United States having jurisdiction of the parties...." 29 U.S.C. § 185(a).

collective-bargaining agreements but also to authorize the development of federal common-law rules of decision, in large part to assure that agreements to arbitrate grievances would be enforced, regardless of the vagaries of state law and lingering hostility toward extrajudicial dispute resolution, see Textile Workers v. Lincoln Mills of Ala., 353 U.S. 448, 455–456, 77 S.Ct. 912, 917–918, 1 L.Ed.2d 972 (1957); see also Steelworkers v. Warrior and Gulf Navigation Co., 363 U.S. 574, 80 S.Ct. 1347, 4 L.Ed.2d 1409 (1960); Avco Corp. v. Machinists, 390 U.S. 557, 559, 88 S.Ct. 1235, 1237, 20 L.Ed.2d 126 (1968) ("§ 301 ... was fashioned by Congress to place sanctions behind agreements to arbitrate grievance disputes"). And in Teamsters v. Lucas Flour Co., 369 U.S. 95, 82 S.Ct. 571, 7 L.Ed.2d 593 (1962), we recognized an important corollary to the *Lincoln Mills* rule: while § 301 does not preclude state courts from taking jurisdiction over cases arising from disputes over the interpretation of collective-bargaining agreements, state contract law must yield to the developing federal common law, lest common terms in bargaining agreements be given different and potentially inconsistent interpretations in different jurisdictions. See 369 U.S., at 103–104, 82 S.Ct., at 576–577.

And while this sensible "acorn" of § 301 pre-emption recognized in *Lucas Flour*, has sprouted modestly in more recent decisions of this Court, see, e.g., Lueck, supra, 471 U.S., at 210, 105 S.Ct., at 1911 ("(I)f the policies that animate § 301 are to be given their proper range ... the pre-emptive effect of § 301 must extend beyond suits alleging contract violations"), it has not yet become, nor may it, a sufficiently "mighty oak," see Golden State I, 475 U.S., at 622, 106 S.Ct., at 1402–1403 (REHNQUIST, J., dissenting), to supply the cover the Commissioner seeks here. To the contrary, the pre-emption rule has been applied only to assure that the purposes animating § 301 will be frustrated neither by state laws purporting to determine "questions relating to what the parties to a labor agreement agreed, and what legal consequences were intended to flow from breaches of that agreement," Lueck, 471 U.S., at 211, 105 S.Ct., at 1911, nor by parties' efforts to renege on their arbitration promises by "relabeling" as tort suits actions simply alleging breaches of duties assumed in collective-bargaining agreements, id., at 219, 105 S.Ct., at 1915; see Republic Steel Corp. v. Maddox, 379 U.S. 650, 652, 85 S.Ct. 614, 616, 13 L.Ed.2d 580 (1965) ("(F)ederal labor policy requires that individual employees wishing to assert contract grievances must attempt use of the contract grievance procedure agreed upon by employer and union as the mode of redress") (emphasis omitted).

In *Lueck* and in *Lingle v. Norge Division of Magic Chef, Inc.*, 486 U.S. 399, 108 S.Ct. 1877, 100 L.Ed.2d 410 (1988), we underscored the point that § 301 cannot be read broadly to pre-empt nonnegotiable rights conferred on individual employees as a matter of state law,[17] and we stressed that it is the legal character of a claim, as "independent" of rights under the collective-bargaining agreement, Lueck, supra, 471 U.S., at 213, 105 S.Ct., at 1912 (and not whether a grievance arising from "precisely the same set of facts" could be pursued, Lingle, supra, 486 U.S., at 410, 108 S.Ct., at 1883) that decides whether a state cause of action may go forward.[18] Finally, we were clear that when the meaning of contract terms is not the subject of dispute, the bare fact that a collective-bargaining agreement will be consulted in the course of state-law litigation plainly does not require the claim to be extinguished, see Lingle, 486 U.S., at 413, n. 12, 108 S.Ct., at 1885, n. 12 ("A collective-bargaining agreement may, of course, contain information such as rate of pay ... that might be helpful in determining the damages to which a worker prevailing in a state-law suit is entitled").

17. That is so, we explained, both because Congress is understood to have legislated against a backdrop of generally applicable labor standards, see, e.g., Lingle, 486 U.S., at 411–412, 108 S.Ct., at 1884–1885, and because the scope of the arbitral promise is not itself unlimited, see Steelworkers v. Warrior & Gulf Navigation Co., 363 U.S. 574, 582, 80 S.Ct. 1347, 1353, 4 L.Ed.2d 1409 (1960) ("arbitration is a matter of contract and a party cannot be required to submit to arbitration any dispute which he has not agreed so to submit"). And while contract-interpretation disputes must be resolved in the bargained-for arbitral realm, see Republic Steel Corp. v. Maddox, 379 U.S. 650, 85 S.Ct. 614, 13 L.Ed.2d 580 (1965), § 301 does not disable state courts from interpreting the terms of collective-bargaining agreements in resolving nonpre-empted claims, see Charles Dowd Box Co. v. Courtney, 368 U.S. 502, 82 S.Ct. 519, 7 L.Ed.2d 483 (1962) (state courts have jurisdiction over § 301 suits but must apply federal common law); NLRB v. C & C Plywood Corp., 385 U.S. 421, 87 S.Ct. 559, 17 L.Ed.2d 486 (1967).

18. We are aware, as an amicus brief makes clear, see Brief for AFL–CIO as Amicus Curiae, that the Courts of Appeals have not been entirely uniform in their understanding and application of the principles set down in Lingle and Lueck. But this case, in which nonpre-emption under § 301 is clear beyond peradventure, see infra, at ___–___, is not a fit occasion for us to resolve disagreements that have arisen over the proper scope of our earlier decisions. We do note in this regard that while our cases tend to speak broadly in terms of § 301 "pre-emption," defendants invoke that provision in diverse situations and for different reasons: sometimes their assertion is that a plaintiff's cause of action itself derives from the collective-bargaining agreement (and, by that agreement, belongs before an arbitrator); in other instances, the argument is different, that a plaintiff's claim cannot be "resolved" absent collective-bargaining agreement interpretation, i.e., that a term of the agreement may or does confer a defense on the employer (perhaps because the employee or his union negotiated away the state law right), cf. Caterpillar Inc. v. Williams, 482 U.S. 386, 398–399, 107 S.Ct. 2425, 2432–2433, 96 L.Ed.2d 318 (1987); and in other cases still, concededly "independent" state-law litigation may nonetheless entail some collective-bargaining agreement application. Holding the plaintiff's cause of action substantively extinguished may not, as amicus AFL–CIO observes, always be the only means of vindicating the arbitrator's primacy as the bargained-for contract-interpreter. Cf. Collyer Insulated Wire, Gulf & Western Systems Co., 192 N.L.R.B. 837 (1971).

These principles foreclose even a colorable argument that a claim under Labor Code § 203 was pre-empted here. As the District Court aptly observed, the primary text for deciding whether Livadas was entitled to a penalty was not the Food Store Contract, but a calendar. The only issue raised by Livadas's claim, whether Safeway "willfully fail(ed) to pay" her wages promptly upon severance, Cal.Lab.Code Ann. § 203 (West 1989), was a question of state law, entirely independent of any understanding embodied in the collective-bargaining agreement between the union and the employer. There is no indication that there was a "dispute" in this case over the amount of the penalty to which Livadas would be entitled, and *Lingle* makes plain in so many words that when liability is governed by independent state law, the mere need to "look to" the collective-bargaining agreement for damage computation is no reason to hold the state law claim defeated by § 301. See 486 U.S., at 413, n. 12, 108 S.Ct., at 1885, n. 12.

Beyond the simple need to refer to bargained-for wage rates in computing the penalty, the collective-bargaining agreement is irrelevant to the dispute (if any) between Livadas and Safeway. There is no suggestion here that Livadas's union sought or purported to bargain away her protections under § 201 or § 203, a waiver that we have said would (especially in view of Labor Code § 219) have to be " 'clear and unmistakable' " see Lingle, supra, 486 U.S., at 409–410, n. 9, 108 S.Ct., at 1883, n. 9 (quoting Metropolitan Edison Co. v. NLRB, 460 U.S. 693, 708, 103 S.Ct. 1467, 1477, 75 L.Ed.2d 387 (1983)) for a court even to consider whether it could be given effect, nor is there any indication that the parties to the collective-bargaining agreement understood their arbitration pledge to cover these state-law claims. See generally Gilmer v. Interstate/Johnson Lane Corp., 500 U.S. 20, 35, 111 S.Ct. 1647, 1657, 114 L.Ed.2d 26 (1991); cf. Food Store Contract § 18.8. But even if such suggestions or indications were to be found, the Commissioner could not invoke them to defend her policy, which makes no effort to take such factors into account before denying enforcement.[20]

---

20. In holding the challenged policy pre-empted, we note that there is no equally obvious conflict between what § 301 requires and the text of Labor Code § 229 (as against what respondent has read it to mean). The California provision, which concerns whether a promise to arbitrate a claim will be enforced to defeat a direct action under the Labor Code, does not purport generally to deny union-represented employees their rights under §§ 201 and 203. Rather, it confines its preclusive focus only to "dispute(s) concerning the interpretation or application of any collective-bargaining agreement," in which event an "agreement to arbitrate" such disputes is to be given effect. Nor does the Howard decision, the apparent font of the Commissioner's policy, appear untrue to § 301 teachings: there, an employee sought to have an "unpaid wage" claim do the office of a claim that a collective-bargaining agreement entitled him to a higher wage; that sort of claim, however, derives its existence from the collective-bargaining agreement and, accordingly, falls within any customary understanding of arbitral jurisdiction. See 53 Cal.App.3d, at 836, 126 Cal. Rptr., at 411.

C

1

Before this Court, however, the Commissioner does not confine herself to the assertion that Livadas's claim would have been pre-empted by LMRA § 301. Indeed, largely putting aside that position, she has sought here to cast the policy in different terms, as expressing a "conscious decision," see Brief for Respondent 14, to keep the State's "hands off" the claims of employees protected by collective-bargaining agreements, either because the Division's efforts and resources are more urgently needed by others or because official restraint will actually encourage the collective-bargaining and arbitral processes favored by federal law. The latter, more ambitious defense has been vigorously taken up by the Commissioner's *amici*, who warn that invalidation of the disputed policy would sound the death knell for other, more common governmental measures that take account of collective-bargaining processes or treat workers represented by unions differently from others in any respect.

Although there surely is no bar to our considering these alternative explanations, cf. Dandridge v. Williams, 397 U.S. 471, 475, n. 6, 90 S.Ct. 1153, 1156–1157, n. 6, 25 L.Ed.2d 491 (1970) (party may defend judgment on basis not relied upon below), we note, as is often the case with such late-blooming rationales, that the overlap between what the Commissioner now claims to be State policy and what the State legislature has enacted into law is awkwardly inexact. First, if the Commissioner's policy (or California law) were animated simply by the frugal desire to conserve the State's money for the protection of employees not covered by collective-bargaining agreements, the Commissioner's emphasis, in the letter to Livadas and in this litigation, on the need to "interpret" or "apply" terms of a collective-bargaining agreement would be entirely misplaced.

Nor is the nonenforcement policy convincingly defended as giving parties to a collective-bargaining agreement the "benefit of their bargain," see Brief for Respondent 18, n. 13, by assuring them that their promise to arbitrate is kept and not circumvented. Under the Commissioner's policy, enforcement does not turn on what disputes the parties agreed would be resolved by arbitration (the bargain struck), see Gilmer, 500 U.S., at 26, 111 S.Ct., at 1652, or on whether the contractual wage rate is even subject to (arbitrable) dispute. Rather, enforcement turns exclusively on the fact that the contracting parties consented to any arbitration at all. Even if the Commissioner could permissibly presume that state law claims are generally intended to be arbitrated, but cf. id., at 35, 111 S.Ct., at 1657 (employees in prior cases "had not agreed to arbitrate their statutory claims, and the labor arbitrators were not authorized to resolve such claims"), her policy goes still further. Even in cases when it could be said with "positive assurance," Warrior & Gulf, 363 U.S., at 582, 80 S.Ct., at 1352–1353, that the parties did not intend that state-law claims be subject to arbitration, cf. Food Store Contract § 18.8 (direct wage claim not involving interpretation of agreement may be submitted "to any other tribunal or agency which is authorized and empowered" to enforce it), the Commissioner would still deny enforcement, on the stated basis that the collective-bargaining agreement nonetheless contained "an arbitration clause" and because the claim would, on her view, entail "interpretation," of the agreement's terms. Such an irrebuttable presumption is not easily described as the benefit of the parties' "bargain."

The Commissioner and *amici* finally suggest that denying enforcement to union-represented employees' claims under §§ 201 and 203 (and other Labor Code provisions) is meant to encourage parties to bargain collectively for their own rules about the payment of wages to discharged workers. But with this suggestion, the State's position simply slips any tether to California law. If California's goal really were to stimulate such free-wheeling bargaining on these subjects, the enactment of Labor Code § 219, expressly and categorically prohibiting the modification of these Labor Code rules by "private agreement" would be a very odd way to pursue it. Compare Cal.Lab.Code Ann. § 227.3 (West 1989) (allowing parties to collective-bargaining agreement to arrive at different rule for vacation pay). In short, the policy, the rationales, and the state law are not coherent.

2

Even at face value, however, neither the "hands off" labels nor the vague assertions that general labor law policies are thereby advanced much support the Commissioner's defense here. The former merely takes the position discussed and rejected earlier, that a distinction between claimants represented by unions and those who are not is "rational," the former being less "in need" than the latter. While we hardly suggest here that every distinction between union-represented employees and others is invalid under the NLRA, see infra, the assertion that represented employees are less "in need" precisely because they have exercised federal rights, poses special dangers that advantages conferred by federal law will be canceled out and its objectives undermined. Cf. Metropolitan Life, 471 U.S., at 756, 105 S.Ct., at 2397 ("It would turn the policy that animated the Wagner Act on its head to understand it to have penalized workers who have chosen to join a union by preventing them from benefitting from state labor regulations imposing minimal standards on nonunion employers"). Accordingly, as we observed in *Metropolitan Life*, the widespread practice in Congress and in state legislatures has assumed the contrary, bestowing basic employment guarantees and protections on individual employees without singling out members of labor unions (or those represented by them) for disability; see id., at 755, 105 S.Ct., at 2397; [23] accord, Lingle, 486 U.S., at 411–412, 108 S.Ct., at 1884–1885.

Nor do professions of "neutrality" lay the dangers to rest. The preempted action in *Golden State I* could easily have been re-described as following a "hands-off" policy, in that the city sought to avoid endorsing either side in the course of a labor dispute, see Golden State I, 475 U.S., at 622, 106 S.Ct., at 1403 (REHNQUIST, J., dissenting) (city did not seek "to place its weight on one side or the other of the scales of economic warfare"), and the respondent Commission in *Nash* may have understood its policy as expressing neutrality between the parties in a yet-to-be-decided unfair labor practice dispute. See also Rum Creek Coal Sales, Inc. v. Caperton, 971 F.2d 1148, 1154 (CA4 1992) (NLRA forbids state policy, under state law barring "aid or assistance" to either party to a labor dispute, of not arresting picketers who violated state trespass laws). Nor need we pause long over the assertion that nonenforcement of valid state law claims is consistent with federal labor law by "encouraging" the operation of collective-bargaining and arbitration process. Denying represented employees basic safety protections might "encourage" collective-bargaining over that subject, and denying union employers the protection of generally applicable state trespass law might lead to increased bargaining over the rights of labor pickets, cf. Rum Creek, supra, but we have never suggested that labor law's bias toward bargaining is to be served by forcing employees or employers to bargain for what they would otherwise be entitled to as a matter of course. See generally Metropolitan Life, supra, 471 U.S., at 757, 105 S.Ct., at 2398 (Congress did not intend to "remove the backdrop of state law * * * and thereby artificially create a no-law area") (emphasis and internal quotation marks omitted).[24]

---

23. We noted that "Congress (has never) seen fit to exclude unionized workers and employers from laws establishing federal minimum employment standards. We see no reason to believe that for this purpose Congress intended state minimum labor standards to be treated differently.... Minimum state labor standards affect union and nonunion employees equally and neither encourage nor discourage the collective-bargaining processes that are the subject of the NLRA." Metropolitan Life, 471 U.S., at 755, 105 S.Ct., at 2397.

24. Were it enough simply to point to a general labor policy advanced by particular state action, the city in Golden State could

The precedent cited by the Commissioner and amici as supporting the broadest "hands off" view, Fort Halifax Packing Co. v. Coyne, 482 U.S. 1, 107 S.Ct. 2211, 96 L.Ed.2d 1 (1987), is not in point. In that case we held that there was no federal pre-emption of a Maine statute that allowed employees and employers to contract for plant-closing severance payments different from those otherwise mandated by state law. That decision, however, does not even purport to address the question supposedly presented here: while there was mention of state latitude to "balance the desirability of a particular substantive labor standard against the right of self-determination regarding the terms and conditions of employment," see 482 U.S., at 22, 107 S.Ct., at 2223, the policy challenged here differs in two crucial respects from the "unexceptional exercise of the State's police power," ibid. (internal quotation marks and citation omitted), defended in those terms in our earlier case. Most fundamentally, the Maine law treated all employees equally, whether or not represented by a labor organization. All were entitled to the statutory severance payment, and all were allowed to negotiate agreements providing for different benefits. See id., at 4, n. 1, 107 S.Ct., at 2213–2214, n. 1. Second, the minimum protections of Maine's plant closing law were relinquished not by the mere act of signing an employment contract (or collective-bargaining agreement), but only by the parties' express agreement on different terms, see id., at 21, 107 S.Ct., at 2222–2223.[25]

While the Commissioner and her *amici* call our attention to a number of state and federal laws that draw distinctions between union and nonunion represented employees, see, e.g., D.C.Code Ann. § 36–103 (1993) ("Unless otherwise specified in a collective agreement . . . (w)henever an employer discharges an employee, the employer shall pay the employee's wages earned not later than the working day following such discharge"); 29 U.S.C. § 203(o) ("Hours (w)orked" for Fair Labor Standards Act measured according to "express terms of . . . or practice under bona fide collective-bargaining agreement"), virtually all share the important second feature observed in *Coyne*, that union-represented employees have the full protection of the minimum standard, absent any agreement for something different. These "opt out" statutes are thus manifestly different in their operation (and their effect on federal rights) from the Commissioner's rule that an employee forfeits his state law rights the moment a collective-bargaining agreement with an arbitration clause is entered into. But cf. Metropolitan Edison, 460 U.S., at 708,

have claimed to be encouraging the "friendly adjustment of industrial disputes," 29 U.S.C. § 151, and the State in Gould, the entirely "laudable," 475 U.S., at 291, 106 S.Ct., at 1063–1064, purpose of "deter(ring) labor law violations and . . . reward(ing) 'fidelity to the law,' " id., at 287, 106 S.Ct., at 1061.

25. It bears mention that the law in Fort Halifax pegged the benefit payment to an employee's wages, meaning that the State Labor Commissioner would "look to" the collective-bargaining agreement in enforcing claims in precisely the same manner that respondent would here.

103 S.Ct., at 1477. Hence, our holding that the Commissioner's unusual policy is irreconcilable with the structure and purposes of the Act should cast no shadow on the validity of these familiar and narrowly drawn opt-out provisions.[26]

III

* * *

[The Court held that Livadas's claim was properly brought under 42 U.S.C. § 1983.]

IV

In an effort to give wide berth to federal labor law and policy, the Commissioner declines to enforce union-represented employees' claims rooted in nonwaivable rights ostensibly secured by state law to all employees, without regard to whether the claims are valid under state law or pre-empted by LMRA § 301. Federal labor law does not require such a heavy-handed policy, and, indeed, cannot permit it. We do not suggest here that the NLRA automatically defeats all state action taking any account of the collective-bargaining process or every state law distinguishing union-represented employees from others. It is enough that we find the Commissioner's policy to have such direct and detrimental effects on the federal statutory rights of employees that it must be pre-empted. The judgment of the Court of Appeals for the Ninth Circuit is accordingly.

Reversed.

Page 1034. Add new Problem:

6. Jack Spratt has been discharged by the Winona Trucking Company. He filed a grievance with the union representing Winona's drivers alleging discharge without just cause. He filed a charge of unfair labor practice with the Regional Director of the NLRB alleging discharge "because of his union and concerted activities" in protesting the assignment of unsafe trucks. And he has filed a lawsuit alleging a violation of state law forbidding retaliation against employees who make safety complaints. The joint union-management grievance committee established under the collective agreement has upheld the discharge as for just cause, for failure to complete an alcohol rehabilitation program. The NLRB's regional director has declined to issue a complaint on grounds of insufficient evidence. And the Company has moved to dismiss the lawsuit on preemption grounds. How should the court rule? Compare Platt v. Jack Cooper Transport Co., Inc., 959 F.2d 91 (8th Cir.1992), with Maher v. New Jersey Transit Rail Operations, Inc., 125 N.J. 455, 593 A.2d 750 (1991).

---

26. Nor does it seem plausible to suggest that Congress meant to preempt such opt-out laws, as "burdening" the statutory right of employees not to join unions by denying nonrepresented employees the "benefit" of being able to "contract out" of such standards. Cf. Addendum B to Brief for Employers Group as Amicus Curiae (collecting federal statutes containing similar provisions).

Part Nine

THE INDIVIDUAL AND THE UNION

I. THE RIGHT TO FAIR REPRESENTATION

A. THE SOURCE AND ENFORCEMENT OF THE UNION'S DUTY

Page 1049. Add after Problems:

In WOODDELL v. INTERNATIONAL BROTHERHOOD OF ELEC. WORKERS, LOCAL 71, ___ U.S. ___, 112 S.Ct. 494, 116 L.Ed.2d 419 (1991), the plaintiff claimed that the local union's discriminatory refusal to refer him from its hiring hall violated the parent union's constitution which required locals to "live up to all collective bargaining agreements." The Supreme Court held the claim to be justiciable in federal court under § 301. It noted that a parent union's constitution was held to be a contract between the parent and the local. Accordingly, the suit could be brought under § 301 by the plaintiff as a beneficiary of a contract between two labor organizations. It also held, following Teamsters Local 391 v. Terry, supra p. 1048, that the plaintiff was entitled to a jury trial on the § 301 claim.

B. THE UNION'S DUTY IN CONTRACT–MAKING

Page 1057. Add after _Strick Corp._:

AIR LINE PILOTS ASS'N, INTERN. v. O'NEILL
499 U.S. 65, 111 S.Ct. 1127, 113 L.Ed.2d 51 (1991).

JUSTICE STEVENS delivered the opinion of the Court.

* * *

This case arose out of a bitter confrontation between Continental Airlines, Inc. (Continental) and the union representing its pilots, the Air Line Pilots Association, International (ALPA). On September 24, 1983, Continental filed a petition for reorganization under Chapter 11 of the Bankruptcy Code. Immediately thereafter, with the approval of the Bankruptcy Court, Continental repudiated its collective-bargaining agreement with ALPA and unilaterally reduced its pilots' salaries and benefits by more than half. ALPA responded by calling a strike that lasted for over two years.

Of the approximately 2,000 pilots employed by Continental, all but about 200 supported the strike. By the time the strike ended, about 400 strikers had "crossed over" and been accepted for reemployment in order of reapplication. By trimming its operations and hiring about 1,000 replacements, Continental was able to continue in business. By August 1985, there were 1,600 working pilots and only 1,000 strikers.

* * *

For many years Continental had used a "system bid" procedure for assigning pilots to new positions. Bids were typically posted well in advance in order to allow time for necessary training without interfering with current service. When a group of vacancies was posted, any pilot could submit a bid specifying his or her preferred position (Captain, First Officer, or Second Officer), base of operations, and aircraft type. In the past, vacant positions had been awarded on the basis of seniority, determined by the date the pilot first flew for Continental. The 85–5 bid covered an unusually large number of anticipated vacancies—441 future Captain and First Officer positions and an undetermined number of Second Officer vacancies. Pilots were given nine days—until September 18, 1985—to submit their bids.

Fearing that this bid might effectively lock the striking pilots out of jobs for the indefinite future, ALPA authorized the strikers to submit bids. Although Continental initially accepted bids from both groups, it soon became concerned about the bona fides of the striking pilots' offer to return to work at a future date. It therefore challenged the strikers' bids in court and announced that all of the 85–5 bid positions had been awarded to working pilots.

At this juncture, ALPA intensified its negotiations for a complete settlement. ALPA's negotiating committee and Continental reached an agreement, which was entered as an order by the Bankruptcy Court on October 31, 1985. The agreement provided for an end to the strike, the disposition of all pending litigation, and reallocation of the positions covered by the 85–5 bid.

The agreement offered the striking pilots three options. Under the first, pilots who settled all outstanding claims with Continental were eligible to participate in the allocation of the 85–5 bid positions. Under the second option, pilots who elected not to return to work received severance pay.... Under the third option, striking pilots retained their individual claims against Continental and were eligible to return to work only after all the first option pilots had been reinstated.

Pilots who chose the first option were thus entitled to some of the 85–5 bid positions that, according to Continental, had previously been awarded to working pilots. The first 100 Captain positions were allocated to working pilots and the next 70 Captain positions were awarded, in order of seniority, to returning strikers who chose option one. Thereafter, striking and nonstriking pilots were eligible for Captain positions on a one-to-one ratio. The initial base and aircraft type for a returning striker was assigned by Continental, but the assignments for working pilots were determined by their bids. After the initial assignment, future changes in bases and equipment were determined by seniority, and striking pilots who were in active service when the strike began received seniority credit for the period of the strike.

[A class of former striking pilots brought suit against ALPA for breach of the duty of fair representation. The district court granted ALPA's motion for summary judgment. The Court of Appeals reversed.]

* * *

III

ALPA's central argument is that the duty of fair representation requires only that a union act in good faith and treat its members equally and in a nondiscriminatory fashion. The duty, the union argues, does not impose any obligation to provide *adequate* representation. The District Court found that there was no evidence that ALPA acted other than in good faith and without discrimination.[7] Because of its view of the limited scope of the duty, ALPA contends that the District Court's finding, which the Court of Appeals did not question, is sufficient to support summary judgment.

The union maintains, not without some merit, that its view that courts are not authorized to review the rationality of good-faith, nondiscriminatory union decisions is consonant with federal labor policy. The Government has generally regulated only "the process of collective bargaining," H.K. Porter Co. v. NLRB, 397 U.S. 99, 102, 90 S.Ct. 821, 823, 25 L.Ed.2d 146 (1970) (emphasis added), but relied on private negotiation between the parties to establish "their own charter for the ordering of industrial relations," Teamsters v. Oliver, 358 U.S. 283, 295, 79 S.Ct. 297, 304, 3 L.Ed.2d 312 (1959). As we stated in NLRB v. Insurance Agents, 361 U.S. 477, 488, 80 S.Ct. 419, 426, 4 L.Ed.2d 454 (1960), Congress "intended that the parties should have wide latitude in their negotiations, unrestricted by any governmental power to regulate the substantive solution of their differences." See also Carbon Fuel Co. v. Mine Workers, 444 U.S. 212, 219, 100 S.Ct. 410, 419, 62 L.Ed.2d 394 (1979).

There is, however, a critical difference between governmental modification of the terms of a private agreement and an examination of those

---

7. "There is nothing to indicate that the Union made any choices among the Union members or the strikers who were not Union members other than on the best deal that the Union thought it could construct; that the deal is somewhat less than not particularly satisfactory is not relevant to the issue of fair representation." App. 74.

terms in search for evidence that a union did not fairly and adequately represent its constituency. Our decisions have long recognized that the need for such an examination proceeds directly from the union's statutory role as exclusive bargaining agent. "[T]he exercise of a granted power to act in behalf of others involves the assumption toward them of a duty to exercise the power in their interest and behalf." Steele v. Louisville & Nashville R. Co., 323 U.S. 192, 202, 65 S.Ct. 226, 232, 89 L.Ed. 173 (1944).

The duty of fair representation is thus akin to the duty owed by other fiduciaries to their beneficiaries. For example, some Members of the Court have analogized the duty a union owes to the employees it represents to the duty a trustee owes to trust beneficiaries. See Teamsters v. Terry, 494 U.S. ___, ___, 110 S.Ct. 1339, ___, 108 L.Ed.2d 519 (1990); id., at ___, 110 S.Ct., at ___ (KENNEDY, J., dissenting). Others have likened the relationship between union and employee to that between attorney and client. See id., at ___, 110 S.Ct., at ___ (STEVENS, J., concurring in part and concurring in judgment). The fair representation duty also parallels the responsibilities of corporate officers and directors toward shareholders. Just as these fiduciaries owe their beneficiaries a duty of care as well as a duty of loyalty, a union owes employees a duty to represent them adequately as well as honestly and in good faith. See, *e.g.,* Restatement (Second) of Trusts § 174 (1959) (trustee's duty of care); Strickland v. Washington, 466 U.S. 668, 686, 104 S.Ct. 2052, 2063, 80 L.Ed.2d 674 (1984) (lawyer must render "adequate legal assistance"); Hanson Trust PLC v. ML SCM Acquisition Inc., 781 F.2d 264, 274 (CA2 1986) (directors owe duty of care as well as loyalty).

ALPA suggests that a union need owe no enforceable duty of adequate representation because employees are protected from inadequate representation by the union political process. ALPA argues, as has the Seventh Circuit, that employees "do not need * * * protection against representation that is inept but not invidious" because if a "union does an incompetent job * * * its members can vote in new officers who will do a better job or they can vote in another union." Dober v. Roadway Express, Inc., 707 F.2d 292, 295 (CA7 1983). In *Steele,* the case in which we first recognized the duty of fair representation, we also analogized a union's role to that of a legislature. See 323 U.S., at 198, 65 S.Ct., at 230. Even legislatures, however, are subject to *some* judicial review of the rationality of their actions. See, e.g., United States v. Carolene Products Co., 304 U.S. 144, 58 S.Ct. 778, 82 L.Ed. 1234 (1938); United States Dept. of Agriculture v. Moreno, 413 U.S. 528, 93 S.Ct. 2821, 37 L.Ed.2d 782 (1973).

ALPA relies heavily on language in Ford Motor Co. v. Huffman, 345 U.S. 330, 73 S.Ct. 681, 97 L.Ed. 1048 (1953), which, according to the union, suggests that no review of the substantive terms of a settlement between labor and management is permissible. In particular, ALPA stresses our comment in the case that "[a] wide range of reasonableness must be allowed a statutory bargaining representative in serving the unit it represents, subject always to complete good faith and honesty of purpose in the exercise of its discretion." Id., at 338, 73 S.Ct., at 686. Unlike ALPA, we do not read this passage to limit review of a union's actions to "good faith and honesty of purpose," but rather to recognize that a union's conduct must also be within "[a] wide range of reasonableness."

Although there is admittedly some variation in the way in which our opinions have described the unions' duty of fair representation, we have repeatedly identified three components of the duty, including a prohibition against "arbitrary" conduct. Writing for the Court in the leading case in this area of the law, Justice White explained:

> "The statutory duty of fair representation was developed over 20 years ago in a series of cases involving alleged racial discrimination by unions certified as exclusive bargaining representatives under the Railway Labor Act, see Steele v. Louisville & N.R. Co., 323 U.S. 192 [65 S.Ct. 226]; Tunstall v. Brotherhood of Locomotive Firemen, 323 U.S. 210 [65 S.Ct. 235, 89 L.Ed. 187 (1944)], and was soon extended to unions certified under the N.L.R.A., see *Ford Motor Co. v. Huffman,* supra. Under this doctrine, the exclusive agent's statutory authority to represent all members of a designated unit includes a statutory obligation to serve the interests of all members without hostility or discrimination toward any, to exercise its discretion with complete good faith and honesty, and to avoid arbitrary conduct. Humphrey v. Moore, 375 U.S. [335], at 342 [84 S.Ct. 363, at 367, 11 L.Ed.2d 370 (1964)]. It is obvious that Owens' complaint alleged a breach by the Union of a duty grounded in federal statutes, and that federal law therefore governs his cause of action." Vaca v. Sipes, 386 U.S., at 177, 87 S.Ct., at 910.

This description of the "duty grounded in federal statutes" has been accepted without question by Congress and in a line of our decisions spanning almost a quarter of a century.[8]

The union correctly points out, however, that virtually all of those cases can be distinguished because they involved contract administration or enforcement rather than contract negotiation. ALPA argues that the policy against substantive review of contract terms applies directly only in the negotiation area. Although this is a possible basis for distinction, none of our opinions has suggested that the duty is governed by a double standard. Indeed, we have repeatedly noted that the *Vaca v. Sipes* standard applies to "challenges leveled not only at a union's contract

---

8. See, *e.g.,* Teamsters v. Terry, 494 U.S. __, __, 110 S.Ct. 1339, __, 108 L.Ed.2d 519 (1990); Electrical Workers v. Foust, 442 U.S. 42, 47, 99 S.Ct. 2121, 2125, 60 L.Ed.2d 698 (1979); Hines v. Anchor Motor Freight, Inc., 424 U.S. 554, 564, 96 S.Ct. 1048, 1056, 47 L.Ed.2d 231 (1976).

administration and enforcement efforts but at its negotiation activities as well." Communications Workers v. Beck, 487 U.S. 735, 743, 108 S.Ct. 2641, 2647, 101 L.Ed.2d 634 (1988) (internal citation omitted); see also Electrical Workers v. Foust, 442 U.S. 42, 47, 99 S.Ct. 2121, 2125, 60 L.Ed.2d 698 (1979); Vaca v. Sipes, 386 U.S., at 177, 87 S.Ct., at 909–10. We have also held that the duty applies in other instances in which a union is acting in its representative role, such as when the union operates a hiring hall. See Breininger v. Sheet Metal Workers, 493 U.S. ___, ___, 110 S.Ct. 424, ___, 107 L.Ed.2d 388 (1989).

We doubt, moreover, that a bright line could be drawn between contract administration and contract negotiation. Industrial grievances may precipitate settlement negotiations leading to contract amendments, and some strikes and strike settlement agreements may focus entirely on questions of contract interpretation. See Conley v. Gibson, 355 U.S. 41, 46, 78 S.Ct. 99, 102, 2 L.Ed.2d 80 (1957); Steelworkers v. Warrior & Gulf Navigation Co., 363 U.S. 574, 581, 80 S.Ct. 1347, 1352, 4 L.Ed.2d 1409 (1960). Finally, some union activities subject to the duty of fair representation fall into neither category. See *Breininger,* 493 U.S., at ___, 110 S.Ct. at ___.

We are, therefore, satisfied that the Court of Appeals correctly concluded that the tripartite standard announced in *Vaca v. Sipes* applies to a union in its negotiating capacity. We are persuaded, however, that the Court of Appeals' further refinement of the arbitrariness component of the standard authorizes more judicial review of the substance of negotiated agreements than is consistent with national labor policy.

As we acknowledged above, Congress did not intend judicial review of a union's performance to permit the court to substitute its own view of the proper bargain for that reached by the union. Rather, Congress envisioned the relationship between the courts and labor unions as similar to that between the courts and the legislature. Any substantive examination of a union's performance, therefore, must be highly deferential, recognizing the wide latitude that negotiators need for the effective performance of their bargaining responsibilities. Cf. Day–Brite Lighting, Inc. v. Missouri, 342 U.S. 421, 423, 72 S.Ct. 405, 407, 96 L.Ed. 469 (1952) (court does "not sit as a superlegislature to weigh the wisdom of legislation nor to decide whether the policy which it expresses offends the public welfare"); United States v. Carolene Products, 304 U.S., at 154, 58 S.Ct., at 784 (where "question is at least debatable," "decision was for Congress"). For that reason, the final product of the bargaining process may constitute evidence of a breach of duty only if it can be fairly characterized as so far outside a "wide range of reasonableness," Ford Motor Co. v. Huffman, 345 U.S., at 338, 73 S.Ct., at 686, that it is wholly "irrational" or "arbitrary."

The approach of the Court of Appeals is particularly flawed because it fails to take into account either the strong policy favoring the peaceful settlement of labor disputes, see, *e.g.*, Groves v. Ring Screw Works, Ferndale Fastener Div., 498 U.S. __, __, 111 S.Ct. 498, __, 112 L.Ed.2d 508 (1990), or the importance of evaluating the rationality of a union's decision in the light of both the facts and the legal climate that confronted the negotiators at the time the decision was made. As we shall explain, these factors convince us that ALPA's agreement to settle the strike was not arbitrary for either of the reasons posited by the Court of Appeals.

IV

The Court of Appeals placed great stress on the fact that the deal struck by ALPA was worse than the result the union would have obtained by unilateral termination of the strike. Indeed, the court held that a jury finding that the settlement was worse than surrender could alone support a judgment that the union had acted arbitrarily and irrationally. See 886 F.2d, at 1445–1446. This holding unduly constrains the "wide range of reasonableness," 345 U.S., at 338, 73 S.Ct., at 686, within which unions may act without breaching their fair representation duty.

For purposes of decision, we may assume that the Court of Appeals was correct in its conclusion that, if ALPA had simply surrendered and voluntarily terminated the strike, the striking pilots would have been entitled to reemployment in the order of seniority. Moreover, we may assume that Continental would have responded to such action by rescinding its assignment of all of the 85–5 bid positions to working pilots. After all, it did rescind about half of those assignments pursuant to the terms of the settlement. Thus, we assume that the union made a bad settlement—one that was even worse than a unilateral termination of the strike.

Nevertheless, the settlement was by no means irrational. A settlement is not irrational simply because it turns out *in retrospect* to have been a bad settlement. Viewed in light of the legal landscape at the time of the settlement, ALPA's decision to settle rather than give up was certainly not illogical. At the time of the settlement, Continental had notified the union that all of the 85–5 bid positions had been awarded to working pilots and was maintaining that none of the strikers had any claim on any of those jobs.

A comparable position had been asserted by United Air Lines in litigation in the Northern District of Illinois.[9] Because the District Court in that case had decided that such vacancies were not filled until

9. Air Line Pilots Assn. Int'l v. United   1985).
Air Lines, Inc., 614 F.Supp. 1020 (ND Ill.

pilots were trained and actually working in their new assignments, the Court of Appeals here concluded that the issue had been resolved in ALPA's favor when it agreed to the settlement with Continental. *See* 886 F.2d, at 1446. But this reasoning overlooks the fact that the validity of the District Court's ruling in the other case was then being challenged on appeal.[10]

Moreover, even if the law had been clear that the 85–5 bid positions were vacancies, the Court of Appeals erroneously assumed that the existing law was also clarion that the striking pilots had a right to those vacancies because they had more seniority than the cross-over and replacement workers. The court relied for the latter proposition solely on our cases interpreting the National Labor Relations Act. See 886 F.2d, at 1445. We have made clear, however, that National Labor Relations Act cases are not necessarily controlling in situations, such as this one, which are governed by the Railway Labor Act. See Railroad Trainmen v. Jacksonville Terminal Co., 394 U.S. 369, 383, 89 S.Ct. 1109, 1117–18, 22 L.Ed.2d 344 (1969).

Given the background of determined resistance by Continental at all stages of this strike, it would certainly have been rational for ALPA to recognize the possibility that an attempted voluntary return to work would merely precipitate litigation over the right to the 85–5 bid positions. Because such a return would not have disposed of any of the individual claims of the pilots who ultimately elected option one or option two of the settlement, there was certainly a realistic possibility that Continental would not abandon its bargaining position without a complete settlement.

At the very least, the settlement produced certain and prompt access to a share of the new jobs and avoided the costs and risks associated with major litigation. Moreover, since almost a third of the striking pilots chose the lump-sum severance payment rather than reinstatement, see n. 1, supra, the settlement was presumably more advantageous than a surrender to a significant number of striking pilots. In labor disputes, as in other kinds of litigation, even a bad settlement may be more advantageous in the long run than a good lawsuit. In all events, the resolution of the dispute over the 85–5 bid vacancies was well within the "wide range of reasonableness," 345 U.S., at 338, 73 S.Ct., at 686, that a union is allowed in its bargaining.

---

10. Even if the Seventh Circuit had already affirmed the District Court's holding in the *United Air Lines* case, the Court of Appeals would have erred in its conclusion that the law was so assuredly in ALPA's favor that the settlement was irrational. First, a Seventh Circuit case would not have controlled the outcome in this dispute, which arose in the Fifth Circuit. Second, even if the *United Air Lines* decision had been a Fifth Circuit case, it was factually distinguishable and therefore might not have dictated the outcome regarding the 85–5 bid positions. In *United Air Lines,* the Fifth Circuit affirmed on the basis of the District Court's finding that the carrier's action was taken in bad faith, motivated by antiunion animus. 802 F.2d, at 898; 614 F.Supp., at 1046. An equivalent finding was by no means certain in this case.

The suggestion that the "discrimination" between striking and working pilots represented a breach of the duty of fair representation also fails. If we are correct in our conclusion that it was rational for ALPA to accept a compromise between the claims of the two groups of pilots to the 85–5 bid positions, some form of allocation was inevitable. A rational compromise on the initial allocation of the positions was not invidious "discrimination" of the kind prohibited by the duty of fair representation. Unlike the grant of "super seniority" to the cross-over and replacement workers in NLRB v. Erie Resistor Corp., 373 U.S. 221, 83 S.Ct. 1139, 10 L.Ed.2d 308 (1963), this agreement preserved the seniority of the striking pilots after their initial reinstatement. In *Erie,* the grant of extra seniority enabled the replacement workers to keep their jobs while more senior strikers lost theirs during a layoff subsequent to the strike. See id., at 223–224, 83 S.Ct., at 1142–1143. The agreement here only provided the order and mechanism for the reintegration of the returning strikers but did not permanently alter the seniority system. This case therefore more closely resembles our decision in Trans World Airlines, Inc. v. Flight Attendants, 489 U.S. 426, 109 S.Ct. 1225, 103 L.Ed.2d 456 (1989), in which we held that an airline's refusal, after a strike, to displace cross-over workers with more senior strikers was not unlawful discrimination.

The judgment of the Court of Appeals is reversed and the case is remanded for further proceedings consistent with this opinion.

It is so ordered.

––––––

In RAKESTRAW v. UNITED AIRLINES, INC., 981 F.2d 1524 (7th Cir.1992), the court upheld, as consistent with the duty of fair representation, two union bargaining positions at United and TWA Airlines: (1) after a strike at United, the union negotiated for relative seniority dates that favored pilot trainees who for the most part honored the union picket lines, over fully qualified pilots who came to work for United as permanent strike replacements; and (2) after TWA acquired the assets of Ozark Airlines, the union "dovetailed" pilot seniority lists according to seniority at either airline company, although this was alleged to disfavor the Ozark pilots, who overall had less seniority and who constituted only a small minority within the union ranks. As to the former case, the court held that even if the union had acted partially out of deep hostility to the qualified pilots for their strikebreaking, its action was nonetheless a reasonable effort to restore preexisting seniority arrangements, and was therefore not a violation of the duty of fair representation. As to the latter dispute, the court held that such "dovetailing" constituted equal treatment and was fair and reasonable, even though it could be viewed as having harsher repercussions for the minority group within the union.

C. THE INDIVIDUAL AND HIS GRIEVANCE

Page 1078. Add to Note on Local 299, Teamsters:

Le'Mon v. NLRB, id., was remanded by the United States Supreme Court— at 499 U.S. 933, 111 S.Ct. 1383, 113 L.Ed.2d 440 (1991)—for reconsideration in light of *United Steelworkers of America v. Rawson,* p. 1080 infra, and *Air Line Pilots Ass'n, Intern. v. O'Neill.* On remand, the Tenth Circuit held that *O'Neill*'s holding, that fair representation applied to "all union activity," vitiated the circuit court's earlier reasoning that the duty did not apply when the union's action affected all the members of the bargaining unit. Nevertheless, the Tenth Circuit accepted the NLRB's position that negligence does not amount to breach of the duty, even when that negligence consisted of urging workers to continue a strike after the union had learned of its possible illegality. Le'Mon v. NLRB, 952 F.2d 1203 (10th Cir.1991), cert. denied, ___ U.S. ___, 113 S.Ct. 93, 121 L.Ed.2d 55 (1992).

II. UNION SECURITY AND THE ENCOURAGEMENT OF UNION ACTIVITY

A. UNION SECURITY AND THE USE OF UNION DUES

Page 1098. Add following Problem 2:

In Int'l Union of Elec. Workers (Paramax Systems Corp.), 311 N.L.R.B. 1031 (1993), the Board rejected the "model clause"—quoted above—approved in Keystone Coat, Apron & Towel Co., 121 N.L.R.B. 880 (1958). It held the clause to be ambiguous, though not facially unlawful.

> [I]t is likely that employees unversed in the intricacies of Section 8(a)(3) and interpretative decisions will literally interpret the clause as requiring full membership and all attendant financial obligations, e.g., assessments. At a minimum, they will be confused about their obligations. Because of this ambiguity, we next consider whether the Respondents, by virtue of their exclusive representative status, are obligated to apprise Paramax unit employees of their actual obligations.

The Board held the duty of fair representation to impose that informational obligation to all employees and not only those facing "imminent discharge" as a result of the invocation of the union security clause. The "statutory evil" to be avoided, the Board opined, is the maintenance among employees of an "erroneous impression" that they do not have a right to resign from the union.

Page 1111. Add after *Beck*:

On April 13, 1992, President Bush issued Executive Order 12800, 57 Fed.Reg. 12985 (April 14, 1992), requiring federal contractors to post a notice informing employees of their rights under *Beck*. On February 1, 1993, President Clinton issued Executive Order 12836, withdrawing Executive Order 12800, 58 Fed.Reg. 7045 (Feb. 3, 1993).

Page 1113.   Insert new Problems 6 and 7.

6.   Mollie Member is a member of the United Auto Workers, which has negotiated an agency-shop provision in the labor contract with her employer. She is active in union affairs, often as a dissenter, and she is often heard on the floor of the union meeting hall and has been an unsuccessful candidate for union office.   She wishes to remain a union member and to exercise these rights—as well as the right to vote whether or not to ratify collective bargaining agreements—but she objects to having a substantial part of her union dues devoted to political causes with which she is unsympathetic.   Mollie has consulted you, and you have informed her that she can secure an appropriate rebate of a portion of her dues if she resigns from membership in the union and invokes the rights given nonmembers under the *Beck* decision.   She, however, asserts that she should not have to be forced, in order to protest and secure a rebate for expenses unrelated to collective bargaining, to forgo the crucial rights of participation afforded to union members.

Does her claim have merit?   See Kidwell v. Transportation Communications Intern. Union, 946 F.2d 283 (4th Cir.1991), cert. denied, ___ U.S. ___, 112 S.Ct. 1760, 118 L.Ed.2d 423 (1992).

7.   Is a union of airline pilots obligated to rebate the portion of agency fees paid by non-members that it spent to support strikes by union members at other airlines?   See Crawford v. Air Line Pilots Ass'n, 992 F.2d 1295 (4th Cir.1993).

Page 1116.   Insert before Problems:

In LEHNERT v. FERRIS FACULTY ASS'N, 500 U.S. 507, 111 S.Ct. 1950, 114 L.Ed.2d 572 (1991), the Supreme Court once again considered the extent to which dissenting fee payers may lawfully be charged their pro rata share of certain union expenses.   Although the case involved a public-sector union operating under Michigan law, the Court—which split into a number of camps, with three separate partial concurrences and partial dissents—invoked its earlier private-sector decisions under the Railway Labor Act.   Writing for five Justices, Justice Blackmun stated:

> Hanson and Street and their progeny teach that chargeable activities must (1) be "germane" to collective-bargaining activity; (2) be justified by the government's vital policy interest in labor peace and avoiding "free riders;" and (3) not significantly add to the burdening of free speech that is inherent in the allowance of an agency or union shop.

The Court held that the dissenting members of the local union could be charged with certain convention, publication and "program" expenditures relating to the state and national affiliates, information services regarding such matters as professional development and job opportunities, and expenses incurred to prepare for a strike that had it taken place would have been in violation of state law; but that they could not be charged with lobbying, electoral and political activities not bearing upon the ratification or implementation of a collective agreement, the union's program to secure funds for public education in Michigan, litigation not concerning the local unit, and public relations efforts designed to enhance the reputation of the teaching profession.

IV. UNION ELECTIONS

Page 1204. Insert after first full paragraph:

In INTERNATIONAL ORGANIZATION OF MASTERS, MATES & PILOTS v. BROWN, 498 U.S. 466, 111 S.Ct. 880, 112 L.Ed.2d 991 (1991), the Supreme Court struck down a union rule that made mailing labels unavailable to candidates for office until after the union's nominating convention. The Court held that section 401(c) of the LMRDA requires the union to accede to such a request if the *request* is reasonable (which the Court found it to be); the pertinent issue is therefore not whether the union *rule* might be reasonable.